TIGER FORCE

"Inward Season Three...Over"

A Vietnam War Memoir
LEO JOSEPH HEANEY

TIGER FORCE "Inward Season Three… Over"
A Vietnam War Memoir

© 2018 by Leo Joseph Heaney.

ISBN: 978-1-7324645-0-6

Cover design by Kacia Kelly.
Cover photo: Leo Joseph Heaney, courtesy of Leo Joseph Heaney

All rights reserved. No part of this publication may be reproduced, stored in a retrieval system, or transmitted in any form or by any means, electronic, mechanical, printing, photocopying, recording, or otherwise, without the prior written consent of the author. Contact: heaneylj@gmail.com

Vietnam map created by Varida P&R, used by permission.

Permission to reproduce the 101st and Tiger Force insignias was given by written consent of the Army Trademark Licensing Office.

Spine: The smaller insignia (an eagle with an airborne tab above it) is the official patch of the 101st Airborne.

Back cover: The larger insignia was designed by Doc Hise and Ralph Mayhew for unit pride among Tiger Force personnel. It was never officially authorized by the Department of the Army, and was worn only while serving with the Force in Vietnam. The graphic created by NordNordWest added the word "RECON" below the eagle.

Dedication

To those who unselfishly wager all
to their tomorrows

Acknowledgements

I had the easy task of composing the narrative portion of the text. The bulk of the labor to bring this work to print belongs to others.

Special commendation belongs to three individuals. Ellen Fisher Heaney was the literary compass for the project and the person most directly responsible for bringing the mission to conclusion. Kacia Kelly designed the cover. Suzanne Hagelin of Varida Publishing and Resources was an unimaginable asset whose guidance and formatting skill were essential to the overall presentation of the book.

Additional thanks go to the following individuals who were instrumental in helping me to prepare the material for publication: Lisa Adams, Sam Carnero, Tom Day, Charlie Evans, Kristin Evans, Pam Flores, Pamela Gross, Shirley Ann Hartz Jacobs, Mark Jordan, Kathy McKeehen, Candy Tingstad, Brigitte Trout, and Melissa Kay Hartz Wadsworth.

A Bit of History

Because Japan had allied itself with Germany, French colonies in Southeast Asia went to the Japanese when the French surrendered to the Germans during WWII. Ho Chi Minh (the eventual leader of North Vietnam) had fought against the Japanese alongside the U.S. in WWII. When the war was over, Ho Chi Minh expected the U.S. to support him in forming the nation of Vietnam. However, a half a world away, Europe was splitting into two major factions: the communists and the West. The future nation of Vietnam was destined to become one of the major conflict areas of the Cold War.

France was viewed as a strategic member to NATO, and the U.S. bowed to French designs to return to Southeast Asia and re-establish colonies in Indochina. So, after fighting the Japanese for 5 years, Ho Chi Minh then had to fight the French. The final deciding battle of the French-Indochina War (First Indochina War) was Dien Bien Phu, where Ho Chi Minh's forces decisively defeated the French. During the conflict, France wanted U.S. air support, but Eisenhower refused. Helping any colonizing attempt would not gain favor for the United States, the free world, or the developing world. Additionally, it would lend credence to the communists' mantra labeling the West as imperialistic.

After the Vietnamese beat the French in 1954, the peace treaty participants met in Geneva, Switzerland. It was decided that Vietnam would be divided at the 17th parallel until a plebiscite (a vote by the people of Vietnam) could be conducted. The people were to determine whether Vietnam would be one unified nation or two separate countries--one communist and one capitalist. The plebiscite never occurred. The communists felt betrayed by the West. The seeds for the Second Indochina War were sown.

Prologue

Tiger Force of the First Battalion, 327th Parachute Infantry Regiment, of the First Brigade (Separate) of the 101st Airborne Division was a counter-guerrilla unit. It combined the battalion's reconnaissance and anti-tank platoons, minus vehicles. The unit's inception is credited to Major (later Colonel) David Hackworth. David Hackworth realized that the typical U.S. infantry line companies, as deployed in Vietnam, seldom commanded the element of surprise. Their organizational equipment, large size, methods of insertion, and normal tactical routine usually gave the enemy knowledge of an American unit's location and intentions. The options to fight or flee then rested with the enemy. Hackworth wanted a combat force that could operate in the enemy's "backyard." His solution was Tiger Force, a tactical element that had both fire power and stealth.

Formed in October 1965, the Force was made up from personnel of three headquarters company components: recon platoon, anti-tank platoon, and the ground surveillance radar section. The first members arrived in Vietnam via ship, and those soldiers affectionately take the label of "Boat People." Later reinforcements to Vietnam arrived by plane.[1] Today there is still a Tiger Force as part of the 327th Infantry.

All Tigers volunteered twice--the first was to go airborne, and the second was to join the Force. Most men came from the line companies. The main prerequisite for joining was prior combat experience. Sometimes (after major engagements when there was a shortage of replacement personnel across the entire battalion) combat experience was waived. In order to "un-volunteer" a Tiger only had to announce his intention to the First Sergeant, and Top would find a job for the soldier in supply, motor pool, orderly room, mail room, mess hall, etc.

In 1966, Tiger Force commander Captain Thomas Agerton summed up the Force's standard operating guidelines in a mission briefing before an operation out of Tuy Hoa. Paraphrased, it went something like this: "When Tiger Force meets an enemy unit, if the enemy unit is smaller than the Force, the Force will overrun it. If it is bigger than the Force, the Force will nip off its head or tail, and keep after it until the rest of the battalion can bring in support."

I served as a combat infantryman in Tiger Force from June of 1966 through October 1967. Sometimes, following an episode of tactical success or some extreme physical endeavor, I found myself humorously commenting to my comrades that someday I should write about their exploits. At that time, my comments were more in the form of a verbal "pat-on-the-back," and not an enterprise I seriously considered. The emergence of a book in 2006 purporting to describe the *true* nature of the Force and the individuals that served in it, compelled me to reconsider my intentions. If I am successful, the following account will leave the reader with an understanding of the history of the Force, its typical composition, how it operated, and (in particular) the character of the individuals that contributed to its uniqueness.

*****

[1] Conversation with Dr. James Wilson (one of original members of Tiger Force who arrived via boat) at a reunion in Deadwood, June 26, 2017.

Map of Vietnam

6 ♦

Table of Contents

A Bit of History		1
Prologue		3
Map		5
Chapter 1	Tigers in the Chow Line	9
Chapter 2	The Diplomat and Warrior	11
Chapter 3	Pistol Poppin' Priest	22
Chapter 4	Operation Hawthorne Heats Up	27
Chapter 5	Tiger Hill	33
Chapter 6	B-52s, Inward Season	48
Chapter 7	Dining with the Montagnards	53
Chapter 8	The Persona of Sergeant Rose	61
Chapter 9	Sergeant Girard 'Discovers' Laos	73
Chapter 10	An Eye for an Eye	82
Chapter 11	The Tuy Hoa Tigers	90
Chapter 12	Hill 51, POW Camps	99
Chapter 13	Base Camp, The Big River Assault	110
Chapter 14	Hot Sauce and Turkey Loaf	124
Chapter 15	Missed the Train	136
Chapter 16	Tiger Six Down	148
Chapter 17	Christmas '66 in Kontum City	155
Chapter 18	The Water Buffalo, Murphy's Law	161
Chapter 19	The Flash, the Cook, and the Chemist	172
Chapter 20	Fire Power Up Front	183

Chapter 21	Doc and Jake	187
Chapter 22	Eight Canteens, The Path Not Taken	193
Chapter 23	A Night Visitor, Waterfalls, The Monk	202
Chapter 24	Blood and Water	212
Chapter 25	Black 'n Blue and Purple	222
Chapter 26	Tiger Valley	231
Chapter 27	An Indifferent Allegiance?	238
Chapter 28	Stone Grenades	249
Chapter 29	The C-Ration Ambush	253
Chapter 30	Night River Crossing and the Old Man	261
Chapter 31	Free Fire Zone?	267
Chapter 32	The Perpetual Can of Fruit	282
Chapter 33	Tunnel Vision	289
Chapter 34	Casualties Mounting	293
Chapter 35	The LAW, 82 Refugees	300
Chapter 36	Final Patrols	308
Chapter 37	Homeward Bound	320
Epilogue	The Orange Time Bomb	322
Glossary		325
About the Author		336

Chapter 1
Tigers in the Chow Line
May 1966

Tigers are generally solitary cats, but in a group they are labeled as a "streak" or an "ambush."[1]

In the hinterlands of Vietnam, two distinct species of tigers prowled the jungles: one four-legged, the other two-legged. Camouflaged, they each stalked silently and with purpose.

I had been in country only a little more than a month, serving as a rifleman in B Company of the 1st Battalion, 327th Parachute Infantry Regiment. The three line platoons of B Company, which had been working separately, were rendezvousing with the rest of the battalion. We were to meet at a large prairie for extraction from the Nhan Co area to a new operating locale northwest of Kontum City.

My platoon was directed to occupy a portion of the perimeter of the LZ (landing zone) and await the arrival of the helicopters. We were told that the turnaround time for the shuttling aircraft would be lengthy. We established security, settled in, and awaited our turn for the choppers. Like many of the troops, I sat down and eased myself into a restful position using my rucksack as back support. I oriented myself so that the sun's warmth could work its best on my soaked fatigues. Sunshine was a rare commodity in the rain forests of the western Vietnamese highlands. We had spent most of the previous three weeks drenched, soggy, and dank. The warmth of the bright, open prairie was both physically and mentally therapeutic.

While we were waiting, the battalion choppered in a mess team with the monthly hot meal. Some U.S. combat units took pride in guaranteeing on a daily basis a hot, mess-hall-prepared meal for their troops. The problem with this practice is that choppers delivering the meals also pinpoint the friendly unit's location for the enemy. The 1st 327th worked clandestinely. We carried five to seven days rations in our rucksacks. We were resupplied weekly, and only about once a month did the battalion deliver a hot, mess-hall-prepared meal to us.

As I was observing the mess team setting up a chow line, I noticed a small element of soldiers behind the mess personnel that were outfitted differently from the rest of us. They sported soft caps rather than helmets, and their fatigues bore a camouflage scheme rather than the customary olive drab. I asked if anyone knew who the troops were that were behind the chow line. One of the short-timers, who took immense pleasure in reminding us newbies or cherries that we were his replacements, replied that they were "Tigers." Sensing that his comment still meant little to me, he followed by adding that it was the battalion reconnaissance unit called Tiger Force. He concluded my instruction on how the battalion was organized with a cadence ditty-- "Just one more month and I'll be home, drinking beer and pissing foam."

Later that day, we were extracted to an airstrip near the junction of the international borders of Cambodia, Laos, and Vietnam. Within a week, the short- timer's predictions were tested. His assertion that he would soon be going home was correct. A few days into the next operation, in a firefight on some nondescript hill, he was killed while we were attacking entrenched North Vietnamese regulars. However, his assessment that I was "his" replacement was incorrect--I ended up as a replacement for one of those Tigers, most of which would also be killed or wounded not far from the hamlet of Dak To at a battle site christened *"Tiger Hill."*

****

[1]www.quora.com/What-is-a-group-of-tigers-called

Chapter 2
The Diplomat and Warrior
June 1966

During World War II, elements of the 101st Airborne Division received the Presidential Unit Citation for landing behind enemy lines in the D-Day Invasion. Also in WW II, elements of the Division received another Presidential Unit Citation following the tenacious stand at the Battle of the Bulge. For action at Dak To, Vietnam, in June 1966, elements of the 1st brigade of the 101st Airborne Division were awarded another Presidential Unit Citation. According to military historians, the fighting at Dak To in June of 1966 was some of the fieriest to date. --General Order 59, Presidential Unit Citation, Issued 21 October 1968

In this action, Tiger Force was more than decimated; it was almost annihilated. –Ward S. Just., To What End: Report from Vietnam.

Early in June, my platoon deployed to Dak To. The hamlet, pronounced "dock toe," lies in the mountainous region of western Vietnam, just east of the point where the borders of Laos, Cambodia and Vietnam meet. Densely forested hills dominate the terrain. The airstrip, oriented east to west, seemed barely large enough to handle transport aircraft. The verdant landscape was punctuated with vibrant orange highlights, where road cuts exposed patches of the underlying soil. The term "outpost" certainly described the tactical arena.

Two of the 1st brigade's three infantry battalions, my unit, the 1/327th (the "First Bat"), and the 2/502nd (the "O-Deuce"), along with other combat support elements, were relocated to the Dak To area. The brigade's third battalion, the 2/327th (the "Second Bat") remained in the coastal area around Tuy Hoa.

Advanced party personnel directed the arriving line units to the portions of the perimeter that each would be responsible for defending. The battalion was in the act of establishing a forward base camp prior to initiating tactical operations in the area. This process usually involved three or four days which afforded the opportunity to shower, exchange fatigues, and enjoy a change of food venue from C-rations to mess hall (actually, mess tent) chow.

The immediate task was to settle in and establish security. Keeping the airfield to our backs, we prepared defensive positions, dug foxholes and prone sleeping shelters, dispatched recon patrols, cleared fields of fire, camouflaged positions, rigged trip flares, set up claymore mines, and dug the ubiquitous slit-trench latrines and emplaced "piss tubes."

To us grunts, Dak To was the name of just another small Vietnamese community which most of us would never visit. The village was a few kilometers to the east of the airstrip, but in the seven weeks that I operated out of that area, I never set foot in the hamlet itself. For that matter, I had never entered the villages of Nhan Co or Cheo Reo, our previous operating bases. My only knowledge of them was by reference to the military airfields where we arrived, and stayed before commencing our field operations.

According to the official records, the general scheme of the initial operation at Dak To (labeled "Operation Hawthorne") was to interdict the flow of enemy personnel and material on the nearby Ho Chi Minh Trail network. The specifics of the operation included relieving the defenders at the outpost at Toumorong, about eighteen kilometers to the northeast, while preventing North Vietnamese forces from attacking the provincial capital of Kontum under the cover of the summer monsoon[1].

Official records stated that the principal opponent in the AO was the 24th NVA regiment. The numerical designation of the opposing unit meant little to me. The fact that we were dealing with North Vietnamese regulars, as opposed to VC militia troops, was significant to me. The regulars would be well trained and armed. Most would be carrying automatic and semi-automatic weapons like AKs or SKSs and backed up with machine guns (RPDs), rocket propelled grenades (RPGs) and 82mm mortars. The VC troops on the other hand, would probably be armed with less sophisticated weapons of World War II or Korean Conflict vintage. Tactically, the militia troops generally hit and ran, while the regulars characteristically gave ground stubbornly. I also noticed that the term NVA had pretty much supplanted the term PAVN, which the leadership personnel had previously employed when referring to the North Vietnamese regulars.

*****

It was here, at the onset of Operation Hawthorne, while on a combat patrol with 2nd platoon, B Company, I encountered the founder of Tiger Force, Major David Hackworth.

Combat operations for my platoon began with a helicopter insertion on the fifth of June. Air time was short and the landing zone was not hot (was not receiving any enemy fire). We encountered no resistance at the landing site. The LZ, however, was at elevation, and we headed downhill on a fairly well defined trail with moderately thick vegetation on both sides. If the platoon had a specific objective other than to find the enemy, I wasn't aware of it. As we progressed, sporadic gunfire from the neighboring hills confirmed that the enemy was about.

My squad was in trail position of the platoon and I was "rear security," the last man back. While the platoon was moving, the implicit mission of the rear security was simple: deny the enemy the capability of surprising the platoon from the rear. The task involved a lot of walking backwards, lingering around bends in the trail and pausing in shadowy areas to see if anyone was following us. Five weeks had passed since I had joined the platoon. I had been mentored well. I performed my tasks with religious fervor, dreading the consequences that might result from complacency. Yet, in the time that I had spent in the field, all the action had generated at the point or flank, not the rear of the platoon. So I was more than a little surprised that day when, on one of my pause-and-wait routines, a small group of personnel rounded a bend in the trail behind me.

About eight armed men in olive drab uniforms came into view roughly forty meters behind us. When their point man spotted me, he stopped. I could tell by their helmets, weapons, and physical appearance that they were American. Normally word was passed back from our platoon leader or platoon sergeant whenever we were operating in proximity of other friendly units. A "friendly-fire" incident is all too easy to initiate in hilly terrain with dense vegetation. But nobody had informed me that an American unit was supposed to be coming up on our rear. At any rate, I waved at their point man and he returned my gesture, but they still maintained their distance. I then moved forward and tapped the man in front of me and told him to send it forward that we had "friendlies" behind us. I remember thinking that the point and slack man of the unit following us looked fairly "old" compared to the average age of most of us on the line.

Our platoon sergeant, SFC Gladstone, was about five men in front of me. When the word reached him, he looked back at me and nodded. Then he dropped back and joined me to check out the situation. After a quick look, he told me that the small element following us was the battalion CP group. The lead man was the battalion commander, and the second man the battalion sergeant major. This was novel to me--a field-grade officer and sergeant major, with packs and rifles, walking point for their element! My short tenure in the Army had generated the impression that field-grade officers were virtual demigods who stayed in TOCs or on helicopters, and ran the war with radios. This CP group was also armed with standard issue M-16s, not some personal side arms of limited effectiveness in a real firefight. At this point in its evolution, the M-16 still had a few bugs in it, but at least the battalion commander and sergeant major were taking the same risks as the rest of us. This commander was certainly different from what I had come to expect.

Shortly after the CP group had come up behind us, my platoon abandoned the trail and turned left down a stream bed. Not long after that, we started taking fire from the high ground to the left. The Battle of Dak To 1966 was heating up.

The incoming fire was not particularly effective. It was sporadic, in short bursts, and passed about three or four feet over our heads. The creek bed was generously endowed with man-sized boulders, affording good cover. However, the boulders also produced an echo, making pinpointing the exact source of the firing a little difficult. Sergeant Gladstone instructed me to recon-by-fire. The purpose of this technique was to draw the enemy's fire, and it worked. I might be understating the situation here. When I squeezed off a few rounds into the area where I thought the firing had originated, all hell broke loose--and, at that particular moment in time, I felt like it was all directed at me.

With incoming rounds ricocheting off the rocks in front of me, I instinctively sought cover behind one of the boulders. I don't recall feeling any pain, but as I reached down to secure a new magazine, I became aware of blood trickling down the side of my nose and dripping into the water. I knew that I wasn't hurt seriously. My right eye felt more like some grit had blown into it. I figured that the incoming rounds had struck the boulders near me and sent some rock sprawl into my eye.

When the shooting started, the squad members near me had responded with a hail of return fire directed at the suspected enemy location. The battalion CP group moved up and joined us. Major Hackworth, the battalion commander, took a position just to my left, where he could provide covering fire for the platoon medic. The medic seemed to materialize out of nowhere and began checking my eye.

I was certain that the wound wasn't serious, but the remedy certainly complicated the rest of my day. The medical procedure for an eye wound involving embedded foreign material attempts to prevent the injured eye from moving, as movement might exacerbate the injury. Since the eyes move in conjunction with each other, first aid required covering both eyes. The medic followed standard medical procedure, and stretched the bandage over both my eyes. I guess the Army felt that an agile eighteen year old paratrooper carrying an eighty pound pack and weapon, should easily be able to negotiate a raging stream strewn with slimy boulders, a trackless jungle, thick with toppled trees and "wait-a-minute" vines, as well as the occasional incoming fire, while blindfolded and holding on to a strap of the rucksack of the man in front of of him. I soon demonstrated the pitfalls in the Army's line of reasoning. After numerous episodes of tripping over fallen logs, careening into low hanging branches, slipping on slick rocks, and stepping off into chest-deep pools of water, the field bandage over my eyes "miraculously" slipped upward toward my forehead. This afforded me some knowledge of where the hell I was--or more accurately--where I was falling.

I understood the medical rationale behind covering both eyes, so I tried to restrict my eye movement by not scanning left or right, just focusing straight ahead. Even so, negotiating the obstacle course by peeking under the field dressing was still no piece of cake. To say that I had some difficulty would be another understatement. Time and again, it was the major assisting me back to my feet. At lunch, and other short breaks, we exchanged the usual information that Americans share when trying to be cordial. The major's demeanor was such that I didn't feel like we were strangers by virtue of the differences of our rank. He had had a pleasant, easy, confident manner about him. In the middle of a war, in the middle of a jungle, on boulders in the middle of a stream, the major's persona telegraphed the message that he was leading a winning team. This field-grade officer was comfortable to be around.

As day wore into evening, most of my physical grace and athletic acumen (assuming that I ever possessed much of either commodity) had gradually deserted me. By the time we settled into our night location, I was ready to call it a day. Fortunately we were near a clearing that would serve as an extraction LZ in the morning. That night, for obvious reasons, I was exempted from guard duty. For the first time in a month, I was not being awakened every two or three hours to pull an hour on guard!

*****

The next morning, the C&C chopper transported me and another wounded trooper to the battalion aid station located on a little rise near the Dak To airstrip. The station consisted of a few medium-sized tents partitioned into two areas, one mostly crammed with canvas cots, and another where treatment was dispensed. I set my rifle and gear down where I could keep track of them and waited my turn. There were other men there, mostly like me. Nothing really critical; no one was thrashing about or dying. The seriously wounded were most likely taken on a medevac flight directly to field hospitals.

After a while, someone directed me to one of the examining chairs. A lean Captain, whom I assumed was the battalion surgeon, read my medical evacuation tag, and asked me what was wrong. I explained that "something" had blown into my eye the day before. He took a quick look and said that he couldn't see anything. Malingering isn't a characteristic of my nature, but I sensed that the surgeon thought that it might be. When I asked him to have another look, he flashed me one of those "whatever" expressions, but proceeded to accommodate my request for reevaluation. Then he muttered something under his breath, procured a tweezers-like instrument from a nearby table, instructed me to hold still, and removed a crescent shaped piece of copper, about half the size of a thumbnail, from under the skin fold in the corner of my eye. I was really lucky. Had the metal fragment struck a centimeter to my right, I'd be sporting an eye patch today. Three inoculations later, I was ready to return to duty. Well, not quite ready. About the time that I was rolling down my sleeve, General Pearson, the brigade CO, arrived. He shook hands with all of us, engaged in some quick talk, we saluted, and then went our separate ways.

*****

At that time and place my temporary reference point in the world was my company's rear defensive area, so I made my way out of the battalion aid station and headed toward B Company's supply tent. The buck sergeant who manned the company supply tent was not a gregarious fellow, so I avoided any engaging conversation. I reported in, informed him that the battalion aid station had released me, and awaited his instructions. He told me to stay nearby, where he could find me easily, and that he'd get me back to the field on the next available resupply ship, probably not before the next morning.

I felt that the sergeant didn't need me cluttering up his tent, so I staked claim in front of the tent close to a drainage ditch (in case I needed to get below ground-level in a hurry) and sat out the rest of the day. This was a rare sense of freedom--not having something to do. I took the opportunity to jot off a letter home, put my APO address on it, wrote "free" where the stamp would be, and dropped it off in the mail clerk's sack. I savored a second full night's sleep, unaware of what was happening to the units in the field. Elements of the First Bat, the O-Deuce, B Battery of the 320th Artillery, along with the 326th Engineer unit were attacked while I slept.

*****

Not long after sunrise I was on board a D-model Huey that served as the battalion C&C ship. Following a short flight, the chopper deposited me and some other resupply items at a bastion called Toumorong. This outpost was being abandoned. I arrived to witness the local ARNV troops busily dismantling the above ground structures. The chief item of interest seemed to be the metal roofing, which the ARVNs were loading onto deuce and a half trucks. The expression, "Chinese fire drill" ran through my mind as I watched what appeared to be extremely underage soldiers directed by "honcho-type" NCOs. The exercise involved a lot of pushing, kicking, and shouting as the roofing on the surrounding structures gradually disappeared, leaving only wooden skeletons above the subsurface excavations. The scene that was emerging resembled something akin to a World War I photograph of trench warfare.

The outpost lay on the side of a hill overlooking a dirt highway, which in grunt-infantry verbiage was a "red ball." To my right, the route stretched ultimately to North Vietnam; to my left, it ran back to Dak To, and then onward to the plateau area of Kontum, and south from there to Saigon. The area was a mountain biker's paradise: verdant, sleepy, and pristine--well, almost pristine. The smoke and napalm scars on the hills to the north and west bore evidence of the recent violence that the area had absorbed.

About that time in my visual assessment of the area, I noticed Major Hackworth off to my right on the road that led to a helipad above the compound. He was alone at the moment and just seemed to be observing the situation. I had located myself away from the ARVN wrecking crews, trying to stay out of everyone's way. When the major noticed me, he made his way over to my "observation post." We exchanged salutes and he asked how my eye was faring. The major amazed me when he addressed me by my surname. He had to have remembered it from the streambed, because the jungle shirt I was wearing bore no name tag. Then, as if I were a visiting general or politician, he proceeded to update me on the tactical situation. Pointing to different pieces of terrain in the distance, he explained that during the early morning hours the artillery, engineer units, and some of the infantry folk had been attacked. The enemy had overrun one of the artillery gun emplacements, which had to be retaken.

I can't quite explain the feeling of awe and respect that I was developing for the major. This senior officer took the time to explain to me, a private grunt, with less than ten months in the military and six weeks in combat, about what was happening tactically. It made me feel that my presence there was an integral part of the battalion's endeavor. Six years later, at the Infantry Officers Basic Course at Fort Benning Georgia, an instructor in a leadership class presented an example of "tact" to us. His description went something like this: "A leader possesses tact, if, after briefing the unit on a pending mission through hell, finds the troops eagerly anticipating the journey." Major Hackworth had "tact."

The major finished summing-up the situation, then told me to sit tight and he'd get me on the next ship heading to my unit. I thanked him, we exchanged salutes again and the major headed back toward the ARVNs. He had managed only a few paces when a second Huey, displaying a brigadier's star, came in and landed on the small helipad beside the ship that had brought me there. Major Hackworth changed his course and headed up the hill to meet the general. That's when some "stay-behind" NVA decided to protest our presence and fired a burst at the outpost.

The incoming rounds were so off-target, no one bothered to duck. But they may have come closer to General Pearson who was further up the hill near the choppers. When I looked up, I noticed the general low-crawling down the road toward Major Hackworth. The major glanced over his shoulder at me. Addressing me again by name, he directed me to quickly return fire. We both knew by the "crack-pop" of the enemy's weapon that the shooter was quite a ways off. And even if I knew exactly where in the tree line he was situated, at this range, my M-16 wouldn't be all that effective.

The odds were better on hitting a monkey than the shooter. Yet, the major said to fire, so I turned downhill, elevated my weapon, and squeezed off several rounds in the general direction of our adversary.

One of the First Brigade's slogans is "Diplomats and Warriors." I believe that I was witnessing the warrior-Hackworth switching to the diplomat-Hackworth. After I had "engaged" the enemy, he reported to General Pearson, who was by then standing and dusting himself off. The Major had conducted a little "save face" exercise, returning fire, making the situation a little more "tactical" than it actually was.

Before long, I was on a resupply chopper heading for my platoon, wherever it was. The helicopter clung to the tree tops and proceeded about two kilometers north until it reached the "red ball." Following the road west for about another five clicks we crossed a large open area, eventually settling down beside two 105mm howitzers. Our paths were crossing again; Tiger Force had arrived there at daybreak.

Brief Summary of Operation Hawthorne[2]

Timeframe: 2 – 21 June 1966
Base camp: Dak To, Kontum Province
Area of Operations: About 18 kilometers northeast of Dak To airstrip
Enemy Situation: The 24th NVA Regiment was operating in the AO
Mission: Search and Destroy and lift siege on outpost Toumorong
Other Considerations: Troops at Toumorong relieved and post vacated
After Action Assessment: 45 friendly KIA, 241 friendly WIA, 1 friendly MIA, 531, enemy KIA, 22 enemy captured, 88 enemy individual and 21 enemy crew served weapons captured

****

[1] Sam Wolf, *"Operation HAWTHORNE, 1 June 1966-21 June 1966."* Freerepublic.com. The Freeper Foxhole Remembers, 5 Feb 2004.
[2] MACV Command History. Cc SEA/Chronology/MACV/_1966.html.

Chapter 3
Pistol Poppin' Priest
June 7-8, 1966

"At 2:30 in the morning of June 7th an estimated North Vietnamese Army battalion of the 24th NVA Regiment savagely attacked an artillery-infantry-engineer position in the valley west of Toumorong. This was the beginning of two weeks of the most violent fighting in the war in Vietnam.

The position was manned by "B" Battery, 2nd Howitzer Battalion, 320th Artillery; Company "A" 2nd Battalion, 502nd Infantry; and elements of "A" Company, 326th Engineer Battalion. The charging enemy was able to penetrate the artillery's perimeter where one of the small dramas of the war took place.

Gun number six came under extremely heavy attack, wherein a small war ensued over the ownership of the howitzer position. Twice the enemy took the position, twice the gun crew, turned infantry, took it back. The battle that had the winner take all climax saw the valiant Americans secure their weapon and fire point-blank into the still charging NVA ranks. As dawn brought light to the exhausted warriors, 86 enemy bodies were counted, 13 of them inside the artillery position." --Sam Wolf, "Operation Hawthorne"[1]

As soon as the skids touched down, I exited the chopper and "thumbs-upped" a nod of thanks to the helicopter crew. I headed for the howitzer section, hoping some the artillery personnel might be able to direct me to my unit. But querying the artillerymen wasn't necessary, for I recognized members of my platoon just beyond the gun tubes. I reported to my squad leader. From him I learned that our task was to take over the defense of this area of the perimeter in order to relieve what was left of the artillery troops. I joined my other team members who quickly provided the specifics of last night's contest for control of the real estate upon which we were standing. The northern-most howitzer position had been overrun twice during the attack.

Our understanding of the engagement was further broadened from conversations with a few of the departing artillery troops, who were gathering their gear around the second gun emplacement. According to these survivors, the tide of battle changed in their favor when the men defending the second gun fired flechette rounds at the attacking NVA. One trooper opined that either the NVA didn't know what flechette rounds could do, or they greatly underestimated the effectiveness of the weapons. At that time, I didn't have a very comprehensive understanding of the flechette round either. I knew it was an anti-personnel munition that had a shotgun effect on advancing enemy. About three weeks later, following a different engagement, I saw firsthand the damage a single flechette blade produced on an American casualty. This trooper explained that when the warning shouts were given that "bee hive" rounds were going to be fired, he had taken cover behind a fallen log. However, his lower leg was exposed and a single flechette cut straight across his calf, cleaving the muscle almost in two.

With the departure of the artillery personnel, our focus returned to strengthening the portion of the perimeter that we had inherited. We were highly familiar with the task. There was a slight variation from our usual defensive routine. Normally, our perimeter was platoon-sized, and circular in configuration. Here we were part of a larger circle, tying in with other units on our flanks. The open area to our rear was large, stretching off a few hundred meters in all directions. The main road from Toumorong, which the resupply chopper had followed, entered our area on the right and curved behind us through the clearing towards the southwest where, depending on your point of view, it crossed a rather large stream or small river. From there the road continued south about eighteen kilometers to the hamlet of Dak To. The ARVNs needed this road to move their trucks (laden with whatever they were salvaging from the outpost at Toumorong) back to Dak

To. A few days earlier, the 1/42nd ARVN Regiment was ambushed on the road to Toumorong, suffering 4 KIAs and 19 WIAs (Hackworth, 536)[2].

*****

Located within our defensive arch were the two, now inactive, 105mm howitzers. From the north, a well defined trail emerged from heavy undergrowth, just to the left of the forward gun position. This was the major avenue of approach into our portion of the perimeter. By the evidence on either side of it, this trail had served as a principle route of egress for the NVA after the battle. In several places, along both sides of the trail, the vegetation was depressed. Litter beside the trail included discarded field dressings and packaging, as well as spots of congealed blood--all evidence that first aid procedures had been administered, and wounded evacuated. Our opponents were not "country bumpkins." They obviously had established procedures for administering to their wounded, and their tactical use of the battle area was sound. Had the fight just been a "slug-fest" with automatic weapons, their attack may have prevailed. Had they overrun the battery, the evacuation of the outpost would have been seriously complicated. As it was, they were withdrawing to their base camps to tend to their wounded and regroup. Most of the 1/327th line units were in pursuit. By the end of the day, Tiger Force would re-establish contact with some of the withdrawing NVA. The next day, all of the battalion's line elements would be engaged.

*****

Eventually, we made an excursion around the fire base and got a better feel for our situation. The road from Dak To appeared to be functional as there were several trucks and jeeps scattered about the area. I couldn't help but notice that most of the deuce and a half trucks had bullet holes in the windshields. There were some brave drivers out there! In that type of terrain, a man in a truck was a pretty easy target.

Not long after we had returned to our perimeter area, a Roman Catholic chaplain drove across the prairie and parked his jeep near us. He established a temporary altar on the hood of the vehicle, then asked us to send the word out that he would soon be administering mass. My friend Eddie Nunez and I secured our helmets, weapons, and web gear, and found a place in the right rear of the "congregation."

My experience with the Army Chaplin Corps was extremely limited. At Fort Benning, on one of my qualifying jumps at airborne school, an old Catholic chaplain jumped opposite door from me. I remember just before the green light activated, he gave us a "thumbs up." The jumpmaster (between the doors) grinned, shook his head from side-to-side, and gave us a "thumbs down." Since we all made it to the ground without incident or accident, apparently they were both correct. Later, we asked our jump cadre NCOs whether the priest was also getting his jump wings. The old sergeant grinned and informed us that the priest in question had the second highest number of parachute jumps in the Army.

The priest conducting the service that morning seemed to have been forged from the same metal as the padre at jump school. We--I should say the chaplain--barely got underway when some NVA on the hillside to the northeast sent a round or two into our perimeter. The chaplain paused in his ritual, produced two 45 caliber pistols from his kitbag, and unleashed about a dozen rounds in the general direction of the hill. Then he turned to us and announced that he was aware that the 45 caliber slugs had no chance of making it to the hillside, but plugging away just made him feel better. He then returned to the administration of his sacraments. This chaplain had to be a few cuts above typical—after all, how many pistol packing, priest paratroopers could there be?

When we returned to our platoon area, I was informed that I would help man an LP (listening post) that night. It seemed only fair since I hadn't had to pull guard the last two nights.

Considering that our perimeter was butted up against pretty thick vegetation which offered our opponents concealment almost to within grenade range of our positions, sending an early warning team down the trail seemed a tactical necessity. I wasn't aware at the time, but a repeat attack on the northern sector of the perimeter that we were manning was highly unlikely. Almost immediately after daylight that morning Major Hackworth had dispatched most of the battalion in a northerly direction in pursuit of the withdrawing enemy. Alpha (Abu) Company, Charlie (Cobra) Company, and Tiger Force were between us and the retreating NVA units. So the listening post was uneventful, and around 02:00 hours, we were called back into our perimeter and took up our original foxhole positions. The entire night passed quietly. Unbeknownst to us, the bloodiest battles were about to begin.

Brief Summary

Timeframe: 7 June 1966, Operation Hawthorne continues

Endnote: At the beginning of Operation Hawthorne, the NVA left their base camps and attacked ARVN and U.S. units. After these initial forays, the NVA shifted their tactics to ambushing American units that were advancing into their core areas. On 7 June the NVA was in attack mode.

****

[1] Sam Wolf. *"Operation HAWTHORNE 1 June 1966-21 June 1966."* Freerepublic.com. The FReeper Foxhole Remembers, 5 Feb 2004. Web. 26 Nov 2013.

[2] David Hackworth and Sherman, Julie. *About Face.* New York, New York: Simon and Schuster, 1989. 536. Print.

Chapter 4
Operation Hawthorne Heats Up
June 8-12, 1966

"When you're up to your ass in alligators, it's difficult to remember that your initial objective was to drain the swamp." – Adage on a psy-ops leaflet

The leaflets and the birddog seemed to have turned up together. As we broke camp and were heading toward the open prairie area, barely two hundred feet above the ground, an OV-1 birddog passed in front of us. The task of the pilot flying the small Cessna was to point tactical aircraft at enemy positions, thus the moniker. Typically this task was accomplished by targeting the enemy position with a smoke rocket. Sometimes an Army artillery FO accompanied the Air Force FAC pilot and coordinated artillery when appropriate.

The psy-ops guys had been busy also: the area had been introduced to a light sprinkling of leaflet literature. The purpose of leaflets varied. Some, written in Vietnamese, gave directions to safe areas for civilians, while others offered safe conduct to enemy soldiers desiring to surrender. Some, however, as the caption above illustrates, were designed for American troops offering a little "brothers-in-arms" humor to the situation. As the birddog passed to our right, the pilot "rocked" his wings, then the little Cessna turned north. In less than twenty minutes we would be following his lead.

*****

General Pearson had taken a position near the spot where the chaplain had conducted services the previous day. He shook our hands as we filed by en route to the helicopter PZ (pickup zone). I don't recall receiving any last minute special instructions. The mission had the appearance of a typical insertion into enemy territory. Fortunately, the insertion LZ was not hot, and we progressed unchallenged down a trail for awhile. Then, at a point where the path elbowed uphill to the left, the NVA made their presence known. A small number of uniformed regulars, occupying hastily prepared spider holes on slightly higher ground to the right, delivered a fusillade of automatic weapons fire on our point element. A "winner-take-all" firefight erupted.

My squad was last in the platoon order of march and not part of the initial response. The first two squads, with machine-gun sections from the weapons squad, were fully engaged. My squad was held in reserve in order to avoid what the older troopers referred to as a "cluster fuck" in the killing zone. When moving, the platoon had maintained a large interval between men. This certainly was a factor in reducing the number of casualties during the first moments of the ambush. Even so, several of our men were down.

By the time the platoon leader committed my squad to the fray, the situation had already started to turn in our favor. Our riflemen and gunners had neutralized some of the enemy positions and were focusing on the few remaining spider holes. Medics were working on several of the wounded who had been pulled to defilade cover. Moving forward, I spotted the lieutenant and his RTO just off the trail. About five meters on their right, a medic was working on one of our wounded—the short-timer, assistant machine gunner, who had told me about Tiger Force a week earlier. He had a stomach wound with about two inches of intestine poking through his abdominal wall. Prior to that day, I had no personal acquaintance with "shock." I knew of it only from descriptions in our first aid classes. The assistant gunner was staring at his exposed intestine. His eyes were sunken. His pallor was waxy. The expression "deer in the headlights," used to describe a panic glare, easily fit the look on the wounded man's face—panic and perhaps a sense of doom as well. I turned away leaving the medic to his job and continued to move forward.

As I was passing the CP group, the lieutenant beckoned me. He was concerned about the loss of the assistant gunner's weapon. When the medics and other troopers pulled the assistant gunner off the line, his weapon was left where he was shot. The LT asked me to keep an eye open for the weapon as I moved forward, and secure it if possible. I knew regaining the weapon was important. With that thought in mind, I resumed my task; actually, I started on a new one—recover the weapon.

The next step was obvious, find the machine gunner, which wasn't all that difficult considering the circumstances. I had started my dash forward running in a crouched position, but before long I was low-crawling. I located the MG quickly and I took up a position about three meters to his right. The rest of my squad had already taken up intervals to his left and were also laying down suppressive fire. The gunner paused a moment to chew me out for not getting down into the "low-crawling form of locomotion" much sooner than I had. If he had not been occupied with fighting a war at the time, he probably would have heaped more vituperation on me. Being an old timer, he had a self-imposed obligation to set my young cherry ass straight. With a nod of my head I acknowledged his advice, and then asked him to point me to the area where his assistant was hit. He managed a quick gesture to my right and then resumed firing. Sure enough, when I looked in the direction he had indicated, there in the open lay an M-16. With the gunner's caveat fresh in my mind, not to mention the organized chaos that was erupting around us, I quelled my first instinct to dash over and grab the weapon. Instead, I low-crawled.

I had snatched up the M-16 and was low-crawling back to the lieutenant's position when I became aware that cartridges were spilling out of the weapon. The rifle had taken a round through the magazine well--probably from the same burst that had hit the assistant gunner. The magazine had ruptured, the pressure spring was dangling down, and cartridges were falling out as I moved. I tried to eject the magazine, but the damage caused from the round passing through it had locked it solidly into the well. I dribbled cartridges back to the LT's position.

After I had turned the damaged M-16 over to the lieutenant and was turning back toward the line, I picked up part of a conversation between the medics working over the assistant gunner. In anguish, one of the medics was asserting that the assistant gunner never should have died, insisting that his wounds were not fatal--but shock was! I quickly made my way back to the firing line. This time, however, low-crawling wasn't required. The machine gunner with the rest of the team had silenced the last NVA spider hole. Some men began checking the enemy positions and bodies for anything of intelligence value. The remaining men either strengthened the security around the site, or lent a hand clearing an area for the evacuation of our casualties. I joined the LZ clearing detail.

With machetes and entrenching tools, we began opening a hole in the bamboo thicket large enough to fit a medevac Huey. The job was pretty much a "no-brainer"—speed was essential, the ships were probably already inbound. So, keeping an eye out for snakes, we set about the task of hacking open a patch of sunlight. As the clearing emerged so did the heat. We had no formal blueprint for a Huey-sized LZ. We just chopped and cleared until it felt right. About the time it felt right, the first medevac ship arrived. If my memory serves me accurately, we evacuated eleven casualties, two of which were fatalities. As the last chopper's rotor noise faded away, many of us paused a moment overcome by the ambiance of silence. Then, reality returned and we drifted back to our respective squads.

I rejoined a few of my team members gathered around the last spider hole on the right, the one nearest to where the assistant machine gunner had been shot. The body of the NVA soldier, which had collapsed back into the hole, was the topic of discussion among several of the squad members standing there. He didn't look Vietnamese. He was very tall and beefy. His face was round. He was balding with a ring of hair circling his head from ear to ear, resembling a medieval, tonsured monk. The consensus was that he was a Chinese advisor. His body type certainly didn't resemble the bodies of the former occupants of the spider holes to our left. They were more of what might be considered typical Vietnamese: short, slender, and thick-haired. Some of the bodies had also sunk down into the holes from which they had been fighting. Other bodies lay just to the side of their final fighting positions.

Another point of discussion soon surfaced among the old timers concerning tactics. Our opponent had set up a linear ambush with his positions parallel to the trail we were following. All his fire power came at our lead element from the right side of the trail; eventually head-on when the first two squads turned on-line to engage him. Some of the old timers pointed out that we could have been in a much bigger bind had the NVA positioned one of their spider holes where the trail elbowed to the left, forming an L-shaped ambush. From there, they could have raked fire on us from a second direction.

In retrospect, fighting from prepared positions had given the enemy a decided, but not necessarily decisive, advantage. The thick vegetation made a flanking maneuver by us impractical. That same dense undergrowth, however, did prevent the enemy from disengaging and making a quick dash to safety. Once our committed elements were on line and engaged in their fire and maneuver phase, the NVA were pinned in their spider holes. Fortunately, there weren't enough of them to overwhelm us. When we suffered a casualty, another man quickly took his place. The NVA, without replacements or an escape route, were doomed in their holes, which ultimately became their graves. True, we suffered some casualties and were delayed for a time, but before long, we were back on the trail again, heading wherever battalion was directing. Other elements of the battalion had also made contact with the enemy. And, Tiger Force was up to its ass in alligators.

Brief Summary

Endnotes: Only the officers were probably aware of what the battalion had in mind for my platoon of B company. We seemed to be running search and destroy operations away from the main action involving the other two line companies and Tiger Force. Perhaps we were screening a flank or in reserve. I can't say that I remember linking up with other battalion units during this phase of the operation. At any rate, I was acquiring combat experience that was a prerequisite for my eventual transition to Tiger Force.

****

Chapter 5
Tiger Hill
June 8, 1966

"I [Ward Just, reporter for the Washington Post] was with a reconnaissance platoon, forty people, deep in the highlands of South Vietnam. We ran into a lot of enemy soldiers. They thought it was somewhere between a battalion and a regiment of enemy. And I think within the space of an hour we had twelve dead and over twenty wounded in this group. We were bunched in very close, with the enemy all around us. Artillery fire was coming in that, in effect, saved our lives; otherwise we would have been overrun in a minute. These were very tough characters I was with, but there were literally hundreds of them, and there were forty of us." — Michelle Ferrari[1]

"The next morning, of the original forty-two Tigers, only sixteen were effective and nine of them were wounded." — Major David Hackworth[2]

"There was an army sergeant there named Pellum Bryant who really saved us that day. If it hadn't been for him, the whole thing would have been gone in fifteen minutes. By all reckoning, we should have been wiped out – the whole platoon should have been killed. But watching him maneuver, I swear to Christ, it was almost like watching a ballet dancer move back and forth. All of us are strung out on this trail, some at the high end, some at the low end, and I'm in the middle with the command post. Bryant is moving back and forth, left and right, firing as he goes. And not firing blindly – firing with purpose. It was somebody with superb confidence in himself and what he was doing. Just as a great musician must understand the importance of what he's playing, Pellum Bryant must have had an understanding in the back of his mind that his actions were going to save a lot of people. And all the time he was doing this kind of dance, back and forth, he did not speak a single word. I'll tell you truly, none of the things I saw in Vietnam had an effect on me like Pellum Bryant." --Christian Appy[3]

In the wee hours of the morning when the artillery base was attacked, battalion headquarters had directed the CO of Tiger Force to abandon his night ambush position and move to a new destination. The task was to intercept the NVA units withdrawing from their assault on the fire base. Abu and Cobra companies were given similar missions. Battalion's plan was to encircle the retreating NVA and draw the noose tight. However, the Tiger Force CO ignored battalion's directions and moved the Force to the artillery fire base instead, thus leaving an escape route open for the enemy. Immediately that morning, Major Hackworth dismissed the CO for not following directions and turned command of Tiger Force over to Captain Lewis Higinbotham. [4]

After a brief update by Major Hackworth, the Force (with its new commander plus a reporter from the *Washington Post*) took off in search of the base camps toward which the NVA units would be withdrawing. About dusk, Tiger Force made contact with some of the retreating NVA. The next day, the 8th of June, the Force entered an NVA base camp and was immediately embroiled in the battle of "Tiger Hill."

A brief aside here regarding terminology...The surviving members of the Force identify with three distinctly different battle sites: Tiger Field, Tiger Hill, and Tiger Valley.

"TIGER FIELD"

On the 7th of February 1966, operating out of Tuy Hoa, the Force, under the command of First Lieutenant James Gardner, attacked across an open expanse in order to take pressure off Bravo Company. Bravo Company was heavily engaged and suffered 19 KIAs and many wounded.[5] The Force suffered twelve casualties, five of which were KIAs.[6] Posthumously, Lieutenant Gardner was awarded the Congressional Medal of Honor for his action that day. The command of the Force then fell upon Lieutenant Dennis Foley.

"TIGER HILL"

On 8 June 1966, at Dak To, the Force, under the command of Captain Lewis Higinbotham, entered an NVA base camp. Of the 42 men, only 7 were not casualties; 8 were KIA, 27 were WIA.[7]

"TIGER VALLEY"

In a day-long battle on 15 May 1967, the Force, under the leadership of 1st Lieutenant Gary Forbes, suffered 22 wounded and 4 KIAs. The supporting helicopter battalion conducting the extraction of the 1/327's wounded reported it as "by far the worst day ever suffered by the Battalion." Eight slicks and seven gunships were hit from intense ground fire.[8]

*****

Following the major's briefing and pep talk at the artillery position, Tiger Force mounted choppers and continued the battalion's effort to re-establish contact with the enemy. After insertion, the Force moved forward on a well-used trail. Indicators of pending combat were abundantly evident. Blood spots, soiled bandages, and recently dug defensive positions all confirmed that the withdrawing NVA units had passed that way. In late afternoon, light contact with the NVA was made. The Force established a defensive perimeter for the night and returned to the search the following day. About noon, the Force reached a point where the trail they were following intersected with another larger path. Captain Higinbotham sent Sergeant Pellum Bryant's element to scout the lower trail to the right; Sergeant Tom Day's team was part of that force. Sergeant Charlie Evans' team was directed to reconnoiter the new branch which progressed uphill. Before long, both elements were taken under fire. A member of Sergeant Evans' force sustained a serious neck wound. Captain Higinbotham recalled Sergeant Day's element and sent them to reinforce Sergeant Evans. The enemy broke contact and withdrew. The Force continued uphill into a large NVA base camp.

The camp complex was secluded under a dense vegetation canopy, making it almost indiscernible from the air. Its size was estimated as capable of housing somewhere between two companies to a battalion of NVA personnel. If the conservative estimate was accurate, if the enemy were still in the area, the Force was outnumbered by at least four to one. Rucksacks were consolidated in one location, and a few Tigers were left to guard them while the remainder of the Force swept the compound.

The camp appeared abandoned: troop barracks, instructional arenas, ammo caches, equipment, uniforms, tunnels, and simmering cooking pots, but no NVA. The enemy apparently vacated the camp in a hurry. The *Washington Post* correspondent wrote that Captain Higinbotham voiced concern for their situation.[9] After the Force had checked out most of the camp, Sergeants Day and MacDonald moved up toward the last rise to clear the remaining area. As the sergeants approached the uppermost crest, a flurry of mumbled "Vietnamese" preceded the NVA's counterattack.

From prepared positions on the surrounding high ground, the NVA had initiated their attack by raking the forward elements of the Force with heavy automatic weapons' fire. Not long into the exchange of fire, a round passed through both of Sergeant Day's lungs. Sergeant MacDonald, also wounded, rolled down hill seeking cover, but he didn't survive the day. The Force was in survival mode. At the time, Army doctrine suggested that an attacking force have a strength ratio of at least three-to-one over a defending force. The strength ratio was in the NVA's favor. Within the first fifteen minutes of fighting, nine Tigers were hit, three of them KIAs. By the end of the first hour, three more Tigers were killed and the friendly WIA count was plus twenty; more than half of the members of the Force had been hit. [10]

The enemy's attack plan was solid. They commanded the high ground on the west, north and east, thus horse-shoeing above three-quarters of the Force. On the west, along with their standard riflemen armed with AKs, they incorporated snipers and RPDs (light machine guns). For the individual members of the Force, cover was a much sought after commodity. Some Tigers were lucky and found vacant "spider holes" dug by the previous tenants of the camp. Behind a small cluster of bamboo to the left of the CP group, Sergeant Evans and his men found some holes to take cover.

The Force's initial advance through the base camp was roughly from south to north. As casualties mounted, the Force retracted its defensive perimeter toward the south until most of the wounded and those still capable of fighting were centered around the CP group.[11]

Following their initial fusillade, the NVA mounted a ground attack, pressuring the surviving members of the Force on all sides. Platoon Sergeant Pellum Bryant rallied the defense against the enemy attacks from the rear. All his men were wounded before the fight was over. Sergeant Evans also held his position protecting the Force's left flank. Although pinned down by machine-gun fire, they managed to repel the enemy force that was trying to advance on the CP group from the west. By the end of the engagement, the bamboo cluster in front of their spider holes resembled gnawed celery. Before the day ended, all of Sergeant Evans' men were also wounded in the encounter.

The NVA overran the position where the rucksacks were consolidated. Two Tigers, SP4 Rockford Goddard and PFC Edward Christie, were killed. CPT Chris Verlumis, Headquarters Company commandant, who had volunteered to accompany the Force on this operation, along with PFC Sam Washburn, went forward to reconnoiter and assist the remaining Tigers at the rucksack location. Washburn and Verlumis killed three NVA, but the captain lost his life in the effort. Washburn barely made it back to the CP location before the NVA launched a direct ground attack on the CP perimeter.

The Force had held out for more than five hours. The main factor contributing to the Force's continuing survival was the judicious and accurate mix of artillery, helicopter gunships, and close air support, employed under "danger-close" parameters.

While the battle raged on "Tiger Hill," C Company and A Company were maneuvering to assist the Force. These companies were also subjected to NVA attacks designed to impede their progress. As daylight was fading, enemy resistance stalled C Company about one hundred meters from the Force's location. The commander of A Company deployed his platoons to take the high ground to the west and north in an effort to cordon off the entire battle site. This relieved the pressure on C Company and they continued their thrust forward. The NVA made one last ditch effort to overrun the Tiger CP group. Here the correspondent, Ward Just, was wounded by grenade fragments. Sam Washburn also had his hand mangled, but he and the remainder of the CP group killed five of the NVA and broke the enemy's advance. C Company's lead platoon arrived with war whoops and hollers and quickly established a secure zone around the Force. The medics went to work immediately. Meanwhile, A Company took over control of the high ground, cordoning off the site. The NVA withdrew to the north and east. The onus of responsibility then shifted to medevacing the critically wounded.

Battalion Operations was notified that eight of the critically wounded probably would not survive the night. They needed immediate medical evacuation to the Mobile Army Surgical Hospital (MASH) at Pleiku. Time was running out. The mission required a volunteer crew to hover a large helicopter with hoist-basket capabilities above the forest canopy, in the dark, about one hundred feet above the ground, and bring up the eight wounded Tigers, while operating within range of enemy gunners on the adjacent ridges. CPT Thomas Agerton, Battalion S4 at the time, started working the theater support assets. An Air Force Search and Rescue crew answered the call and volunteered for the mission. As green Chicom tracers from the nearby ridges arched around them, an Air Force HH-44 HUSKY helicopter extracted the eight critically wounded Tigers and delivered them to the MASH unit at Pleiku. One Tiger was KIA on arrival.

Sergeant Tom Day, who was seriously wounded and thought dead, was evacuated on that HUSKY. The individual **not** evacuated on that aircraft was the *Post* correspondent. For the military, removing a civilian from harm's way is a high priority, particularly if that civilian has already been wounded! Major Hackworth described himself as being in a state of "fury" when he learned that the correspondent was not listed as being delivered to the hospital. Communications with Captain Higinbotham soon revealed that Ward Just had deferred "priority booking" on the evacuation chopper to allow room for a more critically wounded Tiger. Valor and gallantry were obviously not the sole provinces of the military at "Tiger Hill."

The following is Sergeant Tom Day's unedited personal account of his experience at Tiger Hill, with additional insight from Ian Kemp

My name is Thomas P. Day. I was a member of "Tiger Force," the all volunteer Reconnaissance unit of the 1st Battalion, 327th Infantry, 101st Airborne Division. Tiger Force was made up of an A Team and B Team, each team consisting of about 25 men. Rarely did both teams operate together.

On the night of 5 June 1966, the entire Tiger Force was in an ambush position overlooking a well-used trail. Early in the morning we received orders by radio to leave our position and

Tom Day, photo courtesy of Tom Day

move to an artillery battery position that was being overrun by a North Vietnamese Army (NVA) unit. Soon after leaving our position we began to hear the sounds of a terrific firefight. Our guide was the noise of rifles, machine guns and artillery fire which increased as we approached the battle. We halted for minutes on the trail several times. Sergeant McDonald and I discussed what the reasons were for our hesitation. There was no need to consult our compasses, as we could plainly hear the firing ahead. The sun was rising and in the dim light we were now finding bloody bandages and gobs of blood on the trail. A commo wire was found and was cut. It led to the perimeter of the artillery position. The sounds of the fight ahead were diminishing and soon ceased. There were choppers picking up the dead and wounded as we reached the scene of battle. Sergeant McDonald and I figured Tiger Force should have arrived sooner, and we would have, except for all the pauses on the way. There were 16 American soldiers killed and an estimated 87 NVA dead. Most of the NVA dead were carried off by their comrades.

Major Hackworth, our Battalion CO, gathered all the Tigers later that day and gave us a real 'gung ho' speech. He said we will never run across a better location to find and kill the NVA than our current area of operations. He introduced us to our new Tiger Force leader, Captain Higinbotham. I later learned from reading retired

Colonel Hackworth's autobiography, *About Face*, that our platoon leader had been relieved from command for disobedience the same day. That was explanation enough to Sergeant McDonald and me as to why we had not arrived at the artillery position in time to assist them in their defense.

    The Tigers were choppered to a landing zone, "LZ", in the jungle. We exited the choppers into elephant grass at about 12 to 15 feet elevation. The momentum caused me to fall to my knees, and my pack then swung over my head and broke the skin on my nose. I got up onto my feet and looked into the laughing face of the crew chief as the chopper lifted up. We moved into the jungle and soon found a well-used trail system. Our main function on this operation was to find and engage the NVA. This was not a normal mission for the Tigers. We were a Recon Unit, and most of our missions were just that. What we were engaged in now was a Combat Patrol.

    We chose the most heavily used trail and followed it. After several hours of finding numerous abandoned fighting holes, bunkers, and more and more fresh footprints, there was a sudden burst of automatic fire from the rear of our column. It was over in a minute. There was one dead uniformed NVA, his AK 47 and a blood trail into the jungle. PFC Richard Garcia had been shot in the chest. The medic did what he could for him, but he died in an hour. Our location under dense tree cover did not allow for evacuation. That night every third man was awake and on guard. At dawn there was another burst of automatic fire as three NVA soldiers fled hastily down the trail from our position. I had an acute feeling, a foreboding of some terrible danger we were in, as we continued cautiously following the trail in the morning. An LZ was made in a small clearing. PFC Garcia's body, pack, and rifle were put aboard a chopper. At midday as we patrolled a path alongside a small stream about 10 meters wide, we came upon a junction with a wider trail leading up a hill on our left. Bravo Team was directed up the hill. Alpha Team, leaving several men behind with Captain Higinbotham, continued down the river trail. Contact with the NVA was made by both teams about 150 meters on each trail. There were two serious firefights taking place. Bravo had a man down with a serious neck wound, and was trying with great difficulty to carry him up a steep muddy hill. Captain Higinbotham radioed Alpha with instructions to disengage and return to the headquarters element. Packs were dropped and six men were picked to guard them and the rear of the trail. A radio was left with them. I chose PFC Christy to remain with the packs as he was the youngest of my team. I truly believed with all my heart he would be safer as part of the rear element. The remainder of Alpha continued up the trail toward the sound of the gunfire.

The firing died out and the NVA withdrew as Alpha joined Bravo. We entered a commander's fondest dream, one that occurs rarely. Tiger Force was in the middle of a large NVA base camp. There were cases of ammo and grenades, tunnels, fighting holes; there was rice still warm in the pots, pieces of uniform littered about, all evidence of a hasty exit. While some of the men explored, others were trying to make an LZ to evacuate PFC Wilt, who was in serious condition. It was an impossible job with the equipment on hand. There was nothing available other than our personal knives. I chopped on a tree with the circumference of a football with my Bowie knife and then handed over knife and job when I tired.

Sergeant MacDonald, Sergeant Donavon, and I headed uphill to an area that had not been investigated. We were spread several meters apart and continued finding holes with equipment in, and around them. We discussed whether we were in a Company or Battalion-sized base camp. We knew that Tiger Force was vastly outnumbered if the base camp had its full complement of NVA to fill all the fighting holes we found. We heard rustling sounds from uphill and snapping of small branches. One of us, I don't remember who (it might have been me), called out loud enough for everyone to hear "there is movement up hill!" At the sound of the warning, automatic weapons fire and grenades began to fall around us. We returned fire on full automatic.

The Tigers were surrounded. In a short while our artillery rounds were bursting in trees and around our perimeter. I was lying between Mac and Donavan; we were about three meters apart. Donavan begin edging over towards me. I could see machine rounds impacting; dirt, leaves and other debris were being flung up on the far side of him. I began edging towards Mac, he began edging also. The three of us were moving sideways to the left, and trying to stay out of the NVA sight. Mac came up against a tree, pressed his M16 to his chest and rolled downhill. I looked down behind me, and could see only dead and wounded Tigers. I could see and hear the bullets impacting on human flesh. They made a thunk, thunk, thunk sound. I was close to the tree now, and put a new magazine in my rifle. I realized the magazine was from my second ammo pouch, which meant I had fired over 100 rounds.

I was almost ready to roll downhill when I felt a terrific hammer blow to my chest. I put my right hand on my shirt and felt a wound in my left side chest. I told Donavan "I'm hit," and he said "I am too." I could feel blood running down my back and hear the swishing sound of air with every breath. The bullet had gone through both lungs. I placed my right index finger in the hole in my chest but could do nothing to stop the bleeding or air from the exit wound. There was no pain at this time, just a great sense of exhaustion and lethargy. I must have lost consciousness for awhile for I found myself alone when I regained consciousness. I was approximately 10 meters uphill from anyone alive. I called to the guys behind me, I told them I needed someone to stop the bleeding from my back. Sergeant Aikins, a good friend and card-playing partner of mine, said, "Tommy keep your head down." I said, "I need you to stop the bleeding from my back." His reply was, "I can't Tommy, I'm shot in the back and holding Sergeant B's stomach. If I let go his guts will pop out."

I was passing in and out of consciousness. I came to one time and heard the platoon sergeant or someone calling roll. He would call out a name and the reply back would be, "he's dead" or "he's wounded" or sometimes the reply was "here." I heard them call Mac's name, and the reply was "he's dead." I felt so much sorrow, so many of my friends were dead, I wished Mac had stayed with me; maybe he would still be alive. My name was called and the reply was "he's dead." "I'm not," I said, but no one could hear me anymore. I came to again one time and heard someone yell for everyone to get in a hole and keep your head down. We are calling the artillery down on our perimeter, the NVA are inside. The rounds came in, 105's and 155 rounds were impacting inside our perimeter. I could hear screaming from both NVA and Tigers as they were hit. I heard someone yell that Sergeant B had his leg blown off. The rifles firing, the grenades, the artillery…we were now being supported by airplanes dropping 200 and 500 pound bombs. The noise was constant and ear-shattering.

I lost consciousness again and when I came to the firing and grenades had tapered off. Looking up the hill I could see two NVA soldiers peering down at me. They were 15 to 20 meters away looking at me over a fallen tree. Their faces were dispassionate, no emotion whatsoever. They knew I was badly wounded, but alive. I was hoping they would not shoot me again. I believe they were using me as bait, waiting for someone to come to my aid. I was now in pain and distress, not so much from my wounds, but from my ammo pouches and the grenades attached to them. As the ground beneath me became wet with my blood, I would slip down an inch or two. My web belt with the ammo pouches dug into my chest. I had no use of my arms to pull the web belt down, or take it off. Occasionally one or the other of the NVA soldiers threw a grenade downhill. I knew it was only a matter of time before a grenade bounced off a tree limb or fell short. It happened as I knew it would; there was an explosion near me and I felt a sharp pain in my lower back.

Ian Kemp, photo courtesy of Ian Kemp

I (Ian Kemp) heard Sgt. Akins tell me to try and reach a badly wounded Sgt. Day from Alpha Force who lay a very small distance up the slope. I inched up the slope knowing that it was a bad idea, but I had to try. Even then I was hesitant, as I did not know how badly (Tom) Day was hurt, and I could only imagine the terrible pain that he was probably in, and the likelihood of moving him would only make things a lot worse. I was so close to grabbing Day's foot. I had also thought at the time that the NVA were also likely using him as a decoy, and this proved to be the case. The decision was made for me; NVA fire passed between my outstretched hand and Day's foot—just like in the movies I thought, but this was no movie. I was showered with debris but not hit. I slithered back down the slope and told Sgt. Akins that if Day was not already dead, to attempt to rescue him would ensure both of us getting killed.[12]

Author's note: Ian Kemp was born in England and served in our army during the Vietnam conflict. He was awarded a Silver Star for his actions during this engagement at Dak To in 1966.

When next I regained consciousness it was dark and there was a medic working on me. He explained that he could not find a vein, so he would have to do a cut-in. I did not feel a thing. He told me I was lucky to have survived for five hours lying on the hill alone. I awoke again lying in a wire basket being lifted through the trees. There was a chopper hovering above me. I could see the green tracers emerge from out of the darkness as the NVA machine gunners attempted to shoot us down. The chopper evacuated eight of us to a MASH landing pad in complete darkness. There was a quick triage on the pad and five Tigers left in the ambulance. I was left with one live and one dead Tiger lying in the dark. I was cold and shivering. I could look up into the chopper and see that the pilot was crying. He said something to the crewman, who then jumped out of the chopper and placed a blanket around two of us. He said that they had to leave but that someone would come for us soon. When the chopper lifted off the pad it blew the blanket off. I never felt so cold, alone, and abandoned.[13]

Brief Summary of Operation Hawthorne[14]

Timeframe: 2-21 June 1966
Base Camp: Dak To, Kontum Province
Area of Operations: About 18 kilometers northeast of Dak To airstrip
Enemy Situation: The 24th NVA Regiment was operating in the AO
Mission: Search and destroy and lift siege on outpost Toumorong
Other Considerations: Troops at Toumorong relieved and post vacated
After Action Assessment: 45 friendly KIA, 241 friendly WIA, 1 friendly MIA, 531 enemy KIA, 22 enemy captured, 88 enemy individual and 21 enemy crew served weapons captured

****

[1]Michelle Ferrari, "WARD JUST: Getting to the Story," Reporting America at War: An Oral History. Hyperion, 2003. Print.
[2]David Hackworth and Sherman, Julie, About Face, New York, New York: Simon and Schuster, 1989. Print. p. 540
[3]Christian Appy, "Patriots," interview with Ward Just, p. 136.
[4.]David Hackworth and Sherman, Julie, About Face, New York, New York: Simon and Schuster, 1989. Print. pp. 537 & 538.
[5]The Virtual Wall, Vietnam Veterans Memorial, Casualties by Unit, Army, 1/327 Inf Bat, 2 Feb 1966.
[6]Dennis Foley, Special Men A LRP's Recollections, New York, New York: Ballantine Books, 1994. pp. 182-188.

[7] David Hackworth and Sherman, Julie, About Face, New York, New York: Simon and Schuster, 1989. Print. p. 540.
[8] 14 CAB ORL for 15 May 1967, Unit History Information, for: 176 AHC, 14 CAB, 178 ASHC, 1st BDE, 101 ABN, for 15 May 1967, 31 July 1967.
[9] Ward Just, To What End: Report from Vietnam, Houghton Mifflin, 1966. Print, p. 7.
[10] Ibid., p 9.
[11] Charles Evans, Notes and Sketches from conversation with Lewis Higinbotham.
[12] Ian Kemp, unpublished, edited document.
[13] Thomas Day, unpublished, unedited document.
[14] MACV Command History. Cc SEA/Chronology/MACV/_1966.html.

Chapter 6
B-52s, Inward Season
June 13-21, 1966

"If at first you don't succeed, call in an air strike." —Laws of War tee shirt adage

"On Monday morning, June 13th, while the mountain mist was slowly rising from the valley, 24 waves of bombers created a maze of craters below. As the 1/327 and the 2/502 swept into the hills to clean up what was left, they found a systematic series of tunnels, some going as deep as 50 feet, but they also found among the dead and dying, several score who fought on. The final of Operation Hawthorne was ferreting out and killing or capturing the diehards." --SamWolf[1]

The day after "Tiger Hill," the 1/327 continued Operation Hawthorne, but with some intermediate tasks. C Company of the 2/502, under the command of CPT William Carpenter, had also been under heavy attack and suffered many casualties. Abu Company, 1/327 was diverted to help the 2/502.

Sergeant Charlie Evans and some of the Tigers still functioning after "Tiger Hill" were attached to Cobra Company, 1/327. My platoon of Bravo Company had not been diverted to support these units. For the next few days, we continued with what seemed like normal search and destroy missions.

Normal, except we didn't seem to be searching areas in which the enemy was operating. We found no fresh evidence indicating that a large NVA unit was present in our AO. One morning, we started off, made a big circle and ended up pretty much where were started. On another day, we passed through an ARVN unit that had stopped for lunch on a trail. We were moving cross-country, cutting trail, and we proceeded through them at right angles. The pass-through was well coordinated and without incident; however, I was amazed at how much noise emanated from their usage of metal rice cooking pots and mess kits. We heard the ARVNs way before we saw them. And their red scarves didn't lend well to the principle of concealment.

Frequently these cross-country excursions took us right up the sides of some extremely mountainous terrain, usually requiring a lot of scrambling. Often we lost our footing and slid backwards into the man or men behind us. Each day produced nothing substantial; the NVA was not occupying the terrain we were searching. Some troops even debated whether we were searching for the enemy or confirming where he wasn't. Then, one afternoon, without much notice, battalion extracted us to our Dak To base camp.

Back in our company areas, the sergeants told us not to get too comfortable--hit the mess tent and make ready to return to the field in the morning. Brigade had ordered a B-52 strike in our AO. Our mission would be to assess the effectiveness of the air strike. The next morning we were choppered back to the AO.

Before setting us down at one end of the strike run, our choppers paralleled the path of destruction. Different 1/327 units were inserted at various places. Conducting a Battle Damage Assessment, following a carpet-bombing mission, isn't as easy as one might imagine. At least not this one.

The strike had created a unique obstacle to travel. The bombing produced deep, large depressions that could easily accommodate a truck. A mountain line (from ridge to valley floor) that should have been lush with the same green foliage of the surrounding hills, instead looked like a hunk of moldy Swiss cheese, with a patina of grey soil dusting the remaining vegetation that fringed the impact craters. Anything caught in that zone of destruction was pretty much toast. Few critters, man, bird, or mole, are fast enough to outrun that kind of carnage. The bomb pits themselves weren't much of an obstacle. Although the soil was crumbly when dry, it posed only a slight challenge to foot travel, much like negotiating beach dunes. However, the remaining strands of vegetation riming the edges of these craters were a different matter. Each bomb pushed the vegetation (chiefly splintered and shattered bamboo) away from the center of the blast. Where the craters met, the shredded bamboo interlaced like pikes in medieval earthworks. Moving from crater to crater was an effort like passing through briers. To make matters worse, with the trees gone, there was no shade.

What we had been told to look for in this diorama of bark and earth was body parts. But what chance did a human body have of remaining recognizable against a force that shredded huge trees into beauty bark--and then covered everything with grey dust? My platoon found no one, dead or alive. According to Sergeant Charlie Evans, Cobra Company came across a few bedraggled NVA survivors who were more than ready to become POWs.

We stayed in the surrounding area a few more days to insure that the enemy had withdrawn from the zone. According to the military historians, Operation Hawthorne ended officially on 21 June. But our battalion would continue to work out of the Dak To air strip for another month.

*****

Back in our company area north of the air strip, we gathered our duffel bags from the supply tent, and formed around our First Sergeant near the section of the perimeter we had previously been assigned to defend. We seldom stayed in the base camp for any length of time. Three days would be considered long. The routine usually started with a trip to the shower point where we cleaned up and exchanged our soiled fatigues for clean pairs. This was generally followed by a trip to the mess tent for a non-C-ration meal; more important, brewed coffee! Weapons maintenance wasn't an issue; we kept them clean and ready. Sometimes there were a few tidbits of information that the First Sergeant needed to impart. This was one of those occasions.

Top informed us that the battalion reconnaissance element, Tiger Force, which had sustained heavy casualties on the eighth of June, was looking for replacement volunteers from the line units. I didn't toy over the decision long. I liked B Company and the men that I served with, yet something drew me towards the reconnaissance unit. My lateral transfer was quick. I was signed off B Company's roster, walked from their orderly room (tent) over to Headquarters and Headquarters Company's orderly room (tent), reported in, and was picked up on their roster. I shook hands with several NCOs and team members and started to get acquainted with the unit.

So, three days prior to my nineteenth birthday, I had made one of those seemingly insignificant, mundane decisions that end up affecting a person's character forever. Of course, at that age I didn't devote a great deal of time pondering the distant future. Considering the circumstances and the environment, twenty-nine seemed old, and a long way off.

*****

My "get-acquainted" period with Tiger Force lasted one entire night. The next day, Captain Higinbotham, commanding officer of Tiger Force, formed up the platoon and asked whether anyone had any experience with the French language. By the end of the next operation, I could no longer debate the wisdom of my high school counselor for insisting that I included a foreign language in my curriculum. Indeed, I should have challenged myself more in this area, but it was "water under the bridge" by then. At any rate, I had two years of high school French and I was soon to understand why the captain was interested in troops that possessed the rudiments of the French language.

Following "Tiger Hill," the Force was reduced to less than a third of its former complement of experienced personnel. In order to continue the mission of providing reconnaissance to the battalion, the Force would be supplemented with CIDG (Civil

Indigenous Defense Group) troops on loan from the local Special Forces camp. The CIDG forces in this area were largely Montagnard (pronounced: *mountain yard, sometimes montyard*) tribesmen. Quite a few of these local natives spoke French from the period in the early 1950s when France tried to re-establish itself in Indo-China. The tactical concept that the captain had developed was to insert eleven-man reconnaissance teams into the battalion's area of operations. Each would be composed of three Americans and eight Montagnards. The lingua franca, in this case, was "franca" or at least "pidgin franca" augmented with a large amount of "kinesics/gesticulation." The Force put together several of these teams. *"Inward Season"* plus a numerical designator was the radio call sign for these units. I was in the third group; our radio call sign was *"Inward Season Three."*

Brief Summary of Operation Hawthorne[2]

Timeframe: 2–21 June 1966
Base camp: Dak To, Kontum Province
Area of Operations: About 18 kilometers northeast of Dak To airstrip
Enemy Situation: The 24th NVA Regiment was operating in the AO
Mission: Search and Destroy and lift siege on outpost Toumorong
Other Considerations: Troops at Toumorong relieved and post vacated . Hawthorne is merging into Operation Beauregard (Eagle Bait) which commences on 24 June.
After Action Assessment: 45 friendly KIA, 241 friendly WIA, 1 friendly MIA, 531, enemy KIA, 22 enemy captured, 88 enemy individual and 21 enemy crew served weapons captured

****

[1] Sam Wolf, *"Operation HAWTHORNE, 1 June 1966-21 June 1966."* Freerepublic.com. The Freeper Foxhole Remembers.
[2] MACV Command History listed in Wikiedia.org under military operations Vietnam 1966.

Chapter 7
Dining with the Montagnards
June 24-30, 1966

"And here were forests ancient as the hills, enfolding sunny spots of greenery." –Samuel Coleridge, "Kubla Khan"

After the morning formation, we were told to draw equipment and meet back at the staging area, to hook up with the other personnel in our teams, and to receive our mission briefing. The general composition of each team was three U.S. personnel and eight CIDG Montagnards. The veteran Force member on Inward Season Three was John Kado. John easily fit the moniker "quiet giant." He would handle point for most of the operation. The third American on our team was a Specialist Fifth Class whose name I don't recall. He only lasted a few days. Supposedly he had served with MACV (Military Advisory Command Vietnam) Rangers, but it quickly became obvious that his field experience was very limited. In retrospect, I believe that this mission with Tiger Force was his first real combat venture. Regardless, at that point John Kado and I knew nothing of his background. Since he outranked both of us, we figured that he would be the person leading the team. The captain, however, issued me the map, the compass, the radio and sent me to the team leaders' briefing. The Spec-Five got the M-60 machine gun. It seemed a little out of the ordinary, but Tiger Force wasn't your typical line unit. I sensed this early in the game.

The ranking man from the CIDG contingent was a stockily built sergeant about thirty-five to forty years of age, with a gold filling in his front incisor. A white star was formed by the enameled portion of his tooth that was not covered in gold. I always addressed him as "Sergeant," so his surname has escaped my memory. Three of the CIDG troops I can still recall by name.

'Han', about in his late twenties, was related to twin brothers about eighteen years of age, named 'Wien' and 'Huen.' Since I never saw any of their names in print, the spelling here is phonetic. Whenever I went out on patrol, these three troops accompanied me. Two of the other Montagnard troops were considerably older than the sergeant. They displayed no apparent military rank, yet over the course of the next few days, when important decisions had to be made, these two individuals were always consulted. They had particular knowledge about which trails to take, which areas to avoid, or where to find vine bridges across swift streams. I assumed that they were tribal elders. Their advice was considered valid regardless of any military designation.

All of the Montagnards were armed with Second World War and Korean War era American weapons. The M-1 and M-2 carbines were common along with a sprinkling of M-3 grease guns. Some sported conventional green fatigues, while others wore the tiger-striped camouflaged patterns. The tiger stripes were also a favorite among the Americans. I wore a set for awhile, but they had some drawbacks, including the fact they dried very poorly. The Army jungle shirt, however, dried quickly. Bedding down in wet tiger fatigues was like sleeping with a damp towel wrapped around you. They also developed a distinctive odor. I endured the striped fatigues for about a month until sleeping wet, and smelling stale, compelled me back to the Army's quick-drying jungle shirt. I guess that the more experience I gained "in country," the greater consideration I gave to maintaining my "creature-comforts-zone."

*****

In my entire sixteen month stay with Tiger Force, I was never given a typical "sneak and peek," reconnaissance-only mission-- the kind where you were expected to stay hidden and merely observe the enemy. We were expected to damage the enemy; to remove him and his weapon from the field. My first operation with the Force illustrated this concept. Teams were inserted by Hueys roughly a kilometer or two from each other. If a team made contact with an enemy force larger than it could comfortably handle, the team needed to hold on for a while until support arrived. We had a lot of heavy ordinance at our disposal: tactical air, artillery, battalion mortars. Besides these, each of us carried a small arsenal in our rucksacks: claymore mines, plastic explosive, fragmentation grenades, white phosphorous grenades, and light anti-tank weapons to name a few.

After deploying from the choppers, we formed into our line-of-march with John Kado at point and me directly behind him in the slack position. Both of us were armed with M-16s. I also carried the team's PRC-25 radio. The Spec-Five followed us with the M-60 machine gun. Behind him, following in tandem, were the eight CIDG.

Almost from the get-go, the Spec-Five had trouble with his load. His problem was that he wasn't used to "humping," to carrying a load. I understood his plight. Two months earlier, when I first went to the field, I had no rucksack. I had to stuff my five days of C-rations into socks and tie the socks onto my field pack. This "fanny pack" spent most of the day trying to push my backbone out through my navel. I spent the better part of my first couple weeks in the field retying the socks and readjusting my load. I also went into the field with slick soled, Army-issued black stateside "combat" boots. The older troopers facetiously referred to these government-issued, parade ground baubles as "traction masters." I say facetious because traction was a characteristic unrelated to their performance. Every slick, wet, moss-infested rock provided an opportunity for those flat-soled boots to demonstrate their true nature--that they were in fact miniature skate boards. Then one day, after a resupply drop, the First Sergeant called me over to the company CP area and issued me a rucksack and new pair of lug-soled jungle boots. My metamorphosis was instantaneous. I felt as sure-footed as a mountain goat. From that point onward, my days were certainly more comfortable and less exhausting.

The Spec-five, however, had a rucksack and jungle boots. He just wasn't used to "humping-the-boonies." His problem was mostly psychological, and would pass if he gave it time. In the meantime, we were only as fast as the slowest man, so we started to share his load. Most of the gun ammo was dispersed among the CIDG troops. I took the machine gun, some of his ammo, and other military hardware. Eventually, he also gave away most of his C-rations. Fortunately, the area where we were supposed to set up a patrol base was only about four kilometers from the insertion point. Once there, we left the Spec-five in base security with a few of the Montagnards while we reconnoitered.

*****

Our area of operations was pretty much thick vegetation which occasionally gave way to open areas. Most of the open areas contained remnants of habitation, usually some cleared ground and a few unoccupied, dilapidated hooches. The Montagnards seemed very familiar with the area, and I sensed that they formerly lived here before being relocated to the Special Forces Camp at Dak To.

Our patrolling concentrated on trail networks that branched along and out from the local river, the Dak Poko. Except in a few places, the stream was an obstacle to travel. We encountered some vine suspension bridges, all in a sad state of repair. In one or two spots, the river was fordable. As for signs of recent use or military activity, there were none. No smoldering fires, no footprints in the mud, no punji stakes, no domesticated animals, no NVA, and no civilians. In that whole first week, in our area of operations, we encountered not one living soul. Yet, for the first time since I arrived in country, I felt that I was directly contributing to our military purpose. I'm sure that it had a lot to do with my new found sense of autonomy. Captain Higinbotham radioed instructions concerning our mission parameters, but he didn't tell us how to run the missions. We set up the patrol compositions, decided who did the reconnoitering, who guarded the base camp, where to meet, and when to eat. As the fifth day rolled around and we were nearing the end of our standard issue of C-rations, the weather turned sour, and we were informed that no resupply would be possible until the weather cleared. No one was venturing to predict when that might happen.

With only a few cans of C-rations left, and facing the prospect of having to go some time before the next resupply, Kado and I elected to start living off the land. Army training had presented scenarios where we might have to survive on our own resources for a given period of time. Our situation certainly wasn't unique; all of the other teams were in the same predicament. So we set about assessing our options and informing the rest of the team of the resupply situation. In the local Montagnard pidgin dialect "ga" meant food and "ga-ga" meant to eat. So, with our pidgin-franca we conveyed our situation to the Sergeant. He seemed unfazed. The Yards had quite a bit of rice left from their indigenous rations. What we were lacking was protein. The Sergeant suggested "poisson," the French term for fish. We didn't have any traditional fishing gear, i.e. poles, line, bait, or tackle. But, we had a sundry of explosive devices. So, with little ado, John, about four of the CIDG, and I set off to "grenade" some fish.

Not long into our trek we found a deep fishing hole on a small isolated stream that fed into the Dak Poko River. The Yards positioned themselves about twenty meters downstream from the hole at a bend in the stream. The plan was simple. Throw a grenade into the deep hole. The explosion disorients the fish. They float to the surface. The current carries them down to the Yards who are waiting at the bend in the shallow water. The Yards snag the fish and throw them up on to the dry rocks.

John threw the first grenade...nothing happened. Naturally, we suspected that the water had dampened the fuse, so we tried a

Kado grenade fishing by the Dak Poko River, photos courtesy of Leo Heaney

second grenade. Again, nothing happened. While I was giving the situation some thought, I glimpsed over at one of the older Montagnards who we had positioned on the bank for security. He was making a gesture at me not unlike someone back in the States soliciting a ride hitchhiking. He was flicking his thumb up. Finally, nirvana struck and I understood. He was telling me to "spoon" the grenade. In military jargon, the safety handle on the grenade is referred to as the "spoon." The M-26 fragmentation grenade explodes about four and a half seconds after the handle, the "spoon," pops off. One is said to be "cooking" the grenade if they delay throwing the device for a few seconds after popping the handle. In combat, this precludes an enemy from picking up the grenade and lobbing it back at the thrower. The old Montagnard was gesturing to John and me to cook the grenade a few seconds, giving the primer time to ignite before throwing the grenade into the water. The third grenade worked much better than imagined. Fish started floundering to the surface, belly up. The Montagnards at the catch area were working like automatons, cupping fish in their hands and tossing them up on the rocky shore. In that brief window of time, we had procured one hundred and five good sized trout, and lost equally as many. I made a mental note, that the next time we tried this, we would need to improve our harvesting techniques.

Since we were at the stream, I took the opportunity to clean the fish allocated to me. In traditional American manner, I gutted, beheaded, and scaled my fish. The Yards did none of the above. When we got back to base camp, they ran sticks through the mouths of several fish and "kabobbed" them like skewered hotdogs over a small fire; guts, heads, tails and scales still intact. Fortunately, I had my own allotment!

The next day introduced me to another episode of cuisine "culture shock." In the course of gathering some bamboo shoots, the Montagnards procured two moles (or mole-like critters) for the pot. The method of dispatch was two quick thumps to the heart area with the butt end of a bayonet. The critters were then thrown directly into the fire, not for cooking purposes, but for hair removal. Once denuded, the moles were diced up into about eight chunks and stirred into the rice pot. That evening, at the communal pass-the-pot-around, I graciously spooned out my serving of rice while cautiously passing up hunks of mole...claws, snout and all other non-vegetable material. I was hoping that my hosts wouldn't feel that I didn't appreciate their fare. I caught them grinning at each other occasionally during the meal. The Montagnards knew that I was avoiding the mole meat, yet they were too well mannered to display any indignation, if indeed they felt any. Fortunately, in spite of my delicate palette, I wasn't starving. I had rice and sprouts. The weather cleared the next day, but rather than a resupply operation, we were extracted back to Dak To for reshuffling.

Brief Summary of Operation Beauregard (Eagle Bait)[1]

Timeframe: 24 June–15 July 1966
Base camp: Dak To
Area of Operations: nearby Cambodian and Laotian Border region
Enemy Situation: 24th NVA Regiment personnel still in vicinity

Mission: Security Operations along the western border
Other Considerations: Basically a follow up search and destroy operation after remnants of NVA personnel in vicinity. "The concept of the operations was to screen the area west of the DAK POKO River and to deploy deception measures to bait the enemy from suspected hiding places into terrain favorable to friendly forces. Following the first seven days of the operation, the concept was to move west and conduct surveillance, blocking and ambush operations between the DAK POKO River and the LAOTIAN Border. Later in the operation, the Brigade conducted search and destroy operations to exploit intelligence indications and contacts made with the enemy by reconnaissance forces."[2]
After Action Assessment: Not included

****

[1] MACV Command History listed in Wikiedia.org under military operations Vietnam 1966.
[2] National Technical Reports Library, Adjutant General's Office (Army), Washington, D.C., Combat Operations After Action Report, NTIS Report #198104, Publication date 1966.

Chapter 8
The Persona of Sergeant Rose
July 1-4, 1966

"Off the six list; on the shit list." --cliché used by Tiger Force[1]

"Life would be tragic if it weren't so funny." —Stephen Hawking

Another night in the rear gave me a chance to meet more of the unit. Field operations with the CIDG teams didn't present much of an opportunity to get to know many of the other members of the Force. I chatted with Sergeant Holbrook, whom I had met only briefly when I had first joined the Tigers. I believe that he was the ranking NCO in the Force at that time. The Force was regaining strength; volunteers were arriving from the line units. John Kado was moved to a different team. The same squad of Montagnards stayed with me, and we kept the same radio designation, *'Inward Season Three.'* I don't know what happened to the Specialist Fifth Class. I never saw him again. I imagine he "volunteered" for some other unit. His and John's replacements were PFC Rob Tromley and Sergeant Cleve Rose, the new team leader.

The next day we were re-inserted with the same mission parameters, again along the Dak Poko, but to a different portion of the river. Except for the new team members, the operation seemed déjà vu, another week

Rob Tromley, Dak To 1966,
photo courtesy of Leo Heaney

of no contact with other humans—friendlies or non-friendlies. It seemed that the former local inhabitants, as well as the NVA, had abandoned the area. The hooches that we encountered needed repair. Weed-like plants grew in front of entrance ways. There were no fresh signs of human habitation, not even domestic animal dung.

The new operation may have seemed routine, but the new team leader, Sergeant Rose, turned out to be anything but typical. Rose was, to borrow a term, a bit "laid back." To the sergeant it appeared a good cup of coffee was more important than tromping through the monsoon chasing down an enemy that didn't care to fight at the moment. His un-proclaimed philosophy seemed to say that it was going to be a long war. We'd have our share of action, the enemy will surface, if not today, tomorrow… so, be as comfortable as you can today.

His rank was buck sergeant, which next to corporal, is the second-most junior of the NCO grades. Yet his age, time-in-service, and experience suggested that he should have held a higher rank. My guess was that he had either left the service and recently returned (and thus was working his way back up through the ranks), or perhaps had fallen out of favor with a battalion Sergeant Major (or two) and was passed over on the promotion list. As I got to know Sergeant Rose, the second scenario seemed the most plausible. Rose didn't display the exaggerated gung ho attitude so prevalent in the services at the beginning of the Vietnam conflict. The sergeant seemed at home in his skin, and was a comfortable person to be around. Most people readily got along with him. He had light colored hair, stood about medium height, and had a slender build-- the kind that never seems to put on weight. Cleve Rose also liked poker, probably to a fault.

There was a television sitcom in the late Sixties or early Seventies called "F Troop." It featured the antics and shenanigans of a few horse-era cavalry NCOs trying to supplement their meager army wages with harebrained, get-rich-quick schemes. Years after Vietnam, when I first saw reruns of the sitcom, my mind immediately turned to Rose. He was a real life working model of the persona of the sergeants that the TV series tried to portray.

This operation with Tiger Force at Dak To was the first of several times over the next six months that I would be assigned to his team. I always felt that I was being competently led, but the real reward was observing his demeanor. It was a lesson in human nature not equaled in any university psychology course. Any story about the Tigers of 1966-67 would be incomplete if it omitted the exploits of Sergeant Cleve Rose. So, considering the lack of contact with the enemy along the Dak Poko on my second field operation with Tigers, let me introduce some of the character quirks unique to the man who took over leadership of *Inward Season Three*.

*****

One of the first character traits that I noticed about Rose was his gregarious, if somewhat imposing, nature that tended to surface around meal time. I realized he had developed a particular routine. Each evening he would checkout our night defensive posture, making sure we had tied in with the positions on our left and right. Before he departed, he usually pulled out a white plastic C-ration spoon from his shirt pocket. He would then share some friendly conversation and some of our meal, maybe a pork slice and a couple swigs of coffee. After repeating this ritual with two or three other positions, Sergeant Rose consumed the equivalent of a C-ration meal without costing him any humping sweat or preparation time. However, I never resented sharing my food or coffee with the sergeant. On the contrary, I felt that it would have been a demonstration of poor boonie-etiquette if I didn't. Although, I did notice and envy how much lighter his rucksack was in comparison to mine.

Later, as the year wore on and we were working in the coastal area around Tuy Hoa, some of the men, aware that he tended to travel "light," decided to levy some retribution on the old sarge for all the C-rations and coffee that he had sequestered at their expense. They pulled the old "boulder-in-the-rucksack" routine. The rock chosen was not exceptionally large, which would have tipped their hand at the onset. They selected an ostrich egg-sized river stone, something that would wear on a person slowly over the course of the day. And, as if ordained from on high to magnify the drama, the battalion brass had directed the Force to check out one of the tallest hills in the AO. It was a butt-kicker: no shade, no water, just razor sharp elephant grass. Once we reached the top, since it was too late in the day to move on, we started to set up our defensive perimeter for the night.

About one minute into the normal routine of unpacking our poncho liners along with the evening C-meals, all noise discipline was sacrificed by a disparaging string of expletives emanating from Sergeant Rose...he had discovered the "wee pebble!" Everyone feigned ignorance of the atrocity. I really didn't know who actually put the rock in his pack. If I were a betting man, I'd place my wager on: Charley Hartz, Robert Jacobs, Jim Raysor, or all three. It didn't matter though, since no one broke silence and fessed-up to the deed--ever! We were all now subject to certain retaliation. Sergeant Rose was not a vindictive man; neither was he forgetful. He possessed an excellent sense of humor, and I was left with the feeling that he was planning on having the last laugh. Eventually he got even with us on a river crossing operation, but I'll save that incident for later. An interesting side note here, not long after the little rock-in-the-rucksack incident, it seems that Platoon Sergeant Breen came to be victim of the same ploy. There was never a doubt among any of us regarding Sergeant Rose's complicity in this later rock episode!

Another trait of Sergeant Rose was that he liked his coffee hot and often. The supply personnel issued a specific ration of trioxane fuel tablets to C-rations. The tablets burned with a subdued blue flame, but one tablet barely cooked a ration and sufficiently warmed up a canteen cup of coffee. The Army seemed to be stingy with the trioxane. There never seemed to be enough, so substitutes were sought. The plastic explosive C-4 could fill the bill, except to acquire it usually meant cannibalizing one of the team's claymore mines. After awhile the battalion became aware of this, and required that the mine be an "accountable" item that had to be returned to the supply personnel. Failure to do so could result in disciplinary action.

One morning as we were collecting our equipment in preparation for moving out, I overheard Hartz and Raysor muttering something to the effect that "Rose got the C-4 again!" In their hands was the split open, empty shell of their claymore mine. Rose never admitted to anything, he just grinned. The fellows would have to come up with a way to "legally" dispose of the mine or face disciplinary action when they returned to the rear. The next time that we made enemy contact, no matter what the situation dictated, they were going to fire the claymore so they could report it as a legitimate combat loss.

This was line humor among team members. Although people pretended to be angered, no one really took offense. They just waited their turn for the next opportunity at one-upmanship.

On a separate occasion, Rose got pinned down behind a rice paddy dike. What caused him to go out into an open rice paddy was never explained. But Hartz and a few of the other team members were dispatched to go to his aid. While they were hastily picking up their gear to be underway, they were spewing comments about not being concerned about Rose's safety, as they were tripping over themselves to go save his ass. When the team returned to base camp, Hartz filled the rest of us in on what transpired. When they took care of the enemy and finally got to Rose, they found him prone, propped on one side and heating coffee (with C-4 naturally). And, complaining that the rounds that had been chomping away at the rice paddy dike had tossed dirt into his canteen cup. Then he criticized them for taking their time knocking out the enemy gun. Rose was a master at maintaining poise; he was not about to be "rescued." He was not one to stay on the downside of the one-upmanship curve.

On another day during the Tuy Hoa operation, Rose was dispatched to the rear on some administrative errand. We were all a little envious, because we had been in the field for quite some time and the opportunity to get cleaned up enticed all of us. While I was providing security at the landing zone, I asked Sergeant Rose what he planned on doing if he had any free time in the rear. It seems that he had made some money at poker in the field, and he stated he was planning on getting into a game with the battalion Sergeant Major. I made some comment to the effect that he shouldn't take too much of the Sergeant Major's money. Rose's reply was that he planned on *losing* to the battalion's top NCO. He wanted to be in the Sergeant Major's graces when the new E-6 promotion list came out. He was tired of being…"off the six-list and on the shit-list." However, fate was to intervene in the good sergeant's plan.

*****

Before the next promotion levy was due out, Rose was shot in the lower leg. He complained quite a bit to Hartz and Jacobs about them jostling his leg when they carried him to the medevac chopper, but everyone figured he was just "being Rose." It wasn't until sometime later that we received information disclosing the full nature of his wound. The bullet, instead of passing through the leg, followed the bone, splintering it like a fir tree. The medical solution to healing the bone to its former parameters was immobilization. Rose was placed in a full body cast, armpits to ankles, and bedridden. When we got the word of his status from the hospital in Japan, we figured the old sarge was in for a few months of boredom and bedpans. It seems, however, that Rose wasn't ready to accept those conditions, particularly after Bobby Jacobs ended up in the hospital beside him. When Charley Hartz and I took our extension leaves, we hooked up with Jacobs and he plied us with more data on the Rose saga.

It seems that being cast in plaster and bedridden did nothing to change the sergeant's desire to congregate with people for friendly conversation and a drink or two. Rose had devised a plan to get to the NCO club and have a beer. His dilemma was his encasement in a full body cast. This impediment might have dissuaded most individuals, but to Rose it just enhanced the challenge. He borrowed a crutch and used it to "paddle" his bed to the elevator. With the end of the crutch, he negotiated the elevator buttons and successfully arrived on the ground floor. He made it past the admission/reception's desk, which doesn't say much for the hospital's security. However, paddling his bed through the revolving doors proved an obstacle. That's where they got him, stuck in the revolving doors.

Plan "A" may not have been much of a success, but it provided Sergeant Rose with fresh intelligence about the layout of the hospital, and limitations of hospital beds. Although the beds are technically mobile, they are not exactly agile. Plan "B" needed to incorporate a more versatile form of maneuverability--Bobby Jacobs and a wheelchair.

According to Bobby, Plan "B" went something like this. Sergeant Rose had graduated to a less restrictive cast, allowing him to sit in a wheelchair with his leg elevated. Bobby had been shot in the upper thigh and was "crutch mobile," so they could work as a team. The plan was for Bobby to steady himself behind the wheelchair using the handles and push the sergeant to the Class Six liquor store. Once there, they could strap a case or two of beer (actually they managed three) on Rose and make it back to the hospital. Simple plans are usually the most successful and Plan "B" was an initial success. With Bobby hobbling behind, pushing and directing the wheelchair, they made it to the store and secured three cases of beer. The plan came apart on the way back, when Bobby lost his balance trying to negotiate a curb at a busy intersection and

Cleve Rose and Bobby Jacobs, hospitalized in Japan,
photo courtesy of Bobby Jacobs

tripped on a manhole cover. He lost his grip on the handles, and the wheelchair with Rose and the three cases of beer shot out into multiple lanes of traffic. Rose couldn't do much to mitigate circumstances because of the cast and the cases. The lads survived the ordeal largely because Japanese motorists seem adept at swerving around distressed wheelchairs. According to Bobby, they are also adept at expressing sentiments with their vehicle horns.

The hospital administration staff didn't look upon the wheelchair excursion very favorably. Fortunately, cooler heads prevailed. So, in order to avert implementation of the inevitable Plan "C," they moved Jacobs and Rose to the front of the stateside evacuation list and sent them home.

Also during his hospital stay, Rose got a visit from Captain Agerton. It seems that Rose made the E-6 list, but only through the extra efforts of the captain. By coincidence, Agerton was also wounded and hospitalized in a different Japanese hospital when he heard about Rose. He arranged with battalion to have Rose promoted, and Rose's E-6 promotion orders forwarded to Agerton. The captain then purchased the E-6 stripes in the PX, took the 30-minute train ride, and personally delivered them with the orders to Rose, who was still in an elevated cast. He tossed the orders and stripes on his chest, saying, "If you lose those, I'll hunt you down and shoot you myself."[2] Whether Rose managed to keep the rank very long was a point of discussion surfacing at reunion meetings.

Sam Carnero added to Rose's story. Sam was NCOIC in charge of a rifle range at Ft. Sill, Oklahoma, and bumped into Rose years later. He had a pretty noticeable limp because his leg had never properly healed. Given his disrespect for his full body cast in the hospital, failure of his bones to heal correctly is no real surprise. He was no longer infantry qualified, but he didn't want to be discharged. So he and the Army struck a deal. Rose became a mess steward! Considering his appreciation for coffee and creature comforts, his choice was logical. For the record, he had still managed to retain his staff sergeant stripes.

*****

Now, with some knowledge of how Sergeant Rose operated, I can return to where I left off at Dak To in late June of 1966, and finish my story of how my second operation with *Inward Season Three,* under the leadership of Sergeant Cleve Rose, eventually closed.

About the fourth day out, Captain Higinbotham radioed a mission change with coordinates for a rendezvous with other elements for our extraction. Our pick up point was a clearing just southeast of the Highway 14 Bridge that crossed from Vietnam into Cambodia. After checking the map, Sergeant Rose realized that we had no time to waste. We had a long, hard trek, cross country, hacking our way through un-trailed jungle. Making the rendezvous point on time would be a real challenge, if not damn near impossible.

We called over the Montagnard Sergeant to let him know what was up and where we were headed. The Sergeant was good with topographical maps. Basically, it was *"nous sommes ici et nous allons ici"* delivered with my rural Pennsylvania accent while pointing at the map locations of where we were and where we needed to go, augmented with the pickup time in *"heures."* The Sergeant perused the map and offered a suggestion. Since we were to regroup just southeast of the old bridge that crossed the river, why not take the river, which we were near, down to the bridge and make our trek in much less time? This latter bit of information I derived not from my slightly less than excellent understanding of the French language, but from the Sergeant's tracing his finger from our location on the map to the bridge pickup point, while I caught the words: *"les bateaux."* Sergeant Rose asked what was up. My response was that I thought the Montagnards were saying that they had access to boats. Rose eyed the Sergeant and mimicked paddling a canoe. The Sergeant nodded affirmative.

We saddled up, and in about fifteen minutes we were on the river bank. Not really a bank because the jungle ended right at the water's edge. If the old adage, "slow water runs deep" was anywhere near accurate, this stream was deep. If you will remember, I had made the observation previously that the Montagnards seemed familiar with the area where we had worked the week before. Well, this area must have been their backyard. Right about the time my mind was questioning what we were doing there, the twins, being the youngest, stepped off into the chest-deep water. Then they started a routine of taking a deep breath, diving under the surface and re-emerging with a large stone which they threw to the side. Eventually, dugout canoes started bobbing to the surface. The indigenous tribesmen submerge their canoes if they're not going to be used for some time to prevent the sun from drying them out and cracking them. This little bit of surreptitious mooring probably also reduces the chances that someone might "borrow" them.

I won't try to describe the serenity of our river trek. For a short period of time, even though we were right in the middle of it, the war didn't seem to exist. During the previous two months, the intrinsic nature of modern warfare had transported me to places in helicopters, at high speeds, with blazing guns, artillery, and tac air tearing up the real estate. But there, for a few hours on the river, a Neolithic form of transport had eased me through pristine harmony almost like a kind of mental R&R. We made the bridge and the rendezvous on time and without incident. My second operation with the Force was concluded. I felt pretty good about my new unit and my place in it. This was the point in time for me where "Vietnam" was not just a tour of duty during the Cold War. It was morphing into something more than a conflict. It was turning into an adventure.

At the rallying point, we joined other *Inward Season* teams and helicoptered back to base camp at the Dak To airstrip for regrouping. The next operation drew blood.

Brief Summary of Operation Beauregard (Eagle Bait)[4]

Timeframe: 24 June–15 July 1966
Base camp: Dak To
Area of Operations: nearby Cambodian and Laotian Border region
Enemy Situation: 24th NVA Regiment personnel still in vicinity

Mission: Security Operations along the western border
Other Considerations: Basically a follow up search and destroy operation after remnants of NVA personnel in vicinity. "The concept

of the operations was to screen the area west of the DAK POKO River and to deploy deception measures to bait the enemy from suspected hiding places into terrain favorable to friendly forces. Following the first seven days of the operation, the concept was to move west and conduct surveillance, blocking and ambush operations between the DAK POKO River and the LAOTIAN Border. Later in the operation, the Brigade conducted search and destroy operations to exploit intelligence indications and contacts made with the enemy by reconnaissance forces."[5]

After Action Assessment: Not included

****

[1] A cliché used by the members of the Force to describe Sergeant Rose's seemingly perpetual condition of being removed for the Sergeant E-6 promotion list; usually for some indiscretion on the sergeant's part. MFR Journal notes, 18 Sept 2003.

[2] Conversation with Captain Agerton, Deadwood reunion, June, 2017.

[3] Telephone conversation with Sam Carnero, December, 2017.

[4] MACV Command History listed in Wikiedia.org under military operations Vietnam 1966.

[5] National Technical Reports Library, Adjutant General's Office (Army), Washington, D.C., Combat Operations After Action Report, NTIS Report #198104, Publication date 1966.

Chapter 9
Sergeant Girard "Discovers" Laos
July 5-8, 1966

"Gonna' fight all night;
Gonna' fight all day.
Put my money on an M-16;
Young Charlie had an AK!" –Jim Raysor[1]

The next operation started as a night movement into an area somewhere near the Laotian border northwest of Dak To. Although we still had our CIDG components, most of the Force had been inserted in mass and moved as a single unit. The night was bright. Moonlight reflected off a large stream or river meandering through a pronounced valley several hundred feet below the trail we followed. As usual, we were going uphill.

It was the new team leader of *Inward Season Three*, Sergeant Christian Girard, who first mentioned that the terrain didn't seem right--didn't seem to match the place that we were supposed to be. When we stopped, he showed me the map. He was right. If we were dropped off at the correct LZ, the stream on our right to the east should have been on our left. This was before the days of satellite positioning, so we had to wait until daylight in order to confirm our assumption. When morning arrived, the element leaders shot a few back azimuths and confirmed that the choppers had indeed failed to drop us off at the designated landing zone. However, we were not lost; we knew exactly where we were. We had invaded neutral Laos!

After an exchange of radio messages with higher, we were ordered to get back to Vietnam on foot, ASAP! No helicopters would be sent to pick us up, particularly in daylight. That would only be compounding one error with another. That was it, so we headed back the way we came. Several kilometers to the south we found a crossing point and re-entered Vietnam. The Force then broke up into the usual reconnoitering teams and headed out to our assigned patrol areas.

Working in the border region gave me the opportunity to hone up on navigation skills. Without GPS to assess distance traveled, we counted paces. My hundred meter pace was sixty-six left steps. Whenever I wasn't assigned point, I kept pace. Before starting off on a trek, I would break up a dried branch into ten one-inch pieces, and put them in one of my pockets. Every time I reached the sixty-sixth step on my left foot (adjusted for hilly terrain), I discarded one of the twigs. When I threw away the tenth twig, I was roughly one kilometer away from where I had started, and the process repeated. The technique is amazingly accurate. After I left the Army, I used it again on cross-country archaeological surveys back in the states.

*****

About four days later, *Inward Season Three* was directed to meet with another team and secure an LZ for the customary resupply operation. The rendezvous place was an abandoned village. The Montagnards again seemed to be familiar with the area and started gathering some red peppers from plants growing about.

The team we linked up with was headed by a Special Forces NCO. I assumed that the CIDG were from his camp at Dak To. Sergeant First Class Cobley was older than most of us, probably in his late twenties or early thirties, and he had a good no-nonsense air about him. He and Sergeant Girard seemed to get along well. There were one or two other enlisted men who I assumed were Tigers, but I didn't know them. Actually, if a person were talking about "first-name" familiarity, I knew more of the CIDG than I did of the Tigers.[2]

With the resupply came a mission change, and we were given directions to a new operations area. Both teams were to remain together, which put SFC Cobley in overall charge. I was assigned to point and Sergeant Girard took up the slack position, followed by our CIDG element, and then came SFC Cobley and his troops. I'm not sure if we had been advised at the time that we would be working with another U.S. unit, but later that day, we linked up with a platoon of the 17th Cavalry.

As we approached the new coordinates, a subtle but obvious shift in the terrain began to occur. The bamboo forest with its dense fern-like ground cover gradually gave way to slender deciduous trees more open at ground level, and exposing a boulder field of pale grey rocks. A light patina of moss covered just about everything. I stopped to look things over. Something didn't feel right, and Sergeant Girard seemed to sense it also. Just as we huddled up for a little assessment about what it was that didn't seem correct about this place, weapons fire erupted behind us. Not immediately behind us, but about six hundred meters back down the trail we had just followed. The firing was not heavy, but rhythmic. It would die down, then pick up; die down and pick up again. Soon we started receiving radio traffic from higher inquiring whether we could hear the weapons' fire. The sergeants apprised higher of our situation and we were directed to go to the aid of the Cavalry platoon which had sustained casualties. We did an about face. Sergeant Cobley's element took point; I was now rear security and we were moving back towards the bamboo forest.

As we neared the area where the shooting was taking place, Sergeant Cobley left the trail and headed into the thicker vegetation for better concealment. Some of the firing was emanating from directly in front of us, while a second source lay off to our right. Sergeant Cobley was approaching the sources of the fire cautiously, trying to figure out which was the Cavalry's position and which was the enemy's.

When we were almost ready to engage, our team started to drop rucksacks. I radioed Captain Higinbotham of my intentions to leave the communications net and drop the radio until the firefight was over. Following protocol was my mistake. The captain directed me to stay "on-the-horn" and give him a play-by-play assessment of the situation. He called me back a few seconds later to make sure that I hadn't dropped the pack--not that I would have. He told me to carry it, so I did. An order is an order.

It wasn't the radio's weight that was encumbering. When snaking your way through dense vegetation towards an enemy, you want to stay low, moving your head around slowly while trying to figure out the location of the opponent without exposing a lot of yourself. The metal frame of the rucksack with a radio strapped on hinders the raising of the head from the prone position. You have to pretty much do a push-up to get adequate observation. It's not that much of a physical problem, but more of your body is exposed for enemy observation. Another discomforting issue was that the ruck and the radio with its antenna and handset jacks tended to become entangled in vines and foliage. Instead of stealthily

Cleve Rose and Christian Girard, photo courtesy of John Carey

slipping through the undergrowth, I was more like a Tasmanian devil, pulling down a good portion of the jungle as I tried to advance, all too often being hung up in the vines like a moth in a spider's web. Fortunately, I was at the rear of the line-of-march; most of the dangerous action affected the troops with Sergeant Cobley. Because the enemy never directed their fire at me, I was in a good position to observe the situation as it unfolded.

At the time I hadn't given this particular episode very much analysis; it was just a firefight that I had survived. In retrospect, this is what seems to have happened. A small unit of NVA apparently entered the trail behind our Force, but in front of the Cavalry platoon. Whether this was by design (and they were hiding in the thicket waiting for us to pass) or a product of circumstance, is anyone's guess. Ultimately the NVA unit bumped into the point element of the Cavalry platoon that was following some distance behind us. When the fight started, the Cav had dropped rucksacks. In the fight that continued, the Cav took some casualties and established a defensive perimeter for their medics to work on the wounded. Eventually, the NVA worked their way to a point in between the Cav's defensive perimeter and the place where the Cav had dropped its rucksacks. The NVA remained on the trail with the Cav's rucksacks on their right and the main body of the Cav platoon to their front about twenty meters off the trail in the thicket. Unknown to the NVA was that we were approaching through the undergrowth behind them. When the NVA became aware of our presence to their rear, they must have felt pretty much encircled. They probably figured that the Cav had left a security element guarding its rucksacks, so escape in that direction didn't seem feasible. But the Cav had left no security element with its equipment. Had the NVA elected to break contact and exit over the unsecured rucksacks, they would have made good their escape. However, for whatever the reason, the NVA chose to turn and engage Sergeant Cobley's element, and that decision sealed their fate--some of ours also.

As I stated, the enemy never zeroed their fire in on me, so I had a fairly good perspective on what transpired. The heavy, dense undergrowth was like a green fog where periodically one of our men would surface momentarily and then sink back into the verdant haze. The NVA were very close on our right at about the two o'clock position. Sergeant Girard and the Tiger in front of me got a good fix on them when they fired into our lead element. Sergeant Cobley was hit along with one of the twins and about two other CIDG troops. The Montagnards were loyal and brave, but they were too close together for combat that involved automatic weapons. Fortunately for us, the NVA were also packed together. So when Sergeant Girard and the other American with him got a good fix on them, it was over quickly. Both men put about a magazine's worth of fire into the enemy's position and then assaulted it, firing as they advanced. I followed trailing "wait-a-minute" vines in my wake.

Sergeant Girard made a quick search of the dead NVA, then moved right to check out that portion of the trail. The other Tiger moved left down the trail to let the CIDG and Cav know where we were. On the trail were three dead NVA, two armed with AK-47s. The third one had no weapon. Two were lying slumped over on one another, with the third lying a few feet away. Small clusters of cartridge casings indicated that they had worked their way down the trail from the Cav perimeter. Sergeant Girard called me over to where he was standing and pointed out the Cav's rucksacks. As I noted previously, the escape route available to the NVA was down the trail, to the right of the Cav's equipment. I don't know why they didn't take it. If the tables were reversed, and I had just inflicted casualties on two larger enemy units, I would have skedaddled in the best tradition of the "Old Swamp Fox," Francis Marion, and lived to fight another day. My guess is that the initial engagement with the Cav had wounded one or more of the NVA, and they elected not to abandon the wounded.

Sergeant Girard spoke with a pronounced French accent, earning him the moniker: "Frenchy." This operation was the only time we served together. I last saw him in late September when he was leaving Tiger Force for another assignment, which I believe was with an indigenous South Vietnamese unit. I want to believe that he survived the war, but I'm not sure that he did. There is a listing on the Vietnamese War Memorable for a SFC Christian G. Girard, born in 1940, killed in April 1969 while serving with the 5th Special Forces Group, MACV-SOG. It sounds like "Frenchy."

Tending to and evacuating our wounded was our next priority, and here's where the Cav platoon took over and excelled. In no time, using machetes, entrenching tools, bare hands, and whatever else they could muster, they cleared an area in the bamboo thicket large enough to bring in medevac choppers.

The skill and bravery of the air-rescue crews is legendary and the ships that extracted our wounded that day lent full credence to those legends. There couldn't have been more than a helmet's width between the rotor blades of the evacuation helicopters and the standing bamboo along the periphery of the LZ. I found that I had moved to a portion of the cleared space near to the trail so that I had a feasible escape route should a chopper blade catch a tree, and I needed to avoid an aircraft lurching towards me.

To my knowledge, all of our wounded got off the ground alive, but a few days later, we received word that Sergeant Cobley had died of respiratory complications en route to the States. I guess that the nature of our work numbs our perception of time and space, because I felt like I had known Sergeant Cobley for some time, much longer than a few hours and a firefight.

At a Tiger Force reunion in 2013, Jim Raysor, who was one of the old perennial Tigers during 1966 and 1967, asked the group if anyone could recall the name of the Special Forces NCO that was wounded (and later died) near the Cambodian border in the incident involving the 17th Cav. After I recalled that it was SFC Cobley, Jim asked me how I came to know that. I told him that I was there. Jim showed me a scar on his hand made by a bullet in that firefight. He was one of the men wounded during that engagement. At that time, we had only met at the resupply point, traveled to the fight, and then he was medevaced. We would work together for most of the next year, not aware that we had first met the day of that skirmish. And, we didn't discover that item of interest until forty-some years had passed!

Whenever we returned to Dak To, I had planned on dropping by the Special Forces compound to see how the wounded Montagnards were doing, but circumstances got in the way.

Brief Summary of Operation Beauregard (Eagle Bait)[3]

Timeframe: 24 June–15 July 1966
Base camp: Dak To
Area of Operations: nearby Cambodian and Laotian Border region
Enemy Situation: 24th NVA Regiment personnel still in vicinity

Mission: Security Operations along the western border
Other Considerations: Basically a follow up search and destroy operation after remnants of NVA personnel in vicinity. "The concept of the operations was to screen the area west of the DAK POKO River and to deploy deception measures to bait the enemy from suspected hiding places into terrain favorable to friendly forces. Following the first seven days of the operation, the concept was to move west and conduct surveillance, blocking and ambush operations between the DAK POKO River and the LAOTIAN Border. Later in the operation, the Brigade conducted search and destroy operations to exploit intelligence indications and contacts made with the enemy by reconnaissance forces."[4]
After Action Assessment: Not included

****

[1] Jim Raysor, ditty, sung to *Camptown Ladies*.
[2] SFC Warren Cobley was not a member of Tiger Force. He served with the 5th Special Forces Detachment at Dak To which provided the Montagnard CIDG troops that were augmenting Tiger Force until it could rebuild its strength. SFC Cobley was NCOIC of one of the Inward Season teams, which included eight Montagnard troops and two Tigers.
[3] MACV Command History listed in Wikiedia.org under military operations Vietnam 1966.
[4] National Technical Reports Library, Adjutant General's Office (Army), Washington, D.C., Combat Operations After Action Report, NTIS Report #198104, Publication date 1966.

Chapter 10
An Eye for an Eye
July 9-15, 1966

"There is some good in this world, and it's worth fighting for." -- J.R.R. Tolkien

Butt-busting mountains and punji stakes characterized our final operation out of Dak To.

Following the medevacs that carried SFC Colby and the other wounded Americans and Montengards from the battle area, another *Inward Season* team, lead by SSG Tyrone Watson, rendezvoused with us, and the units were reshuffled. Sergeant Girard took charge of what remained of SFC Cobley's element. I was assigned to Sergeant Watson's element. For most of the following week we covered a lot of real estate without finding any signs of recent enemy activity. It appeared that the NVA had indeed vacated the area for sanctuaries in neighboring Cambodia and Laos. Our battalion was also preparing to vacate the area. It was getting ready for operations back along the coast near the town of Tuy Hoa. Of course, those of us in the field were unaware of the pending redeployment. We continued with business as usual.

In the four weeks that passed since I had joined the Force, I had worked alongside three different veteran NCOs (Rose, Girard, Watson), each demonstrating a distinctive leadership style characteristic of their individual personalities.

The most obvious trait of Sergeant Watson, immediately recognized by anyone serving with him, was his reticence. I wouldn't label Tyrone Watson as anti-social, but he certainly was quiet. Idle banter for the sake of cordiality was not his style. We shared a kinship of geographic sorts, since both of us hailed from

Pennsylvania. Frequently, he'd address me as "Home." Tyrone possessed that unique ability of appearing never to be overly bothered by anything. Overt excitement, frustration, and paranoia were not part of his demeanor. No matter how difficult the terrain or stressful the situation, nothing seemed to faze him. He stayed intent on the task at hand and displayed no emotion. No matter how challenging the environment, he never seemed to be annoyed. I don't recall him ever uttering an expletive out of frustration. Even in those trying moments when some of us sought temporary solace by heaping invective upon the Army or the top brass for concocting up some obviously ill-conceived strategy that delivered us to some piece of gonad-crunching real estate, Tyrone just adjusted the straps on his rucksack and moved on.

One day, around the middle of July, our team was directed to scout ahead of C Company. We rendezvoused with the company around midday and passed through them while they were chowing down. Not very long after, we reached an open, grassy area which was infested with punji stakes.

These sharpened laths of bamboo were designed and employed to cause injury to the lower leg or foot. We usually encountered punjis in areas that could serve as helicopter landing zones. These NVA defensive obstacles were certainly labor intensive, sometimes covering acres with a surface density of about five or six stakes per square foot. In knee-high grass, some of the stakes were virtually invisible. Earlier in Operation Hawthorne, while still serving with B Company, I had witnessed a futile attempt to cross through a field seeded with punji stakes. The plan was to have the lead man pull out the stakes as he proceeded down the trail through the field. After about the seventh impaled point man, the effort was abandoned and we swung way around the punji area. I say "way around" because our opponents foresaw the possible end-run scenario and extended the stakes well into the forest on all sides.

Finding a safe way through the field in front of us didn't seem all that promising. If the area were a mine field, we would have stopped cold and backed cautiously out of it. But static punji stakes don't conjure up the same cautionary impulse that bounding mines do, so we continued gingerly down the trail that passed through the open area. That was a mistake. At first we did well, and had progressed about twenty meters into the field. Then I heard Sergeant Watson say that he had struck a stake. I turned to see how he was doing and struck a stake myself. Tyrone's was more of a laceration than a puncture. The stake ripped through his boot lace and cut the front part of his foot. The stake that I hit passed through the inside upper of my boot as I was turning and ran up into the calf muscle. As I lifted my leg off the stake, the color of my green jungle boot faded into maroon. Once the bleeding subsided, we traced our steps back out of the field. It was one of the "water-under-the-bridge, spilt-milk" situations. I knew Tyrone wouldn't curse, so I uttered enough for both of us.

C-company's medics cleaned and bandaged Tyrone's laceration. They confirmed that I would need surgery. A couple hours later I was transported to Dak To in one of the battalion's shuttle runs.

At the aid station, I was assigned a cot and informed that I would be sent to the surgical hospital at Pleiku the next morning. Nothing else was done for the wound. One of the staff medical personnel told me that the surgical procedure for a punji stake injury was to open the wound, clean it out good, pack it with gauze, and let it drain for awhile and then stitch up the wound. He said the procedure involved inserting a chrome rod up the wound and then opening the muscle down to the rod. It was purported that the enemy treated the stakes with animal dung, so the medical concern was infection. If the wound remained free of infection, recovery time would be around six to eight weeks.

After the initial surgery at the MASH unit at Pleiku, I was transported to a field hospital at Qui Nhon. There I had a second operation and my leg was closed with wire sutures. I was slated for convalescence out of country where sanitation conditions were more favorable towards preventing infection.

*****

Before my eventual plane ride to Japan, I remained a few days at the Qui Nhon hospital--not a very exciting place. I would skip this rendition of my Vietnam experience, except for a few exceptional acquaintances that I made at the hospital.

The first was Joe Hennessey. He was recovering from a bout of malaria. We soon discovered that we were both from the same battalion. Not only was Joe from my battalion, but he was in my old unit, B Company. We knew a lot of the same people and had tramped over some of the same terrain. I must have really "sugarcoated" my appreciation for my Tiger Force experience because, when Joe later returned to B Company, he acquired a transfer to Tigers and became one of the Force's perennial icons over the next year. We became virtual shadows of each other.

Joe "acquired" his transfer in a manner typical of Joe; I think of it as the 'Hennessey style.' When the company's First Sergeant denied Joe's initial request, Joe (refusing to take "no" for an answer) wrote directly to the brigade commander, General Pearson. The First Sergeant probably didn't appreciate Joe's bypassing the chain of command, but what could he do about it-- the general had already approved the request! When my leg healed and I returned to the Force, Joe was there and we served together for well over a year. But I'm getting ahead of myself; back to the hospital.

Other nationalities and service members occupied the ward with us including Koreans and Vietnamese soldiers. One particular Vietnamese male drew my attention because he didn't seem to be sick or wounded. Joe and I had bunks near the entrance of the ward, and just across from us were two Vietnamese children: a girl (about five years old) and her brother (around ten). Each child had one eye bandaged. Eventually, we learned that the particular Vietnamese male turned out to be the father of the children.

Each morning, teams of two or three doctors and nurses made the rounds, checking charts and patients. The treatment for the two Vietnamese children involved removing the bandages and then extracting a strip of gauze dressing about six feet in length from the vacant eye socket of each child. The gauze pieces had caked, dried blood on them and it was obvious that the procedure was very distressing to the children. Yet, the only indication of discomfort that the children displayed was a wince or bodies tensing as their wounds were reopened and cleaned. They gave all of us observing their morning treatment ritual a lesson on enduring pain.

I couldn't help wonder what caused the exact same malady, the loss of same eye, to each of these siblings. So when an opportunity presented itself, I asked one of the medical personnel if he had any background information about the nature of the children's injuries. He did. He told me that the Viet Cong militia operating near the children's village wanted to make an example for anyone serving with the ARVN forces. So they dug out an eye of this brother and sister because their father was a South Vietnamese soldier. It wasn't an easy realization to acknowledge--that humanity is capable of such cruelty. Naïve I was.

*****

Before the week was out, I found myself in a hospital at Johnston Air Force Base, Japan. The fear expressed by the Army surgeons at Pleiku and Qui Nhon about the possibility of a developing infection proved warranted: an infection did set in. It popped a few of my stitches and extended my overall stay another two weeks, via a detour through the hospital's isolation ward.

As my recovery improved, I enjoyed a great deal of freedom which I certainly used to my advantage. I don't recall withdrawing any more money from finance than I usually did at the end of each month. However, I was able to visit most of Japan's tourist attractions. Over several weekends I toured the gardens of the Imperial Palace, shopped in the Ginza, hit a few cocktail lounges in Yokohama, visited the Hilton to check out the koi ponds, attended a Noh play and a kabuki performance, was serenaded by German-speaking Japanese in a ratzkeller, found a few excellent fish & chip-type restaurants on the waterfront, and reconnoitered the countryside around the air base on a bicycle lent from special services. I spoke few Japanese words, only the common courtesy terms and phrases, but that seemed adequate. The Japanese people were amazingly honest, friendly, and helpful, particularly at redirecting me around train stations and menus.

During the week I played chess and checkers with other personnel recovering from wounds. I did a lot of reading, and even tried some oil painting with materials provided by the hospital Special Services personnel.

One morning, near the end of my hospital stay, two brigadier generals (one Army and the other Air Force) entered the ward and headed towards my bed. I should say my beds because the staff had allowed me two: one to sleep in and the other for my project. I was finishing up a model of a P-51 Mustang. It was remote controlled with a gas engine. I constructed it from a kit that the Special Services volunteers had provided me. The hospital staff had converted the second bed into a workbench by placing a sheet of plywood over it. I needed the large work space because the model had a wing span of over three feet.

Even though the ward was pretty much vacant, as the generals approached my project, the thought occurred to me that they might consider my second bed acquisition a misappropriation of government property. So, I stood quietly at attention beside my bed and waited for their inquiries. They made some favorable comments about the model and asked the usual questions about how I was doing and what unit I came from. I responded that I had healed well and felt that I should be returning to the "Hundred and First" pretty soon. With that, one of the generals asked me a "loaded" question, "Was I ready to get back to my unit?" I replied with the expected response, "Yes, Sir." One of the generals countered to the other that the Hundred and First lads are always ready to go back. The irony was that I really was ready. I had enjoyed my visit to Japan, but I never felt comfortable in those blue hospital pajamas. They didn't fit the image of myself that I had been slowly honing over the last year. I had two months of the good life. I needed to get back to where I felt I belonged.

I had left Vietnam in late July of 1966. I returned to Tiger Force in early October, after Operation John Paul Jones concluded and Operation Seward was underway. It was during Operation John Paul Jones that Sergeants Bryant, Walker and Private Wanamaker were killed in a minefield early in the operation in the Tuy Hoa area.

Brief Summary of Operation John Paul Jones[1]

Timeframe: 21 July–5 September 1966
Base camp: Tuy Hoa
Area of Operations: Along Route 1 from Vung Ro Pass to Vung Ro Bay, later in the Ky Lo Valley
Enemy Situation: 95th and 18B NVA Regiments of the 5th NVA Divisions
Mission: Secure vital terrain to protect engineers working on Route 1, relieve the 2d Korean Marine Brigade, be ready to exploit b-52 strikes. Later expanded to conduct search and destroy operations between the Ky Lo Valley and Vung Ro Bay, and to protect civilians during the initial harvesting of rice in Tuy An.
Other Considerations: Brigade elements started moving from Dak To on 15 July and were completed by the 21st of July. This movement required 181 sorties on C 130 aircraft. Operation John Paul Jones ended on 5 September when the Brigade began Operation SEWARD to protect the Tuy Hoa rice harvest.

****

[1] Combat After Action Report – Operation John Paul Jones, 1st Bde, 101st Abn Div, 27 March 1967, PDF file AD No. 388882.

Chapter 11
The Tuy Hoa Tigers
Late September 1966

"...nine inches above the left shoulder..." --Sgt. Evans

I caught a hop on an Air Force C-141 from Japan to Vietnam. I was beginning to appreciate MAC (Military Airlift Command): just check in, show them your orders, and wait for an aircraft. Usually the wait was short. Besides, I really had very little else to do. I could always find a book, and there's no such thing as an Air Force Base without coffee. The transportation was usually a cargo craft of some kind, which I found more comfortable than the over-air conditioned commercial airliners which seemed to enjoy a monopoly of the normal troop hauling contracts. However, in comparison to the real meals that the civilian airlines served in that bygone era, the MAC-way offered lunch in a paper bag: usually a sandwich, chips and a can of pop. Yet, for some reason, I found the military transports preferable. Perhaps it was the availability of parachutes positioned about the aircraft.

In retrospect, I was forming a regimen that I would employ over the next two years whenever I returned to Vietnam. Usually I entered country at Saigon or Bien Hoa. The first thing I'd do was to try to find out where the "Hundred and First" was deployed. After that, if I needed to drop off any personnel files, I'd catch a hop to Phan Rang and turn in whatever paperwork the military needed to the 1st Brigade's Administration Center. To prevent any chance of being listed AWOL, I would sign in with my unit's rear area detachment. Sometimes the rear area folk had transportation going to the forward area. Other times, it was back to MAC and grab a ride with one of the ubiquitous C-123s or C-130s. Once I snagged a ride on an old C-47 carrying a load of ammonium hydroxide to a Special Forces compound. Fortunately it was a short hop and well ventilated! If I was ahead of schedule or had no files to surrender, I'd skip the diversion to Phan Rang and go straight to the forward area and find my unit. At this particular time, I was on my way to a place named Tuy Hoa.

Tuy Hoa, which sounded like "Too dee Wah" when a Vietnamese national pronounced it, is on the coast, north of Nha Trang, south of Qui Nhon. On our landing approach I noticed (close to the airfield) a rather spartan bivouac area, which had the earmarks of an airborne infantry battalion's forward area. Each company had a few GP medium tents, a few hex tents with pup tents in rows behind. A two-and-a half ton truck heading that direction gave me a lift. A piece of painted plywood sheeting displaying the phrase "Above the Rest" with the appropriate logos confirmed the accuracy of my initial assumption. I was at the base camp of the 1st battalion, 327th Infantry (Airborne). I made my way to the left, past the line-companies orderly room tents, and found the guidon with HHC on it. I was home.

I say "home" with ambivalence because home is a place where an individual usually feels at ease and familiar. As I approached the GP medium tent that served as the company orderly room, I wasn't experiencing the "familiarity" sensation. When I was wounded, Tiger Force was not operating as a single reinforced platoon as the name implies. Rather, it had been divided into several small reconnaissance elements often augmented with indigenous CIDG troops borrowed from the Special Forces camp at Dak To. Almost my entire experience with the Tigers at Dak To was in the field. I only knew a few members of the Force. I remembered Captain Higinbotham, the Force leader. I knew Sergeant Holbrook and a few of the team leaders whom I served with: Sergeants Girard, Rose, and Watson, and some of the enlisted men. Now I was a stranger to most of the Force. At Tuy Hoa I was about to become formally acquainted with the whole unit for the first time. I don't really remember what I was anticipating, but Sergeants Girard and Watson mastered-the-ceremony.

Both were in the headquarters area, and they dispelled my apprehensions immediately. Sergeant Girard inquired about the condition of my leg. Sergeant Watson remembered that we both hailed from Pennsylvania and gave me a big, "Welcome back, Homey." The ice started to melt; I felt like I was again among kin. They updated me on the Force which was coming in that afternoon to clean up. The men had been in the field for quite some time, so they were being extracted for a shower run. I would go back to the field with them the next day. That was the good news. The not-so-wonderful news was that Sergeant Girard was moving on to a new assignment. Naturally, I wished him the best. Inwardly, I nursed a mental sigh. I suspected that I would never see him again, and I never did. As I mentioned earlier, he apparently was killed in a helicopter crash in Cambodia in 1969. Over the course of the next six or seven months, Sergeant Watson and I would participate in several operations together. In 1970, on a subsequent tour, he also was killed in action while serving in the 173rd Airborne Brigade. It wasn't until several years later, however, that I learned of their deaths. Until then, I had thought they had both survived the war.

Desmond Hanakai,
photo courtesy of Leo Heaney

Not long after I had drawn my field equipment and weapon from the supply tent, members of the Force started trickling into the company area. I spotted John Kado who introduced me to his friend Jim Potts. I think they knew each other before the Army. Other introductions followed. To name a few, there was Dennis Crowley from Maui. Charley Hartz and Jim Raysor hailed from Pennsylvania, as well as Neil "Joe" Hennessey. Robert Jacobs was from Norwalk, Connecticut and Ervin Lee from Aniston, Alabama. Doc Deffenbaugh and Jimmy Clark were also present. The NCOs included SFC Flynn, SSGs Evans, Kratzberg, and Hanakai, with SGTs Rose, Carnaro and Budd. The Force had two company grade officers, Captain Thomas Agerton and Lieutenant John Carey, but I do not recall meeting them on my first day back. What I do recall is that there was no "shower run." In typical Tiger fashion, the Force headed off to the South China Sea for a splash in the salt water and a barbeque on the beach. I retired that night well fed, feeling clean and content.

The next day we were airlifted to Hill 51. The Force had operated from this area for quite some time, and most of the men were familiar with the hill and the surrounding territory. The Army liked to defend from high ground, so a double-humped mound rising fifty-one meters above the surrounding rice fields met the military's criteria for defensible terrain. The choppers dropped us off in the saddle between the humps and we made our way up to the higher of the two. There was a tree with a sandbagged bunker beneath it, some two-man fox holes, scrub brush, and not much else. Very little concealment and no water, only a modern army with helicopter resupply capabilities would consider this a piece of defensible terrain. I felt like bait, but the battalion wanted the enemy to make contact with us. That was our job in the fall of 1966. We were to take on any enemy regardless of their size. Captain Agerton put it to us kinda' like this: "If the enemy force was smaller than us, we'd overrun them. If it was bigger than us, we'd bite off the head or tail and then hang on until the battalion could move in and finish it off." The Old Man's mission statement was clear and concise. It left no doubt.

John Kado and Malcolm Budd,
photo courtesy of John Carey

I was assigned to Sergeant Malcolm Budd's team, and I shared a two-man fighting position with Jim Potts. At this time the Force was organized into two sub-units, Alpha Force and Bravo Force. There was also the command post (CP) group which included the officers, platoon sergeant, radio operators (RTOs), artillery forward observers (FOs), and if we had them, tactical air liaison personnel and interpreters. Medics from the medical platoon were usually assigned to each one of the sub forces. Later, as Tiger Force grew in number, a third element (Charlie Force) was created.

These three sub-elements (Alpha Force, Bravo Force, and Charlie Force) most often patrolled independently. Each of these forces was further divided into two rifle teams of about six men each, plus a machine-gun section. Usually each of these forces was led by a staff sergeant (E-6), and each team by a buck sergeant (E-5). The teams, referred to as Alpha 1 and Alpha 2, habitually rotated point and rear security duties on consecutive days. On patrol, Alpha Force might be organized as follows: point man, slack man, sergeant, grenadier, two rifleman, staff sergeant, artillery FO, radio men, medic, and machine-gun section, followed by the rear team, which mirrored the first six men and would swap rear security duties for point responsibilities the next day. It would not be unusual for either Force to further divide into light and heavy separate patrol teams, the heavy one having the machine gun attached. My first action in Tuy Hoa came on light team patrol.

Since Hill 51 was surrounded by flat open terrain, leaving it in daylight meant that the enemy knew a patrol was going out. However, once into the tree line, the team became shadows. A kilometer away from the hill, and with a few direction changes, it regained the element of surprise.

On this particular day, Staff Sergeant Evans, the Force leader, had accompanied Sergeant Budd's team. There were about six of us. I was rear security. We were paralleling a well-used trail that ran on a raised dike of an irrigation canal. The thick brush beneath the levy trail gave us some fairly good concealment. Our noise discipline was excellent; the enemy's wasn't. Vietnamese is a tonal language, making it virtually impossible to mistake it for English. The chatter emanating from down the trail alerted us to the presence of Vietnamese. The trail broadened as it made a dogleg left. At the wide area, a squad of VC riflemen and an officer had stopped to rest. The men were on the dike and the officer had drawn a hammock between two trees just along the trail. Sergeants Evans and Budd directed us into position with hand signals. The point element sealed off the escape route down the dogleg. Sergeant Budd covered the center, and Sergeant Evans maneuvered down the right side. Crowley was backing up Budd and I was securing our rear while "rubber-necking" the rest of our team. When the enemy became aware of our presence, their situation was already hopeless.

Three of the VC made a vain effort to get to their weapons, in this case Mauser 98Ks, which they had stacked in a classic textbook "teepee-structure" on the dike. They never made it. Two others, further from us and realizing the futility of that course of action, tried to escape down the trail. Our point element took care of them. The officer, armed with a handgun, died in his hammock. In what amounted to a few short bursts of M-16 fire, the engagement was over. Six enemy were dead. We captured five rifles and a revolver. No one had to be told what actions to take; indeed, no Tiger had even uttered a word until the area was secured. Obviously I had been assigned to an experienced team. Being rear security, my job was to prevent someone from surprising us from that direction. I hadn't fired a shot. I don't believe Crowley had either. The point team and the two sergeants took care of business. After we secured the area, we radioed in the contact, picked up the weapons and any material of an intelligence nature, and proceeded on to a rendezvous point in order to link up with other elements of the Force.

On a low hill which afforded good observation of the neighboring dry rice paddy and dike network, we married up with other elements of the Force. Except for the foliage along a small river on our left, the area was pretty much open. We were directed to take up hasty blocking positions. The Battalion's C-Company was moving towards us and they might "push" something our direction. Sergeants Evans and Budd had settled into a position about twenty meters to the right of me. Before long I noticed them passing a pair of binoculars back and forth. I heard Sergeant Evans request that someone go get one of the captured Mauser 98Ks which had more accuracy at longer range than our M-16s. After the weapon arrived, Sergeant Evans made an adjustment on the rear elevation sight, took up a prone supported firing position, and squeezed off a round. I strained my eyes in the direction that the rifle was pointing. About half of a kilometer or more down range, I made out two

Charlie Evans, photo courtesy of Charlie Evans

individuals running across the open from left to right. They were well out of effective M-16 range. I assumed they were Sergeant Evans' target and that his shot had missed. I was incorrect. Within a few minutes C-Company radioed in confirming a kill to Tiger Force. Their point element had just come upon a lone VC with his back to a tree and his weapon leaning against it. He had a single bullet hole above his heart.

Later on, Sergeant Budd filled us in on the missing segments of the story. He and Evans had observed through the binoculars three VC, one with a weapon and two unarmed stopping for a rest in the shade of a tree. The armed man had set his weapon beside the tree and rested himself up against the trunk. The two unarmed men remained standing on either side of him. To allow for wind and distance, Sergeant Evans had aimed about nine inches above the left shoulder of the seated man. The range was about six hundred meters. The rest is history.

This day's action was rather typical of the encounters that we had while operating in the Tuy Hoa area. Because of the way we maneuvered in quiet, small groups, we tended to meet the enemy in chance encounters. As often as not, we literally bumped into each other. Since we were operating in our opponent's backyard, most of us carried our weapons in our hands at the ready. Whereas, the VC more often than not, had theirs at sling arms or balanced on their shoulders like a farm implement. The quick, ensuing gunfights usually ended in our favor.

Brief Summary of Operation Seward[1]

Timeframe: 5 September-25 October 1966
Basecamp: Tuy Hoa
Area of Operations: Tuy Hoa and Ninh Hoa areas
Enemy Situation: the PAVN 18B Regiment, the 95th Regiment and the 307th Battalion
Mission: to protect the rice harvest in the Tuy Hoa and Tuy An areas, search and destroy, provide security from Vung Ro Bay to Tuy Hoa

Other Considerations: Operation Beauregard rolled right over into Operation Seward which was considered a success because 90 percent of the rice was harvested with minimal interference from the enemy. On 3 October, 1/327th liberates 23 Vietnamese nationals held as prisoners by the enemy.[2]

After Action Assessment: 239 enemy KIA, 27 friendly KIA

****

[1] John Carland, (1999), *Combat Operations: Stemming the Tide, May 1965 to October 1966 (PDF),* Government Printing Office, p. 254, ISBN 9780160873102, Cited in Wikipedia.org, 2/15/18.

[2] Combat Operations After Action Report, Operation Seward, (RCS: MACV J3-32) (U), 6 Nov 1966.

Chapter 12
Hill 51, POW Camps
Early October 1966

"In the 101st Airborne, the battalion recon platoons had always been elite units... they gave a man an opportunity to see more combat than a Lurp had any business seeing." —Kenn Miller, LRRP[1]

I was developing an understanding of the different types of reconnaissance units within the 1st Brigade of the 101st. The term "reconnaissance" didn't conjure up a stereotypical meaning. Lurp (Long Range Reconnaissance Patrols) teams generally consisted of five or six men, and usually operated well in front of the advancing line battalions. They became shadows. Their missions involved observation and stealth, referred to as "sneaking and peeking." Discovery by the enemy could easily be catastrophic to the success of their mission and the safety of the team members. On the other hand, Tiger Force was designed for offensive action. Tiger Force, like its four-legged namesakes, was designed to pounce from the shadows with potent ferocity.

*****

In the fall of 1966, the general mission of the battalion was to secure a stretch of the coastal highway and keep it open. This was related to protecting the rice harvest. Denying the enemy access to a piece of terrain meant controlling real estate. A geographical high point like Hill 51, rising above the surrounding rice paddies, provided an excellent observation platform of the converging valley system. It also served as a base camp for deploying combat patrols. Life on Hill 51 developed a regimen. Some teams patrolled and some stayed behind and defended the hill. During the defensive episodes, I got to make the acquaintance of the other members of the Force.

On the other side of the only tree, just below the military crest of the hill, was a position manned by Robert Jacobs and Charles E. Hartz II. No description of Tiger Force in Tuy Hoa of 1966 would be complete without addressing these two individuals. On a morning that we had not been assigned a patrolling mission, I moseyed over to Hartz and Jacobs' foxhole and traded the usual salutations that people extend when they don't really know each other, but want to be polite and cordial. Hartz came from my home state, Pennsylvania, so we had some common ground. Jacobs, also referred to as Jake or Bobby, had an accent that I would have taken for New York. It turned out that he was actually from Connecticut.

While we were sharing tidbits of back home gossip, I noticed that Hartz was taping hand grenades to branches. Each branch was about an inch in diameter and roughly a foot and a half in length. He then arranged them neatly along his side of the foxhole. Without giving it much thought, I asked him why he was doing this. He replied that he was lengthening the lever arm to give him more leverage, so he could throw them farther. He even demonstrated his technique of snapping the stick like a whip right before he'd release it. It made sense. Later, I discovered that he had thrown the javelin in high school competition. I would come to know him (and later his family) quite well. The term "secure in your own skin" certainly applied to Hartz. He was someone I came to admire immensely. His optimism was contagious. That fellow from Nazareth would have called him Peter. I valued his

Charley Hartz,
photo courtesy of Bobby Jacobs

comradeship more than I can express in words. Of course, like most of my revelations concerning humanity, I hadn't realized how valuable I considered his presence on this planet, until it was gone.

Bobby Jacobs was a counterbalance to Hartz's flamboyant optimism. Missouri might be the "Show Me" state, but New Englanders seem to own the "show-me" copyright. On that particular morning, as Hartz was finishing up his stick-grenades, Jacobs chimed in with the hazards associated with these latest "Hartz-weapons." Jake's pessimism covered possibilities like the stick grenades hanging up in the brush around the foxhole, tape failure due to sun and elements, or simple separation from the stick due to Hartz's manly effort to "snap-launch" the grenade. The resulting effect, Jake pointed out, was that the stick-grenades more than likely would land closer to his position than to an intruder. Hartz continued with his taping task as if he heard none of Jake's criticism.

Bobby Jacobs,
photo courtesy of Bobby Jacobs

I came to realize that when the Force moved under what might be considered trying circumstances, Hartz and Jacobs were usually selected to walk point. I also noticed that they had developed a unique profile or silhouette. Men on patrol normally maintain a fairly dispersed distance from each other to minimize casualties in explosion and ambush situations. The point element was an exception to the normal dispersion rule. Because the point and slack men worked rather closely together, they tended to maintain a slightly closer interval than the rest of the unit. Hartz, however, tended to close the interval between himself and Jacobs to where at times he appeared to be looming over Jake. The distance between them was much closer than most point teams prefer, but it worked for them. I also noticed that Hartz's persistence to be where he could support Jake sometimes meant that when he engaged the enemy, his muzzle burst was right in Jake's ear. Quite often, if Hartz was on the left, the hot, spent shell casings from Hartz's weapon were ejected right down the back of Jake's neck. On more than one occasion, I overheard Jacobs castigating Hartz for one of these breaches of firefighting etiquette.

But that's how they were. The Force felt confident when these two were on point. They complemented each other and protected each other. When Bobby was wounded, Hartz wasn't with him. I believe that the situation might have been different had the two old comrades been working the point in their usual manner. But I'm getting ahead of myself, for that action occurred in Phan Thiet about five months down the road.

*****

One day near the end of October, the officers called certain elements of the Force together for a special operation, a raid. The mission was to take and secure a VC prison compound. While I was still in Japan, the Force had taken two other such camps, rescuing more than twenty Vietnamese civilian and military personnel imprisoned by the VC. So, for most of the Tigers, this was to be their third operation of this type. Since Jake was on the assault team of the previous raids, I plied him about those two operations. Also, the 1st Brigade's weekly news paper, *Diplomat and Warrior*, carried a front page article on the second operation in its 14 October 1966 edition. So, between Jake's account and the newspaper's rendition, I will attempt to reconstruct those operations.

Around late September, or early October, the Force had raided and destroyed a prison camp in the mountains southwest of Tuy Hoa. On that engagement, the element of surprise was lost. During the ensuing firefight, (before their egress routes could be cut off), the Viet Cong had managed to evacuate most of their prisoners to a different compound about two miles away.

The Army learned the location of the second POW camp when three prisoners escaped from a work party and made their way to the American lines. These escapees agreed to lead U.S. forces back to the place where they had been held. During the mission to the second POW compound, the lead element of the Force was being directed by Lieutenant Carey. Tigers were supported by the first and third platoons of B Company. The line platoons from B Company ensured that there was enough staying power on hand should unforeseen contingencies arise and the units have to make a stand and wait for reinforcements. The enemy was bound to be on the lookout; only about a week had elapsed since the first raid. More so this time than the previous operation, surprise was essential.

John Carey,
photo courtesy of John Carey

The Force covered about six miles clandestinely. A good portion of the trek was uphill over large algae encrusted boulders. Moving three platoons surreptitiously up the side of a mountain and avoiding trails that might be watched by the enemy was the task at hand. Lieutenant Carey's solution was to dispatch a small scouting party well forward of the main body. The scouting element stood a better chance of remaining undetected and could warn the main Force of any threats ahead. The main problem would be enemy patrols using trails that the raiding party might need to transect in route to the objective. According to the newspaper article[2], the Force encountered and evaded three VC patrols that day, each composed of 8 to 9 men. The Brigade's newspaper account painted the operation with the customary commando-like efficiency; however, Jake's version reflected more of the Tiger-like reality.[3]

As I noted previously, when the Force faced special circumstances, the officers tended to prefer having Hartz and Jacobs walk point. Sergeant Rose, whom I had patrolled with at Dak To, was their team leader. The weather that day was particularly miserable. At one point, as they were nearing the location of the camp, Lieutenant Carey had the scouting element hold up for awhile. The element had just reached an area where they had fairly good observation of a trail crossing their intended line of travel. Sergeant Rose took this opportunity to brew some coffee. Actually, Sergeant Rose never needed much of an excuse for whipping out the ol' canteen cup. "Coffee break" seemed to be his default setting.

As the three of them were sitting there waiting for the coffee to cool off, and the lieutenant to radio in further instructions, Jake looked up to witness a squad of VC entering the trail above them. Cautiously and quickly the scout element slipped back into the surrounding bushes to await the passing of the VC patrol. However, in the rush for concealment, no one remembered the cooling canteen cup still sitting on the stove in the open. Right about the time that reality was sinking in, Sergeant Rose whispered to Jake to crawl forward and get the coffee, and while he was at it, to fetch "Jake's" M-16 which was lying beside the coffee. He distinctly said to Jake, "your rifle." Jake turned to Sergeant Rose and informed him that he had "his" rifle. Hartz also had "his" rifle. The only weapon Rose held at that moment was a white, plastic C-ration spoon that he had used to stir the coffee. So much for commando-like efficiency!

Fortunately, the "Victor Charlies" were themselves not models of efficiency: the M-16 and canteen cup went undiscovered. The enemy passed and the mission continued.

The camp consisted of three huts nestled among large boulders. The prisoners, twenty-three in number, were tied shoulder-to-shoulder on a platform in the middle of the compound. The point element had already entered the camp, and was waiting for the support elements to take up their blocking positions on the perimeter, when one of the guards started firing. The return fire from the point element hit two guards who dropped their weapons and fled the scene leaving blood trails. In the initial confusion, one of the VC guards while trying to retreat, turned and shot one of the prisoners in the foot. The point element moved in immediately and the firefight ended almost as fast as it began.

The area was quickly secured; four weapons were collected. The medics, with the help of the interpreter, gave each of the former prisoners a quick check over. The prisoners represented a cross section of Vietnamese society, and consisted of eighteen males and five females of various ages. As was later learned, some were farmers, soldiers, tailors, medical personnel and school teachers. Their length of incarceration varied from five to thirty months. They were mainly used by the VC as laborers, carrying commodities, usually rice, from the lowlands to the highlands. All were half-starved and maltreated. All had been subjected to interrogation sessions which usually terminated with a beating. Three were so weak that they needed to be carried by members of the Force.

As soon as accommodations were made for transporting the infirm and wounded, Lieutenant Carey had the Force move out into the dense jungle. He chose to avoid trails and roads, the most likely spots to encounter VC patrols.

The lieutenant probably realized from the start that the former prisoners were in no shape to make a quick forced march to the rendezvous point before dark. Accordingly, after he put some distance between the camp and the Force, he set up a defensive perimeter and held up for the night. The normal dead silence usually associated with a Force defensive position was not prevalent that night. Instead, tonal Vietnamese delivered in murmured cadence emanated from the center of the defensive perimeter where the former prisoners were placed for safety. Most of the night, they whispered quietly among themselves. According to the interpreter, the crux of their conversations centered upon finally being released. The next morning, the Force delivered the Vietnamese to the extraction point where helicopters transported them back to freedom.

An additional part of Jake's account of the raids on the prisoner camps stuck with me because of its uniqueness. As Jacobs and Hartz entered the camp and started taking fire, they sought cover behind obstacles that they thought were logs. Sometime during the ensuing firefight, Jake became aware of a pair of feet sticking out of the end of the log that he was hiding behind. It turned out that he and Hartz had taken cover behind stiff matting that had been wrapped around cadavers in preparation for burial. About a year later, up north in the I Corps, I would encounter this unique practice again. At any rate, having absorbed what I could about the first two prisoner camps, I, along with the rest of the Force, made ready for an assault on camp number three.

*****

For those members of the Force who were part of the first two prison compound raids, the third venture must have felt like deja vu. Again the Force traveled on foot for several kilometers before starting uphill. I was in Sergeant Budd's team, walking my old rear security position. We were following a stream of fairly fast flow, which was littered with large boulders, some the size of jeeps. To our left lay a veritable sea of impassable, razor sharp elephant grass about twelve feet high. To our right, a wall of thick undergrowth blocked our advance. Any attempt to pass in that direction would require a lot of loud machete work. The stream offered the path of least resistance; however, it wasn't a "red ball." The rocks were slick, they had to be negotiated gingerly in order not to dislodge them and make noise. Branches and elephant grass overhung the water course, retarding progress.

By late afternoon it became obvious that we'd either have to push on and take the camp with a night attack or hold up there in the streambed. The decision was to hold up. At that place security wasn't a real issue; nothing was going to come at us through thick elephant grass and undergrowth. We couldn't even push the vegetation back far enough on the banks to make sleeping positions for ourselves. So we grouped together on the largest boulders and tried to stay dry. The only approach at us was from the way we came, and that avenue offered no tactical edge to an enemy. The undergrowth would canalize them into the streambed beneath us, leaving us with an uphill advantage. Feeling we could easily control any ground attack from the rear, we established a single guard position covering that direction and tried to get some sleep.

For all of us, it was a rather restless night. Sleeping on large boulders in the middle of a rushing, cold stream is not conducive to promoting a restful sleep. As the night progressed, the Fates acquainted me to several variations of the "falling reflex." I slid from my rocky perch on my stomach, on my back, caressing my rucksack, sometimes catching my footing, sometimes not. About the time that I was conjuring up a mental "Why me?" a splash followed by muffled expletives confirmed that Destiny had not targeted me alone. When dawn finally arrived, we were more than ready to get out of that streambed. In no time we were at the objective.

We followed the stream to a well-established trail. About forty meters on the uphill side of the trail lay the camp. By the time I got to the trail, the forward elements were already moving into the compound. Sergeant Budd motioned to me to take a position to the left. I concealed myself just off the trail where I could cover that approach and the open area to the left of the camp. In a very short period of time, the Force withdrew down the trail to the right. The camp had been abandoned. The only item of note left behind was a light weight motorcycle. My most poignant memory of the operation turned out to be the cold, sleepless night in the stream. It wasn't, however, to be my last night spent with Tiger Force in a stream.

Brief Summary of Operation Seward-continued[4]

Timeframe: 3-25 October 1966
Basecamp: Tuy Hoa
Area of Operations: Tuy Hoa and Ninh Hoa areas
Enemy Situation: the PAVN 18B Regiment, the 95th Regiment and the 307th Battalion
Mission: to protect the rice harvest in the Tuy Hoa and Tuy An areas, search and destroy, provide security from Vung Ro Bay to Tuy Hoa
Other Considerations: Operation Beauregard rolled right over into Operation Seward which was considered a success because 90 percent of the rice was harvested with minimal interference from the enemy. On 3 October, $1/327^{th}$ liberates 23 Vietnamese nationals held as prisoners by the enemy.[5]
After Action Assessment: 239 enemy KIA, 27 friendly KIA

****

[1] Kenn Miller, *Six Silent Men*, The Random House Publishing Group, New York, 1997, p.183.
[2] PFC Luis Callender, *327 Frees 23 More Viets*, Diplomat and Warrior, Vol. I, No. 21, October 14, 1966.
[3] Robert Jacobs, personal conversation, October 1966.
[4] John Carland (1999), *Combat Operations: Stemming the Tide, May 1965 to October 1966 (PDF)*, Government Printing Office, p. 254, ISBN 9780160873102 Cited in Wikipedia.org, 2/15/18.

[5] Combat Operations After Action Report, Operation Seward, (RCS: MACV J3-32) (U), 6 Nov 1966.

Chapter 13
Base Camp, The Big River Assault
Late October, Early November 1966

"The best laid schemes of mice and men go often askew." —Robert Burns, 1785

I enjoyed the Tuy Hoa area of Vietnam because it was drier than the other areas I had previously worked. Since it lacked the triple-canopy vegetation of the highlands, the sun quickly dried us out even after a downpour. At times, however, it was too dry, and obtaining drinking water became a problem. Initially I only had two canteens, which were barely enough, but eventually I acquired additional ones. On several occasions, before moving into a night location, we had to fill our canteens with water from stagnant rice paddies or irrigation canals. Under these circumstances, I added a third purification tablet even though the directions only called for two.

While pulling up the rear on a patrol, I stopped to fill my canteen from the green, scum-coated waters of an irrigation channel that paralleled the trail. As I glanced up, I was startled to observe the head of a crocodile staring back at me. The animal possessed an extremely long, slender snout with teeth curving out along the sides of its mouth. I did not know that there were crocodiles in Vietnam! I backed up the levee bank and scurried forward to Ervin Lee and told him to check out the croc. Of course by then, the critter had submerged. Lee just flashed me one of those dubious looks that are usually accompanied by an "…if you say so" qualifier, and continued on his way. Sometime later, I found literature on these "fish-eating" crocs. Apparently they are not a danger to most adults. At the time, however, I immediately upgraded the acquisition of additional canteens to a higher priority status, as well as becoming more cautious about where I filled those canteens. Likewise, fording deep streams added a new layer to my strata of apprehensions. Naturally my croc-epiphany arrived just prior to the largest river crossing assault operation of the war (at least up to that time), and Tiger Force was to lead the way.

*****

For over ninety days the battalion had been running tactical search and destroy operations to remove the opposition forces from the farming area around Tuy Hoa, and to secure a portion of Route 1. A change in tactical operations was coming. Intelligence had located an area where local VC forces seemed to be regrouping, and the mission changed from search and destroy to a battalion-sized raid. We were extracted to the forward area base camp for a few days prep time before the pending operation.

The battalion was bivouacked near the air strip, just across the bridge leading into the city of Tuy Hoa. The South China Sea was a ten minute walk. Protocols in the rear necessitated the assumption of a garrison look, or at least a quasi-garrison look. As we arrived back into the company area, we secured our duffel bags from the supply tent and made our way to the designated platoon location. The first order of business was to scrape out shallow two-man prone shelters about two feet deep, aligned in neat rows. Then each of us provided one half of the standard Army pup tent. The halves were snapped together and erected over the prone shelters. Air mattresses went into the pits. Poncho liners were tossed in upon the air mattresses. Weapons and rucksacks followed off to the sides.

With our sleeping quarters established, the next priority was to shed our grimy field clothes and get cleaned up. There were basically three options here. After a visit to the shower point, some troops preferred changing into standard issued fatigues with non-subdued, state-side patches and emblems. Others just "D-Xed" (direct exchanged) their soiled field fatigues for clean jungle fatigues at the shower point. The third option was to draw clean fatigues from the supply tent, procure a bar of soap, make your way over to the beach, and clean up in the sea. I favored the latter option. The salt water and sun seemed to have a remedial effect on the body, particularly where blisters were an issue.

In the rear, shaving was a requirement that presented a problem. The issue wasn't the lack of razors, but the scarcity of mirrors. Anything made of glass didn't survive well in the field. Metallic signal mirrors didn't fare much better than those made of glass. Before long the metal surfaces became too marred to be of much use in providing a clear reflection, rendering them about as effective as a C-ration peanut butter tin. For my morning ablutions in the rear, I generally tried to find a vehicle with an intact mirror and performed my shaving ritual near it.

Finding a vehicle, however, was not as easy as one might expect. The very nature of a parachute unit restricted the number and type of vehicles that it could be allocated--i.e. they have to be "parachuteable" or in Army jargon, air-deployable. The quagmire called Vietnam further limited the effectiveness of the usual complement of vehicles a unit could maintain in its forward areas. The bottom line meant that the few vehicles available were a valuable commodity and in use most of the time running military errands. If necessity dictated that we needed another vehicle, and an opportunity arose, we cloned another unit's unattended vehicle. We would take it back to our motorpool, paint over their bumper number, and replace it with ours. Now there were two identical "HHC 1" vehicles—twins—which were never allowed to coexist side-by-side. Once we moved on we would abandon the vehicle so it could make its way back into the system.

My shaving relationship with the company's deuce and a half truck probably prompted the First Sergeant to select me for the laundry-run work detail on my first full day back. It really wasn't bad duty. The First Sergeant had contracted the company's laundry out to local Vietnamese entrepreneurs. We delivered bags of the company's soiled fatigues collected at the shower point to a civilian facility downtown, and picked up any processed laundry.

After walking about the countryside for several weeks, the ride into town was a rare comfort, not unlike a sightseeing tour in the states. Our truck, its bed laden with a carpet of sandbags to mitigate the possible effects of an encounter with a land mine, crossed a long trestle bridge spanning the estuary south of the town. Into the quaint coastal community we lumbered. I busied myself snapping pictures with the twenty-dollar camera I had purchased from the PX. Since this was my first and only visit into the town, I hadn't the slightest idea of where we were going. However, as we turned down one street, I spotted a familiar landmark…Sergeant Rose, walking alone. I waved, he waved, and we both continued on our separate ways. His, no doubt, was destined to eventually rendezvous with a deck of cards. My destination, as it turned out, was just down the street. We unloaded the dirty laundry at a Vietnamese shop and waited for the supply person in charge to give us further instructions. When he found out that our clean laundry wouldn't be ready for awhile, he told us to meet him back there at a designated time. Off he went on another of his list of errands, leaving us a few hours on our own to reconnoiter the local terrain.

In strange localities there are certain establishments (i.e. bars, restaurants, laundries) that military personnel seem to be able to locate without any prior directions. Before long I found myself standing in front of the Four Seasons Restaurant. Jim Potts and Dennis Crowley had mentioned the name a few times, and there were a few members of the Force already there. I joined some of the fellows at an outdoor table, and indicated to a waiter that I would try some of what the other customers were having. I wasn't interested in displaying my naiveté with menu handling and food course recognition; I pointed to a salad and a meat dish. I had forgotten what fresh tomatoes were like! The Army in Vietnam wasn't big on fresh anything; just about everything seemed to come out of a can. The gourmet theory of food presentation was a concept as foreign to me as the language of the waiter, but the effects were obvious. Just viewing the fresh vegetables had me salivating. I waited with baited anticipation. Fortunately the cooks were speedy.

The salad was everything I had expected and more, but the meat dish was an enigma. It wasn't chicken. It was dark like beef, but tasted something like (but discernibly more palatable than) the lamb entrees from the indigenous rations that the Army provided the Montagnards. After a few pieces, I made the error of asking what I was consuming. This afforded Ervin Lee, seated at a nearby table, the opportunity to jest with a Yankee. In his best Alabama brogue, he asserted that I obviously wasn't very familiar with the flavor of dog. My man-of-destiny, groomed-paratrooper façade dictated that I finish my plate without comment or reservation. I continued with the meal, preferring to believe that the odd tasting meat item was water buffalo, a mentally acceptable, bovine substitute, and that Lee was just "pulling my leg." The "fly in the ointment" of my logic was that Ervin Lee was one of the most dead serious people I had ever met.

*****

At the appointed time I was back at the laundry, reunited with the supply honcho, and finished loading the truck. On the way back to the battalion, just prior to crossing the bridge out of town, we drove past what appeared to be a vestige of the French occupation: a formidable looking, Second World War-type, concrete pillbox. Mentally I started processing how it could be tactically neutralized if ever I found myself confronting something like it. I don't think that I entertain, nor ever had, much of an appreciation for static defenses. I knew that I'd preferred to be outside of structures like pillboxes where I could maneuver or escape if necessary rather than being trapped inside of one. We got back just in time for evening mess call.

Some members of the Force never bothered with the mess tent food, choosing instead to heat Cs in their squad areas. Others, myself included, enjoyed the change in routine and the type of meals available at the mess tent. Since I don't possess what one might call a "delicate palate," Army mess hall food was okay with me. I also found myself acquiring Sergeant Rose's penchant for coffee, and the mess personnel prepared it substantially better than anything derived from a C-ration packet. On occasion, when in the rear, I would make my way to the mess tent before sunrise and sample some coffee as it was being freshly prepared. These pre-dawn sojourns to the mess tent were unique, quiet, almost nostalgic periods void of the daytime chaos associated with our military presence. Coleman lanterns hissed and gas stoves hummed as various mess personnel busied themselves with breakfast preparations, and were pretty much unconcerned with my presence in their bailiwick. Another bonus with my coffee habit was that it afforded me access to the front of the chow line.

After breakfast we were told to stick around the company area, because there would be a battalion formation later that day where we would receive word on the next operation. Our stay in the rear area seldom lasted more than three or four days, so most of us returned back to our sleeping areas to ready our equipment. I wanted to pick up another canteen or two, plus any extra LRRP rations that I could get my hands on. The LRRP rations, short for Long Range Reconnaissance Patrol, and pronounced "lurp," were lightweight, freeze dried meals that only required the addition of water. They were pretty tasty to boot. The problem was they were in high demand and scarce. I tried to carry at least two extra LRRPs to supplement the usual complement of Cs in case unforeseen events extended the customary five-day resupply interval.

Back at our pup tents, while waiting for the word to come down to form the battalion, we busied ourselves checking our equipment. Weapons were always maintained at a high state of readiness, so they required very little attention at that time. Some of the fellows mentioned that Captain Agerton had dropped by the previous evening and reminisced over a few beers. My predilection for an undisturbed, full night's sleep caused me to have missed the gab session with the "Old Man." The conversation that transpired among those Tigers that had chased a few beers with the captain only reconfirmed my opinion that we were lucky to have an officer of his caliber in command of the unit. A social partition, primarily designed to enhance discipline, existed between officer and enlisted ranks. The captain had a manner that kept the partition from becoming a barrier. My experiences over the next few months only strengthened this assessment of our commanding officer.

Eventually the battalion formed in an open area before what appeared to be a large billboard with a canvas curtain draped over it. This was new. Normally we received our mission statements from our immediate unit commanders. On this day, the battalion commander presented the mission and scheme of maneuver himself. The curtain was dropped to reveal a rough map of the area where we would be operating. As usual, the battalion's mission was to surprise, surround, and annihilate some VC regiment. The irony here is that Army doctrine dictated that an attacking force should have a numerical advantage of three-to-one over the opposing force. A regiment is normally composed of three battalions. If the enemy were to present itself at full strength, we would certainly be the underdog, a picture the brass seemed to enjoy creating about itself. Actually, with the supporting weapons that we could draw upon, we probably were well capable of handling an enemy force much larger than ourselves. This premise was not tested on the forthcoming operation, however. The VC did not respond in regimental strength, but the "fickle-finger of Fate" did put in a more than adequate appearance.

The operation plan was simple enough to understand. With other allied units in blocking positions, our battalion was to conduct a river-crossing assault into the local VC regiment's backdoor. A large scale feigning operation (to divert attention from the crossing site) was employed by trucking most of the battalion's maneuver elements, Tiger Force included, off in several different directions to secluded dismount points. From these locations the combat units navigated to the river crossing site where a pontoon bridge was to have been erected. The Force would lead the assault into the enemy's backyard, so to speak.

Stealth, speed, and surprise were the catch words. Here's where the concept-of-the-operation becomes questionable. While the infantry units were to be making their way to the crossing area, the engineers were to be hastily constructing the pontoon bridge. As evening settled in, one detachment of combat engineers was to anchor a steel cable across the river at the crossing area. Upstream, another detachment of engineers was to start drift-paddling pontoon bridge sections downstream to the crossing area. The idea was to snag the individual bridge sections on the steel cable and slide them laterally into position forming the bridge decking.

To me, with virtually no experience in river crossing operations, the plan sounded okay. However, some of the experienced NCOs raised an eyebrow or two when this portion of the plan was delivered. As we made our way back to our platoon assembly areas, Sergeant Rose mentioned that he never had much luck with water crossing exercises. He commented that while in Germany, on a river crossing maneuver, his amphibious APC (Armored Personnel Carrier) sank. Then, as an afterthought, he added that the track sank because the crew had not re-installed the drain plugs after cleaning the vehicle. Another one of those little inconveniences that kept Sergeant Rose off the promotion list, I assumed. At any rate, the mission we were embarking upon wouldn't have any tracked personnel carriers or drain plugs to worry about. The bridge sections would pose enough of a dilemma.

As part of the deception plan, we were trucked away from the point where the bridging activity was scheduled to occur. We had about a six kilometer hump from the dismount point to the location where we were to lead the battalion's assault across the river. The deception and maneuver phase of the operation worked well. The problem developed at the bridging site. The bridge wasn't there. Actually, all the pieces were there, just not in "bridge format." The bridge sections, which looked like narrow rectangular skiffs united with cross bracing, very much resembling outrigger canoes, were clustered in a shallow eddy on the near side of the river. I don't know if the steel cable spanning the river was ever installed. I saw no sign of it. To construct the bridge in conventional manner would take hours in daylight, and it was already night. However, "they who get paid to think" were hard at work with an alternative plan which ultimately proved to be less complex than the original bridging concept: fill two of the "outrigger" bridge sections with Tigers, paddle across the river, and secure the far bank. Whatever the overall strategy was, I didn't know, nor did I need to know. At my level on the "make-it-happen" chain, the big picture wasn't important. I might as well add here that the bridge never did get constructed. Of course we didn't question the feasibility of success or failure as we launched two of the pontoon sections, with five men in each, towards the far shore. Technically, our bridging operation had just turned into an amphibious one, but these military semantics are only important to the historians.

I was in Sergeant Budd's team in the lead section. Sergeant Rose's team, accompanied by Captain Agerton, was off to our right, on the upstream side, and a little behind us. I believe Rose and Budd had exchanged a little bit of a challenge concerning which team would make it to the opposite shore first. Knowing these two, a wager was probably involved.

In the calm eddy area, we only had about three inches of freeboard between the top of the pontoons and the waterline. When we hit the swifter current about mid-channel, water started to splash up over the sides and into the pontoons. Some of us started fishing through our rucksacks for canteen cups and B3 cans to use as bailers. About that time, the other team came up beside us. After a quick exchange of words, Sergeant Rose transferred his rucksack and weapon to our pontoon section and jumped into the water, hanging on to our craft. His team continued on past us having gained more buoyancy by the removal of Sergeant Rose and his rucksack. The additional rucksack didn't help our situation any; we were now rapidly taking on water. Soon we were awash and lost the ability to maneuver the section. Sergeant Budd issued an "over-the-side" directive and we all entered the water. Luck hadn't abandoned us all together since our feet touched bottom. We had drifted onto a sand bar and were in about chest-deep water. Cautiously we inched our way along the bar until the water was only about waist deep and then started bailing water out of the nearly submerged pontoon sections. Slowly the section acquired more buoyancy as the water was removed, but it was obvious that we would not be able to negotiate the swifter current loaded again with six packs and men. Here, Rose offered a suggestion. He would swim back and return with a second pontoon section and we would finish the crossing, three men to a section. It sounded good; none of us had any better idea at the moment. Besides, he was the ranking man. He pushed off on his back, rolled over and headed towards the friendly side of the river.

Our immediate problem became one of anchoring the bridge section in place. Although the current at our portion of the river was not swift, it was persistent. We needed to hold our position so we could make it straight to the other side when we continued the crossing. Otherwise we might have trouble locating Captain Agerton and Sergeant Rose's team, which should have made it over.

About ten minutes into this "hang loose and wait" phase of the operation, the fireworks erupted. Red tracers, green tracers, and some odd colored silver-like tracers started buzzing around the far shore directly across from us. Only the red tracers were ours. Rose's team had made contact with some of our opponents. Two of the battalion's machine guns behind us threw in some supporting fire and raked the far bank to the right of the initial firefight. The shooting ended as abruptly as it started, but as it was closing down, red tracers seem to have dominated the display. We felt pretty sure that our team on the other side was in control. Then we waited. We would need the other bridge section that Sergeant Rose swam back for, in order to get all of our weapons and equipment over. Without these items, we wouldn't be much help securing the far bank. So for the moment we impatiently put our faith in the return of Sergeant Rose.

As the minutes drew into quarter-hours, which seemed like individual fragments of eternity, we waited. Patience can be a virtue or a curse, depending on your position with respect to the proverbial "rock" and "hard spot." Finally we succumbed to what Sergeant Rose would have done. On one of the flat areas on the bridge section, under a poncho, we set up a stove, and cooked up a B-3 can of coffee. Everywhere was quiet. The only sounds were those made by water. We passed the coffee around and waited. Perhaps another half hour passed, and then, after weighing his alternatives out loud, Sergeant Budd made the decision to return to the near shore, find out what became of Sergeant Rose and the other pontoon section, and check on the status of the operation.

We beached our pontoon section about a hundred meters downstream from our initial cast off point, donned our rucksacks and set out with Sergeant Rose's equipment, looking for its owner. There were troops everywhere. Most were rolled up in poncho liners sleeping. All of the line companies appeared to have made it to the bridgehead, but a bridgehead without a bridge is a chokepoint. Tactically it was a critical situation, the enormity of which would become even more evident at first light. If our adversary had possessed the means or capability to deliver mortar, rocket, or artillery fire on us in that confined space, concentrated as densely as we were, we would have been hard pressed to avoid a heavy volume of casualties. Fortunately, the night proceeded without interruption from our opponents.

We eventually found Sergeant Rose, wrapped in a wet poncho liner, huddled with some other troops brewing coffee. He looked pretty soggy and tired. He said that the bridge crossing fiasco was scrubbed and that we should find a vacant spot and get some sleep. We handed over his ruck and rifle and chided him for leaving us out in the middle of the river. His rebuttal was that he knew we were smart lads. We would have figured out that the mission had changed when the element of surprise was lost, without him having to swim back out to tell us. He was correct in that respect. We wouldn't have stayed out there "twiddling our thumbs." As a group we were resplendent with the positive side of impatience—not sitting around waiting for fate to intervene. If things weren't going as planned, we usually adapted to the new situation quickly. Tigers were exceptional at regrouping and trying a different approach. So we found a spot to rest awhile, and at first light, rose to resume the war again--along with the rest of the battalion.

*****

During those wee-hours, the operations officers in the battalion S3 shop must have been working the handsets off their radios trying to arrange helicopter transportation by dawn. Remember, at that time, the battalion had to acquire helicopter support from other units. As morning dawned, CH-47 Chinook helicopters arrived on scene to airlift elements of the line companies across the river and out to blocking positions ahead of us. The Force, however, didn't get a helicopter ride. We were provided small black rubber rafts to continue the crossing operation. The rafts at this point in the operation were probably more of a "photo-op" rather than a tactical necessity. At least this time we were supplied with actual watercraft replete with paddles. It's amazing how well issues resolve when the proper tools are available! Once across the river, we reunited with the Captain and Rose's advanced team that had been stranded after the aborted bridging attempt.

Our mission had changed. Instead of leading a surprise attack against a VC unit, we were pursuing and evading enemy, hopefully pressuring them into ambush positions that the line companies ahead of us were preparing. For the remainder of the day we were following footprints, some barefooted, and some displaying the distinctive tire-tread imprint of Ho Chi Minh jump boots. It wasn't until we set up our night perimeter that the opportunity arose where I could query Hartz and Jacobs regarding their action the previous evening.

According to Jake, the team had set themselves into a concealed position where they could wait for the rest of us to complete our crossing. However, within a very short period after their arrival, a party of VC arrived on scene. The enemy seemed completely oblivious of the activity that was taking place on the other side of the river. Bathing seemed to be their mission. They started washing up where a small stream joined the river. Jake felt that the best course of action was to stay concealed and just observe for the time being. But Hartz held a different opinion. As Hartz saw it, the mission was to secure the crossing site. VC bathing in vicinity of the crossing site was a threat to the mission. The VC had to go. With no objections from Captain Agerton, Hartz (along with Harold Jacobs on the machine gun) let go with everything they had. The VC returned fire, but then two of the battalion's MGs chimed in from across the river, spraying the undergrowth to the left and right of Hartz's location. That was the firework-tracer display that we had observed from our perch in the middle of the river. Our adversaries, opting for the discretion side of valor, elected to relinquish the contested piece of real estate and took off. Hartz had accomplished his mission: the far bank was secure!

Brief Summary of Operation Geranimo[1]

Timeframe: 31 October–4 December 1966 (officially)*
Base camp: Tuy Hoa.
Area of Operations: Phase I started 50 kilometers southwest of Tuy Hoa. Phase II shifted to the mountainous area northwest of Tuy Hoa.
Enemy Situation: Phase I targeted the PAVN 18B Regiment. Phase II shifted to the base camps of the PAVN 95th Regiment.
Mission: Search and Destroy
Other Considerations: This was a joint operation initially with the 1st Brigade and elements of the South Vietnamese ARVN 47TH Regiment of the 22nd Division, along with the South Korean 28th Regiment of the 9th Division. Later in Phase II, U.S. 4th Infantry Division joined in support of the operation.
After Action Assessment: Intelligence indicated that most of the PAVN 18B had evacuated the AO before the operation commenced. The PAVN 95th Regiment vacated the AO to the west after losing its base camps. Enemy losses were 150 KIA, with 76 POWs.
*The 95th had actually abandoned the area by the 24th of November.

****

[1] *George L MacGarrigle, Combat Operations: Taking the Offensive, October 1966 to October 1967, Government Printing Office, 1998, p. 79. ISBN 9780160495403, cited in Wikipedia.org, 2/4/18.*

Chapter 14
Hot Sauce and Turkey Loaf
Greater Part of November 1966

> *"Not twice this day*
> *Inch time foot gem.*
> *This day will not come again*
> *Each minute is worth a priceless gem."*
> —Takuan, Zen Teacher

We spent the ensuing days wearing tread off our jungle boots trying to re-establish contact with an adversary dead set on remaining elusive. The earth seemed to have swallowed them up. A footprint here, a whiff of a bamboo fire there, but solid contact remained illusory. Time itself seemed to have slowed down to keep pace with the lack of activity. In the absence of the punctuated "rattle of battle," the war seemed to have withdrawn into the earth. Days dawned, coalesced and decayed into night without incident. And then, on a morning when the weather was fairly decent, reality resurfaced.

We had been following a well-established trail through a lightly canopied forest, and had just started heading downhill into fairly open brushland, when the point element tripped an explosive device of some kind. Residual evidence, along with opinions of senior personnel, suggested that the device was a booby-trapped M-26 fragmentation grenade.

The trail switch-backed beneath me from left to right; most of the Force was below me. I was above the activity, overlooking the point element as they hurried into their routine. Those of us removed from the activity set up security immediately. There wasn't much else for us to do at this time. The people affected by the blast and its aftermath went about their jobs in preparation for the medevac. The sound of the explosion had seemed uncharacteristically muffled. A whiff of dark smoke had hovered above the scene but dissipated rapidly. I initially felt that the situation probably wasn't very critical, considering that the noise of the explosion seemed so "weak." Unfortunately, I was wrong. As the medevac chopper arrived on station, the word made its way back along the line, informing us on the top of the hill that the Force had suffered a KIA. Then, with the medevac barely departed, a new point team moved up and the Force resumed its mission. The whole episode seemed to have taken less than ten minutes.

Eventually, the word filtered back along the line that the Tiger killed was Jerry Ruiter.

Once we resumed the march and snaked our way down to the place where the explosion had occurred, I was amazed at how undisturbed the scene appeared. I had expected to see a charred hole scaring the ground, but there was virtually nothing indicating that a life had just been forfeited on that very spot several moments before. Violence, although seldom benign, can be subtle.

Jerry Ruiter and I had been on Hill 51 at the same time, yet we served in different teams, so I knew him only by "Hello" and "How's it going?" However, from the informal eulogies that emanated from the members of the team that had worked with Jerry, I gathered that the Force had lost a highly respected and well-thought-of member.

*****

For several days battalion intelligence seemed convinced that we were in hot pursuit of a routed adversary. On the ground the signs weren't all that decisive. Yet we continued at a determined pace. We "human chained" across swollen streams. We moved all day and set up defensive positions late into the night. A few days into our forced march, as twilight was degrading into darkness, Captain Agerton brought the Force to a halt in an open area. We had humped the entire day, traversing a grueling twenty-six kilometers. The tactical situation was that we had 'walked off' the edge of the map sheet. Battalion told us to hold tight until they could provide us fresh maps in the morning. In the absence of accurate topographical maps, accessing and directing combat service-support assets, medevac evacuations, or appraising friendly units of our location would be extremely limited.

The captain directed us to defend in place until morning. We fanned out from the trail and, because of the openness of the terrain, we dispersed our positions further apart than usual. The machine guns were placed to fire down the trail in both directions. Since there was a rural curfew in effect throughout Vietnam, the only persons using the trails at night would be those ignoring the curfew. The strategic purpose of the nationwide curfew was to curtail the insurgents' use of their customary infiltration routes under the cover of darkness. We frequently set up night ambushes on trails. The Air Force, likewise, stalked the trails with gunships. The captain directed everyone not to stand up during the night, and anyone that was standing would be assumed to be an enemy and fired upon. I can personally aver that a man can empty his bladder while lying on his side.

*****

Often, when the Force took a break for lunch or some other necessity, Captain Agerton had the habit of wandering off to recon the surrounding area. His little jaunts impacted his two RTOs, because one of the radios needed to be near him at all times. (One radio was on battalion's frequency, the other on the Force's push.) It wasn't until a 2014 reunion in Nashville that Agerton learned of an ongoing wager between his two radio operators. His old RTO, Roger Phillips, said they would flip a coin to see which unlucky operator had to cut his rest period or lunch short, and follow the captain.

At the Deadwood reunion in 2017, Tom reminisced that Phillips provided him some of the best entertainment and stress relief moments. As they marched along, Phillips was full of constant complaints, yet to Tom they were not insubordinate ones. He took them as humorous quips that managed to keep Tom sane under the worst of circumstances. In his head, he still hears Phillips muttering, "Here we go again…We're all gonna die…Why do I have this job…He's gonna get us killed."

Trying to get himself killed wasn't beyond the captain's attempted feats either. On the raid to the POW camps Agerton assumed point to insure that the Force was heading in the prescribed direction. Santana (Sam) Carnero followed as his slack man. As they were skirting a small rise they encountered an armed VC sentry. Facing away from the patrol, the VC hadn't initially noticed the captain or Sergeant Carnero. Eventually, sensing their presence, the VC spun around towards the captain. Agerton immediately attempted to engage the target.

Roger Phillips,
photo courtesy of Roger Phillips

As he moved his index finger forward to release the weapon's safety, reality set in—the safety selector wasn't where he was accustomed to finding it! Like most of us, the captain had qualified on the M-14. On that weapon, the safety selector is located forward of the trigger. But the weapon he had in his hands was an M-16! Enlisted personnel had a week of familiarization with the M-16 at Proficiency Training; officers weren't required to take the course. The safety switch on the M-16 is on the left side of the weapon and designed (for a right-handed person) to be manipulated with the thumb. It's a small mental adjustment, true. But small mental adjustments can become monumental when confronting an enemy drawing down on you. The captain quickly slipped into crisis mode and called in backup.

"Sergeant Carnero, shoot the *&#@!" Sergeant Carnero quickly moved around the captain and fired a few rounds into the VC, who tumbled down into the ravine below them. As the situation stabilized, Captain Agerton asked why it took so long for Sergeant Carnero to shoot! Obviously, two seconds can seem like a long time when your life is passing in front of you, and you can't get your weapon to fire. Sergeant Carnero, a man of few words, glanced down at the fully functional, unfired weapon in the captain's hand and said, "For a moment, I thought that you were gonna kill him with your knife!"

*****

Not long after we were re-mapped, we finally re-established contact with our elusive adversary. We had departed the dry paddy areas and were moving on a well-used trail passing through a section of broad-leafed woodland. A small stream paralleled the trail on the right. We hadn't proceeded very far down the trail when the Captain called a ten-minute break, while the CP group could take down and digest an incoming battalion directive. Sergeant Budd and most of the squad were in front of me on the trail. I moved off the trail to the right a few paces, leaned back against a tree beside the stream, and waited for the order to move out again. As I stared blankly down the stream, two Vietnamese seemed to materialize from out of thin air. There they were, about thirty meters downstream, heading straight at me. Both wore faded fatigue uniforms and were carrying rucksacks. The lead one had a flop hat and an M-3 grease gun slung horizontally near his right hip. The other one had an M-1 carbine slung on his right shoulder. When they spotted me, they made no panic moves. They just stopped in place and stared. My impression, since they did not make any offensive move when confronted by a Caucasian soldier, was that they were Special Forces CIDG troops. I issued the customary palm downward beckoning gesture common to the culture, and they started towards me.

The next few minutes provided two additional pieces of evidence confirming that I was not my parents' smartest offspring. First, I had just unknowingly invited two VC to join me. The moment of realization occurred when these individuals lifted their feet out of the water to step over a rock. Instead of the standard black canvas tennis shoes issued to the CIDG troops, these men sported sandals fabricated from used tires—Ho Chi Minh jump boots! Second, I had leant my M-16 against the tree that I was currently using as a backrest. My weapon was behind my right shoulder, and not easily reached without telegraphing my intentions. The lead VC had his M-3 slung under his arm about waist level, his forearm resting on the weapon just above the safety cover. If the "proverbial gunfight" were to start at that moment, he would probably get rounds off first. As I started snaking my right hand behind my back, fishing for my 16's pistol grip, fate intervened on my behalf. About twenty yards from me the VC stopped, looked at each other, then back at me, and then bolted for the thicket to their right. The first individual made the thicket before I brought my weapon around, but the other was a little slower. As he was disappearing into the trees, I got two quick shots off.

As I gave chase, Sergeant Budd and a few other Tigers joined with me. Budd asked me what we had. I gave him the essentials: two uniformed VC, with weapons, one probably wounded. Almost immediately we picked up a blood trail…a great deal of blood. After ten yards, we found his weapon. Another ten yards, we found his gear. Another ten yards, we found him. He was in pretty bad shape from loss of blood. One round had creased his side in the muscle area near his lower ribs. Not much more than a flesh wound. But the second shot did a lot of damage. His left arm must have been crooked in a V-position when the round hit him. The bullet passed through his bicep then through his forearm—four holes! We carried him back to the CP area where the medics went to work. They stopped the bleeding, administered morphine, treated for shock, and started intravenous transmissions of blood expanders. After the second unit of blood expander was used and the individual still hadn't stabilized, a third unit was administered. The medics felt this was risky because blood expanders aren't designed to do the job real blood does. But the consensus among the medical personnel was that he wouldn't make it without the third unit. The third unit of expander worked. He seemed stable and alert for transport, so we made a poncho litter and carried him back to a spot along the trail wide enough for a Huey to airlift him to a hospital. Then we rejoined the Force and continued the war.

*****

As the operation waxed on, the idea that we were in hot pursuit of an evading enemy merged into the old recon-search-and-destroy scenario. One day near the end of the month, Captain Agerton stopped the column and told us to take a break. This was not uncommon, particularly when the battalion had a change of mission coming down and maps had to be consulted. We had just crossed a clean, fast moving stream, so the NCOs sent a few of us back to top off our depleted canteens. I had collected canteens from several members of the team and headed back towards the stream. As I passed back through the CP group, I overheard the captain saying into the hand set, something on the order of, "No thanks, the men have turkey loaf and hot sauce." Turkey loaf was a C-ration meal. Why the Old Man was discussing it over the battalion net seemed a little strange. Finally, as I finished filling the canteens, I associated turkey with end of November and concluded that the conversation was about Thanksgiving. The U.S. military makes a big deal over this holiday. Every soldier gets his slice of turkey and pumpkin pie, even if the pumpkin filling is really derived from canned sweet potatoes. My non-tactical assessment of the situation was that the battalion was getting ready to provide us a warm turkey dinner. But why did the captain say, "No thanks, the men have turkey loaf?"

Thomas Agerton,
photo courtesy of Thomas Agerton

When I got back to my team, we were told to move out and find a place suitable for an LZ. It didn't take long before we came upon an adequate clearing. We fanned out into our regular security envelope and waited for the team leaders to brief us on the new plan. I felt pretty certain that a hot meal was coming our way. As it turned out, I had it backwards; the deal was for us to go to the hot meal.

If someone wanted the inside "poop" on the tactical situation, by virtue of their positions in the Force, the captain's RTOs were the sources to consult. Normally, Jimmie Clark or Roger Phillips carried the radios for the captain, so they were the individuals to go to in order to find out what was coming down. According to the RTOs, the battalion had radioed down an invitation for the Force to join them for dinner and photo op at the TOC CP (Tactical Operations Center Command Post). That meant that we had to "hump it" to the top of the mountain that the TOC was situated upon, dine, and then hump back down to our AO and continue our mission. The captain declined the excursion, opting for "turkey loaf and hot sauce," unless the battalion would provide a means to taxi us to their location. Thanksgiving being what it is in the Army, the battalion elected to ferry the Force up to the TOC with the C&C ship, one lift at a time.

I was extracted on the third-to-last lift, and there were still about a dozen Tigers left at the LZ location. The chopper dropped us off on a grassy knoll slightly above where the battalion CP and mess line were located. The chopper immediately turned around to go back for another of the remaining two lifts. The Force (minus the two missing lifts) was dispersed in the vicinity of the LZ. We were waiting for everyone to come in before we moved down to the chow line. Another Huey was parked off to the right. I sat down, leaned my back onto my rucksack, and waited.

The sensation that something was amiss preceded the arrival of the ferrying chopper. Word came in that the aircraft had taken fire on lift off and was returning damaged with wounded onboard. Most of the Force started moving to the area where the chopper would touch down. The two unknowns plaguing the experienced troops were the condition of the casualties onboard the chopper and the status of the team still at the LZ. Captain Agerton was a "first in, last out" type of commander. He wouldn't be on the second-to-last ship out; he'd be on the last ship out. This meant that he and about four or five men were on their own until an effort to extract or reinforce them could be mounted.

As the senior NCOs were weighing the tactical options while crossing their fingers, the C&C ship came into view and made its way directly to the landing panels near us. When the chopper touched down, Doc Deffenbaugh and Sergeant McKennedy exited on my side, a little cut up, but otherwise they appeared okay. I noticed a small amount of blood on the cabin floor but nothing like you would expect to see had there been serious wounding. Another good sign, the chopper wasn't issuing any smoke or oozing fluids either. However the windshield did have a few bullet holes in it.

The rounds that passed through the windshield probably sent shards of Plexiglas and metal fragments about cutting people. It could have been a lot worse. The question still remaining was, "How were the men faring at the LZ?" The pilots of the damaged C&C chopper declared that their ship was not fit for a return trip. Options were dwindling. Any quick response required another helicopter.

At this point in the drama a true hero appeared. The warrant officer piloting the other Huey parked on the side of the LZ beckoned some of the team leaders over to his ship. The CW3 had probably been monitoring the radio exchanges, so he was apprised of the general situation. He produced a map and asked the sergeants to pinpoint the location of our team. After this information was exchanged, he told us that he had enough fuel and would make a run to the LZ. Hearing this, about half of the Tigers present made an effort to scramble onto the chopper. I didn't even try. There was no way a mere private was going to unseat any of those senior NCOs. However, the old warrant did. He reminded our enthusiastic hoard that he would need an empty aircraft in order to extract the team on the ground. So off he and his crew went, heading for a compromised LZ, only large enough for a single "sitting duck" ship. It was a place where the enemy, a few minutes earlier, had demonstrated their capabilities by sending several rounds through the windshield of the previous aircraft attempting the same operation.

Back at the LZ, Captain Agerton readied his RTOs and Harold Jacobs' machine-gun section for extraction. Here fate intervened favorably again for the Force. The commander of a flight of Australian B-57 Canberra bombers came up on Captain Agerton's internal push and offered assistance. According to Jacobs, the old man's plan went as such: The captain would step out on to the LZ and fire a few rounds to draw fire. When the enemy responded, Harold saturated the area with fire from his '60 while the others beat a path to the chopper. As the chopper "slow-flighted" along the ground, the men jumped aboard. As the pilot pulled pitch and made haste to vacate the LZ, the Australian bombers delivered their ordnance immediately behind the chopper. In about ten minutes flight time, the old warrant officer delivered the captain and the other Tigers unscathed to the TOC for Thanksgiving dinner.[1]

When the dinner and PR were over, we donned our rucksacks, humped back down to our AO, and continued our normal search and destroy operations. With the rice harvest no longer in jeopardy and Route 1 secured, those individuals capable of designating mission accomplished, did so. In a matter of days, we were on C-130 aircraft heading back to the Central Highlands and Christmas in Kontum City.

Brief Summary of Operation Geranimo (continued)[2]

Timeframe: 31 October–4 December 1966 (officially)
Base camp: Tuy Hoa
Area of Operations: Phase I started 50 kilometers southwest of Tuy Hoa. Phase II shifted to the mountainous area northwest of Tuy Hoa.
Enemy Situation: Phase I targeted the PAVN 18B Regiment. Phase II shifted to the base camps of the PAVN 95th Regiment. The 95th had actually abandoned the area by the 24th of November.
Mission: Search and Destroy
Other Considerations: This was a joint operation initially with the 1st Brigade and elements of the South Vietnamese ARVN 47TH Regiment of the 22nd Division, along with the South Korean 28th Regiment of the 9th Division. Later in Phase II, U.S. 4th Infantry Division joined in support of the operation.
After Action Assessment: Intelligence indicated that most of the PAVN 18B had evacuated the AO before the operation commenced. The PAVN 95th Regiment vacated the AO to the west after losing its base camps. Enemy losses were 150 KIA, with 76 POWs.

****

---

[1] Author's notes, conversation with Thomas Agerton on 24 June 2016, and "1st Battalion, 327th Infantry Regiment," *1/327th History Vietnam '66*, 1 Jan. 2004, Web. <http://oldsite.327infantry.org/first/1_327th_history_page.htm>.

[2] *George L MacGarrigle, Combat Operations: Taking the Offensive, October 1966 to October 1967*, Government Printing Office, 1998, p. 79. ISBN 9780160495403, cited in Wikipedia.org, 2/4/18.

Chapter 15
Missed the Train
Late November, Early December 1966

"Not all those who wander are lost." —J.R.R. Tolkien

The trail wasn't normal. At places there were parallel routes running alongside it, then farther on, intersecting and joining with it. Frequently the trail left the riverbank and entered the stream, only to emerge again onto the bank several meters downstream. It split around large trees. It possessed all the earmarks of a deer trail except for its breadth and compactness. An inexperienced, uninitiated urbanite might stand on a deer trail and not be aware of it, but this trail was so obvious a blind man could follow it from a helicopter. That was precisely the problem.

A battalion staff officer had diverted us on a cross-country azimuth. We trudged through thick brush, across swollen streams, and over rolling terrain to check out trail networks near a river. The trails were not depicted on any topo map, but readily observable in flyovers…elephant trails! We knew it, but the battalion personnel questioned our assessment because of the extensiveness of the trail network. When we eventually arrived at the rear end of a trailblazing elephant, they finally accepted our premise. Being assigned a mission to recon (what would ultimately turn out to be elephant trails) would happen several times while we were working in the central highlands around the city of Kontum. But "recon" was after all, one of our purposes for existence. Fortunately for us, elephants tend not to scale cliffs.

Just a few days earlier we had been airlifted to Kontum City to set up a forward base camp just off the runway. We were inside an ARVN perimeter. The South Vietnamese troops had deployed a light tank section to secure the portion of the airstrip near our bivouac area. The terrain was pretty open, firm, and flat-- a good place for armor to operate effectively. I, however, wasn't operating effectively.

I don't recall if the pain started onboard the transport aircraft or on the ground, but by the time we reached our designated company area, my whole body was aching and my head pounding. My self-diagnosis was that I was being introduced to malaria. If I hadn't ached so much, I might have been angry that the Army medical service had failed me. Each Monday I had fervently downed the large, orange malaria tablet that many troops avoided because of the diarrhea that normally followed after ingesting the pill. For a time, medics were required to watch each man swallow the orange tablets to insure that they didn't spit them out. I also took a daily dose of the small white dapsone pills that had originally been introduced to prevent leprosy. Dapsone had also been deemed beneficial in warding off malaria. I had applied mosquito repellant liberally. So why did I feel like the proverbial freight train was running through my head?

Jim Potts sensed my problem (probably because of all my whining and moaning), and told me to give him my poncho and shelter half. He would take care of constructing the hooch and digging our prone shelter. I couldn't muster enough strength at the time to even feel guilty

Jim Potts,
photo courtesy of Leo Heaney

about leaving Jim with my half of the labor. I did recognize the debt that I owed him.

I started the night shivering under a poncho liner. Somewhere I drifted off into a deep, restful sleep. When I awoke, the pain was gone. I felt completely normal again, almost like the previous day had been a dream. I experienced no lingering after effects. Again, I tried to apologize for leaving him with my portion of the entrenching and shelter constructing tasks the previous evening, but he just shrugged it off. On the line, expressing and receiving gratitude is a quick thing; neither party flaunts it. Be where you're supposed to be, do what you're supposed to do, when you're supposed to do it, and somewhere down the line you'll get a chance to pay it back or pay it forward. I didn't push the thanking thing. Jim knew that I truly appreciated his favor. We procured some "Army" coffee from the mess tent and waited for the mission statement, which the battalion delivered in short order. Before the morning could creep into noon we had been "heliborned" into our new AO…back with the NVA.

*****

In the central highlands more caution was required when selecting LZs because many of them were seeded with punji stakes. I figured that the battalion operations officers might have suspected this, and that was the reason they had inserted us at the base of the mountain. They then directed us to hump up, rather than drop us farther up the mountainside. My analysis was not entirely correct, but the reason for the lowland insertion wouldn't become obvious to us until we rose higher in elevation.

An archaic trail (not elephant produced) headed up the mountain in the direction we had been assigned. That was the good news. The bad news was that we had a butt-kicking climb in store for us. The brown contour lines were so close together that it looked as if someone had smeared chocolate on the maps. As we gained elevation we encountered fog--actually clouds on the ground. For the next few days we would not see the sun. A perpetual, cold dampness pervaded everywhere. A layer of moss shrouded everything, covering rocks and logs, dangling from branches like stalactites. The landscape reminded me of those old black and white horror flicks where a prehistoric creature that time forgot emerges from out of the primordial mist. Except where we passed, the area was undisturbed, and had been that way for quite some time.

When the terrain leveled out near the summit, we moved off the trail into a standard defensive perimeter which became our patrolling base for the next several days. What passed during this reconnaissance phase might easily qualify as the most uncomfortable weather episode that I had experienced while in country. Our thin jungle fatigues and light poncho liners were not up to the task of keeping us warm. The high altitude, cold rain, perpetual dampness, and no sunshine left us shivering most of the time. It wasn't unbearable. No one was going to freeze to death, but comfort was a fleeting commodity to say the least.

Nights were more difficult than days. During the day we could warm a C-ration or brew coffee. We dried ourselves off and warmed up a little by cooking our Cs between our legs with a poncho liner wrapped around us. We resembled little teepees with heads sticking out. Those wearing traditional jungle fatigues dried out pretty fast in the poncho oven teepees. The camouflaged, cotton, tiger striped fatigues took quite a bit longer. The fuel tablets we used for heating our rations were always in short supply, and now we were expending them at an accelerated rate. The claymore mines were packed with C-4 plastic explosive which could be substituted for cooking fuel when the normal trioxane tablets were unavailable, or in this case, becoming rare. Actually, the C-4 was preferred over the standard heat tablets because it seemed to burn hotter--which translated into faster coffee.

Joe Hennessey and I had dismantled our claymore and scavenged the C-4. We didn't give it a great deal of thought. The claymores were expendable items; they were expected to be used. Harold Jacobs, our former machine gunner, had taken a job in supply. We figured we would just draw another claymore from him when the operation ended. We retained the empty casing and canvas carrying sack so that everything would appear normal. No use in inviting criticism from our platoon leaders who might object to the cannibalization of a defensive weapon.

At night Mother Nature seemed adamantly determined to defeat our most ardent shelter erecting efforts. Cold drips and driblets found their way through our defenses and homed in on us as we slept. The person on guard duty suffered even more. Maintaining light discipline meant that nights were cold. Morning brought with it the ability to produce some warmth by lighting up a fuel tablet or a hunk of C-4. I say morning, not daylight. There was no sun for the three days that we were marooned in that defensive position in the clouds.

Charley Hartz and Bobby Jacobs were manning the position to the right of mine. On the second day I moseyed over to chat and complain about the weather. Hartz was preparing some coffee with his normal "confident-self" grin. The cold rain seemed to have no effect on Hartz. Just inside their poncho hooch sat Bobby Jacobs wrapped in a standard issue woolen blanket, the only person clever enough to carry one with him! On closer scrutiny I realized that underneath his camouflaged fatigue shirt, Hartz was clad in a light weight, olive drab sweater. I gave up the idea on complaining about the weather. No use drawing attention to my lack of experience and forethought.

Whatever the reason the battalion had for our sojourn into the clouds, it was never revealed to us. If our officers knew, they didn't share the wisdom. But as the routine resupply day neared, it was obvious that we needed to relocate out of the fog to a place where the pilots could land, or at least drop supplies to us. This was probably the reason that they couldn't insert us at the top of the mountain at the start of the operation. On the morning of the fifth day, as unceremoniously as we arrived, we withdrew back down to the lowlands. Near the end of our descent, where the land flattened, we passed through C Company heading up the trail. During a brief pause while the COs exchanged information, we had the opportunity to do the same with some of the line troops. They, like us, had found very little sign of the enemy. Within ten minutes we were on our distinct ways: we to a resupply LZ in the sun, and they up into the damp and gloom.

*****

The resupply chopper brought with it a change of venue and a caveat from the battalion commander. The battalion staff was on to the C-4 drain! Henceforth, the claymores were to be considered an "accounted for" item and needed to be returned to the ammo sergeant at the completion of the operation. The threat of battalion level, non-judicial punishment, in the form of an Article 15 from the battalion CO, was not even remotely disguised!

Tom Rosales and Joe Hennessey, photo courtesy of Tom Rosales

Joe Hennessey and I got the message and Joe's response was classical Hennessey. "What are they going to do, send us to Vietnam?" I took the matter with a little more apprehension, but considering that we had just been delivered another five days of rations, I figured we had some time to work out a plan to legitimately "expend" the empty claymore shell that I was carrying. Then the word came down to prepare for extraction—we were being pulled back to provide security for the battalion tactical operations center. Maybe I didn't have five days!

*****

As usual, the battalion TOC was situated on a bald hill offering fields of fire for the troops providing security, while requiring enemy infantry personnel to traverse large expanses of open ground. I didn't have a lot of experience at battalion operation centers, but the presence of two 105mm howitzers at the TOC CP was new to me. In my past experiences, I encountered them in a single battery formation of six guns.

I really appreciated the immediate, accurate support that artillery provided. The disadvantage, if you are around the howitzers, is that they are noisy and they tend to draw enemy mortar and rocket fire. Three of us were directed to establish a listening post in the bunker farthest downhill, just below and slightly to the left of the howitzer section. I believe Joe Hennessey and Bob Stanczyk completed our threesome.

The listening post was well constructed with overhead cover stout enough to withstand a direct hit from an 82mm mortar. Obviously the previous occupants had access to a lot of building material and some well-engineered plans. Although the structure didn't leak, it wasn't what a person would call warm and dry. Dank and damp would more accurately describe our sandbag bungalow. But it afforded us the opportunity for a change of venue. We familiarized ourselves with our area of responsibility. We readied our night vision starlight scope. We set up a cook stove to prepare some coffee during the night watch, a luxury not available to us in our normal defensive posture out under the stars. The crescendo and concussion of the artillery tubes just to our right pretty much insured that no one would fall asleep, either on guard duty, or off guard duty for that matter. We cursed in unison when the coffee can toppled off the stove, and the floor of the bunker seemed to rise up and toss us a half a foot into the air. Also, considering the ringing in our ears, we were a listening post in name only. As far as we were concerned, the extraction of the guns the next morning by helicopter wasn't soon enough.

No one seemed to know how long we were destined to provide security for the TOC, but that lack of information didn't really have any effect on our situation; we were where we were. When the sergeants gave us the word, we would pack up and leave. Since we were stationary, I planned on using the respite to write a few letters home. Christmas was only a few weeks away. I had procured some writing paper and envelopes from the sundry package that accompanied the last resupply. I got comfortable by the forward aperture of the bunker and set about my composition task.

In the area where I grew up in eastern Pennsylvania, we customarily sent Christmas cards depicting the three Magi following the Star of Bethlehem. The first of such cards to arrive was placed above the entrance way and was said to bring good luck throughout the year, something akin to placing a horseshoe above the door in new homes. My Aunt Teresa and my mother were especially close. Since my aunt and uncle had no children, my mother encouraged my brother, sister, and me to be sure to remember their birthdays and holidays, as well as helping out with certain chores like mowing the lawn or running errands. Early in my card writing career I took on the mission of sending my aunt and uncle the traditional good luck Magi card. So, on a grey cardboard C-ration box, I sketched three soldiers in tiger fatigues and hats following a large star. The accompanying stanza that I included went something like this:

> "For nineteen years, I followed this star.
> It's brought me adventure and taken me far.

> And now I find it has delivered me here,
> to join with these Tigers in their Christmas prayer."

I don't know what my aunt did with the numerous inexpensive vials of eau de toilet that I purchased for her as Christmas and birthday gifts, but I do know what she did with that handmade Christmas card. Many years later, when my aunt had passed away, my brother and I were sorting out some of her estate items. We came across that card pressed into the photo album with her and Uncle Frank's wedding pictures.

While we were laid back, enjoying the respite that our bunker duty was providing us, we were aware of (but not paying much attention to) the helicopter activity taking place up the hill. The TOC was leapfrogging to another location. Since the Force was the security element, we figured that we would be the last to be evacuated, assuming we were being heli-borne out and not walking. At any rate, our rucks were ready for the moment the team leaders gave us the word to move out. When we scribbled the last "free" on the corner of the envelopes where the stamps would go, I collected all the letters that we had finished, and headed up hill to put them in the platoon sergeant's mail pouch.

A sound similar to a flag snapping in the wind registered first. The sound was from a discarded poncho draped over a ridgepole, flapping in the breeze. If isolation can be a sensation as well as a condition, I was experiencing it. The TOC, the Force, everyone was gone. I then noticed in the valley to the east, a helicopter evacuating an artillery piece by sling. I returned to the bunker and appraised the other two Tigers of our situation. If we sat tight and hoped someone with the Force noticed our absence, we lost the window of opportunity for reaching the artillery in the valley. How long would it be before someone in the Force noticed we weren't present? We were missed in the pack count going out. What if the Force went into a hot LZ? It might be some time before our absence crossed anyone's mind. There was also the possibility that some of the local NVA might come scavenging around. Joe Hennessey wasn't the type of person to sit around and wait to be rescued; neither was I. So Plan A (to stay in place and wait) was scrubbed. We were going to head east for the artillery position, an estimated distance of six kilometers.

We assessed our odds of covering the distance to the artillery position before it was completely evacuated. If it was a full battery of six guns, and they had just started to redeploy with one ship ferrying the tubes, then we might be able to get there before all the personnel were extracted. It was almost a direct line downhill on a good trail. Without a map or a radio, the artillery position was our only known location of "friendlies" in the area. At that moment, it was the only game in town. If we didn't make it in time, we'd be left with the old proverbial "Plan C," which we were still working out. Heading north or west would put us deeper into territory controlled by the NVA. To the south lay more highlands, which meant slower going and we only had about five days of rations on us. After that it would be bamboo sprouts and whatever. To the east, the land dropped and opened up: easier going and in a friendlier direction, less densely populated by our adversaries. We could probably cover a pretty fair distance in five days, and maybe intersect a major north/south highway near the coast or even hit the coast. From there we would turn south. Plans B and C were definitely east.

The familiar "wap-wap" sound of a Huey's blade slapping air proffered Plan C. The slick emerged out of the overcast and touched down just ten meters to our left. The pilot on the left side slid back the Plexiglas and beckoned me over to him. He said, "Are you Heaney?" When I nodded, he motioned for us to get onboard. I flopped onto the metal deck behind the pilot. I preferred the floor rather than the web seating. The view to the rear was better than facing forward trying to catch a limited glimpse over the control console. I sometimes envied the door gunners, but only momentarily. They were easy targets; so were the helicopters. The ground offered more protection. However, I wasn't in a particular hurry to have the chopper ride end. The fact that the pilot had addressed me by name had not escaped me, nor did I consider it a propitious omen. I had observed in my short career in the Army that when someone calls your name, it frequently means you're on a list. More often than not, when your rank is private, the list is a "shit list." I had the feeling that Platoon Sergeant Flynn would want to speak with me when we alit from the aircraft. Actually, he started the one-sided conversation before we had even cleared the aircraft.

Sergeant Flynn was an experienced, competent leader that I highly respected. He had every right to be angry. Catering to my creature comforts, I had missed an extraction and redeployment, not to mention that we could have easily become a missing-in-action statistic. Since I was the ranking PFC, the responsibility was mine. When wrong, shut up. That's what I did. I offered no excuse; I had none. I just stood there waiting for the tirade to cease so I could rejoin my team and later face the extra duty assignments that most certainly would come my way when we returned to base camp. Digging ammo pits and burning shit cans were definitely in my immediate future. But Sergeant Flynn wasn't ready to let me off quite yet. He inhaled and started delivering a second volley. Captain Agerton, who had been observing off to the side, tactfully put an end to the verbal castigation with a comment to Sergeant Flynn that it appeared that we had "received" the message.

As we turned to head off to Sergeant Kratzberg's force, the captain queried us about where we were heading when the chopper intercepted us. The pilots must have reported that they picked us up as we were departing the old TOC location. We told the captain that since we didn't have a map or a radio, we were going to try to make our way down to the artillery unit that was in the process of redeploying. If we didn't get there in time, then we would continue east to the South China Sea and then south, hoping to run into friendly forces. The captain commented that he probably would have done the same. His response eased the moment.

Brief Summary of Operation Geranimo[1]

Timeframe: 31 October–4 December 1966 (officially)*
Base camp: Tuy Hoa
Area of Operations: Phase I started 50 kilometers southwest of Tuy Hoa. Phase II shifted to the mountainous area northwest of Tuy Hoa.
Enemy Situation: Phase I targeted the PAVN 18B Regiment. Phase II shifted to the base camps of the PAVN 95th Regiment.
Mission: Search and Destroy
Other Considerations: This was a joint operation initially with the 1st Brigade and elements of the South Vietnamese ARVN 47TH Regiment of the 22nd Division, along with the South Korean 28th Regiment of the 9th Division. Later in Phase II, U.S. 4th Infantry Division joined in support of the operation.
After Action Assessment: Intelligence indicated that most of the PAVN 18B had evacuated the AO before the operation commenced. The PAVN 95th Regiment vacated the AO to the west after losing its base camps. Enemy losses were 150 KIA, with 76 POWs.
*The 95th had actually abandoned the area by the 24th of November.

****

[1] *George L MacGarrigle, Combat Operations: Taking the Offensive, October 1966 to October 1967*, Government Printing Office, 1998, p. 79. ISBN 9780160495403, cited in Wikipedia.org, 2/4/18.

Chapter 16
Tiger Six Down
Second Week of December 1966

Things that go bump in the night.

A few days after that little introduction to humility, as we were easing into a defensive position, battalion directed the Force to prepare for a night movement which would involve passing through B-Company's perimeter.

Jacobs and Hartz were selected for point; I was rear security. Dallas Rogers was the man in front of me. Dallas was new to the Force, and this might have been his first night operation in country. I fastened my open compass to his rucksack so I could follow the luminous dial as he moved. Fortunately the vegetation was not particularly dense, so we could snake our way between trees without resorting to machetes. Mother Nature provided little ambient light, so it was extremely dark. Normal tactical dispersion was impossible without running the risk of breaking contact with the man in front of you. We moved literally right behind each other. If a person got a second or two ahead of you, they vanished into the darkness. This was the era before satellites, GPS, and night vision goggles, and we were not on a trail. Jacobs and Hartz were moving cross-country, following a compass azimuth to B-Company's night position.

Our progress was slow but constant. I wasn't paying attention to time. My focus was on the compass dial on Dallas's pack. About the time that I started feeling comfortable maneuvering within the inky milieu, the luminous dial disappeared. Almost simultaneously there followed thrashing sounds. The Force had made a left turn to avoid a rather steep, wide gully. Dallas missed the turn, went over the edge, and down the embankment. Fortunately he arrested himself in some thick brush about fifteen feet down the face of the gully. I looked over the edge and could barely see him. I gave him a hand getting up, and I took the lead to regain contact with the Force.

The Force had already dissolved into the dark...and no one in the Force was aware that we were no longer with them. I had always felt that one of the Force's greatest tactical assets was its ability to move silently. That night I would have appreciated a little noise to help me relocate it. Stumbling around in the night, without a radio, in close proximity to an American line company was not a prospect I welcomed. We needed to get reattached to the Force.

Dallas Rogers,
photo courtesy of Sam Carnero

Logically, Jacobs would skirt the rim of the gully until it was shallow enough for him to safely cross over and regain his original heading. Dallas and I needed to re-establish contact with the Force quicker than ASAP. In what felt like eternity (but was probably less than five minutes), our luck changed for the better, and I bumped into the last man in the element. Actually, our luck had doubled down, for we not only found our way back to the Force, but we reunited at the very moment our point element found B-Company's outer perimeter. Then the firing started. Someone in B-Company didn't get the word about our passing near their perimeter, and sent a line of red tracers across our front.

Maintaining noise discipline was no longer an issue. Radio crackle and Captain Agerton's voice punctuated the night. The tracers had emanated on our right. The muttered expletives drifting back towards me confirmed that the Captain had taken off in that direction. The wait to move wasn't very long. We kept B-Company to our right and moved over a small ridge and into defensive position. The next morning, Jacobs revealed that when the shots were fired, he and Hartz (like the rest of us) had hit the ground. Jacobs, however, landed directly in front of one of B-Company's command detonated claymores. Fortunately for Jake, and all the tigers around him, by the time the situation was under control, cooler heads prevailed.

The next day we resumed normal search and destroy operations. The purpose of the night move was never made known to us.

*****

Within a few days, the Force was directed to link up with the Battalion CP group again. It looked like another TOC security mission. However, when we arrived on the scene, it was obviously not the typical TOC location. Instead of selecting a defensive position on the military crest of a hill (where they could control the high ground), the battalion command group was scattered on the side of a hill, in a fairly open area with wooded terrain above them. Tactically the position was poor, and it was compounded by the lack of dispersal of the battalion personnel. They were clustered just off both sides of the only trail passing through the area. The Force was moving through the battalion gaggle, uphill towards the place where the battalion staff was gathered.

Joe Hennessey and I were about ten men back from Hartz and Jacobs, who were on point. Getting a security element up the hill into the tree line seemed tactically essential at that moment. About the time that Joe and I had reached the center of the battalion mass, a halt was called. Word came down to send our "six" forward to meet with the battalion staff officers. Six (6) or zero six (06) is the call sign suffix that designates the unit commander. Joe and I stepped off the trail to allow room for Captain Agerton to pass through. As the captain passed by, he muttered some disdainful comment regarding the tactical prowess of the individual that had selected that particular location for the TOC. It was something on the order of, "Whose fucking idea was this?"

Knowing that these officer powwows could sometimes take awhile, Joe and I assumed our customary "wait-a-minute" posture: sitting down, resting on our rucksacks, facing each other, so we could cover each other's back.

The shot echo generated little more than an inquisitive reaction from us. We weren't sure if it was incoming or outgoing. We did not hear the normal crack-pop of a round whizzing nearby. As we were trying to process the peculiar nature of the shot, Sergeant Kratzberg shouted, "Agerton's been hit." That caveat initiated a reaction. Two of our Force medics flashed past Joe and me as they darted for the captain. The point team of Hartz and Jacobs started racing towards the tree line. Joe and I instinctively slipped through the nearby battalion personnel and took up a position about twenty meters to the right, where we could cover a small gulley that led towards the CP group. The senior NCOs of the Force quickly set up a defensive perimeter around the battalion group. Off my left shoulder, I picked up the familiar figures of Hartz and Jacobs leading the rest of the point team into the tree line. Joe and I had moved up the hill a little, so the medics were behind us as they assisted the battalion surgeon with the captain. One of our medics asked the surgeon if he thought the captain should be turned over onto his wounded side. First aid doctrine for a chest wound prescribed laying the wounded person on the side with the injury to prevent blood and fluid from running into the good lung and drowning the individual. The medevac chopper arrived; the captain was out of there. And we all felt numb.

Sergeant Kratzberg delivered the news that we would be setting up a defensive perimeter with the battalion CP group for the night. Joe and I were to stay where we were, and the sergeant would send over another man to make guard shift easier. Just two men, pulling 'one hour on' and 'one hour off,' makes for a long tiring night. Before long, the point team returned. Hartz and Jacobs had chased down and dispatched a lone enemy armed with an AK-47. Say what you will about vengeance being the purview of the Lord's; it can be extremely satisfying to mere mortals as well. Sergeant Kratzberg returned later to check out our position and update us on the captain's status. The captain made it to the hospital alive. Sergeant Kratzberg directed us to cover the small gulley that led into our area. This gave Joe and me a potential opportunity to legitimately "expend" our C-4 deprived claymore. Hopefully we would be presented with a reason to use it!

Tigers almost never fired their weapons at night unless they had a valid target. Joe and I were betting that the battalion personnel would be a little jumpy after the day's activity. We just needed to wait until someone let loose a burst, or a trip flare went off, or some other incident arose so we would have an excuse for firing our claymore. The trick would be detonating a claymore that had no explosive in it! To this end, we defused an M-26 fragmentation grenade and replaced its blasting cap with the claymore's cap. We taped the grenade to the backside of the plastic claymore shell and ran the electrical cord back to our position where we hooked it up to the claymore's M-57 firing device. Also, we set out some trip flares. We ran a separate wire from the flare in front of our claymore directly back to our position, so that we could trip the flare ourselves. We set up behind a large log and waited to see what the night presented.

About two hours into the watch, someone uphill from us let off a burst, followed by another. A quick jerk on our trip flare wire ignited the flare in front of the claymore. We then fired our claymore--or more accurately--our grenade. We figured that we just insured our chances of being omitted from the battalion commander's Article-15 list. However there were three small glitches in our reckoning. One, a fragmentation grenade doesn't leave the same odor as a claymore. Two, a claymore sounds about five times louder than a grenade. Three, Sergeant Kratzberg was in our position almost before the flash waned. He was doing his job checking on our situation. We told him that the flare in front of the claymore went off, so we fired the claymore. He rather quizzically responded with, "That was the claymore?" The sergeant was a pretty experienced old timer. He let it go. One claymore expended and accounted for, and Joe and I had avoided inclusion on another shit list! I still had Sergeant Flynn to face when we got back to base camp for my missing-the-chopper incident at the last TOC.

The next morning, the Force swept the hillside above the TOC. A well-defined trail displaying very little recent use ran across the ridge above the battalion's location. There were no signs of any permanent facilities in the area, so we speculated that the individual who shot the captain was probably in transit. As he passed above the battalion assembly area, he took a quick shot at the officer that he perceived as most threatening. Of the several battalion officers clustered for their powwow, the captain was the only officer in camouflaged fatigues, and the other battalion officers would have appeared to have been waiting for him to arrive. The enemy's logic was sound: of all the officers present, Captain Agerton was the one who would personally bring the war to him. The captain survived his wounds. I met him again about three years later at Ft. Bragg while he was a major serving with the Eighty-Second Airborne Division. We still correspond, and every year or two we reminisce at the Force reunion.

Major David Hackworth may have designed the Force to "outguerilla the guerilla," but Captain Thomas Agerton gave the Force its standing directive: to seek out and attack the enemy no matter what their size. We left the battalion CP on the side of that hill and carried the captain's directive into the mountains of Kontum Province, moving towards Christmas of 1966.

Brief Summary of Operation Pickett[1]

Timeframe: 6 December 1966-19 January 1967
Base camp: Kontum City near air strip
Area of Operations: Started near the Cambodian border, after Christmas truce, moved to an area north and east of Kontum City
Enemy Situation: 1st and 10th NVA Divisions supposedly in AO
Mission: Search and destroy. Executed in three phases: movement to Kontum from Tuy Hoa, search and destroy operations near border, then shift to AO north and east of Kontum City
Other Considerations: Concurrent with tactical operations, the brigade conducted airborne refresher training at base camp for proficiency jump in area near Kontum City
After Action Assessment: Intelligence indicated that several of the enemy regiments had recently moved across the border into Cambodia. 62 enemy confirmed KIA.[2]

****

[1] Combat After Action Report—Lessons Learned, HQ, Operation Pickett, 1st Bde, 101st Airborne Division, 17 March 1967.
[2] List of Allied Military Operations in Vietnam 1966, en, Wikipedia.org.

Chapter 17
Christmas '66 in Kontum City
December 1966

"...when your heart wants lifting, think of pleasant things..." —J.R.R. Tolkien

Bright and early on my first morning back in our base camp near the Kontum City airfield, I was directed to report to First Sergeant Kazmin. Naturally, I assumed Sergeant Flynn had not forgotten (nor forgiven) my wee indiscretions during the last operation and had reserved a place for me on the extra duty roster.

I arrived at the orderly room tent to find four or five other Tigers already gathered there. As the First Sergeant emerged from the back of the tent, a large toothy grin spread across his face. My mental wager on what our extra duty might include waned from burning shit cans to digging latrines or grenade sumps.

The First Sergeant was a person I liked and respected. He served with the Hundred-and-First in World War Two. He had a Screaming Eagle patch on his left shoulder with the eagle facing forward, and a Screaming Eagle combat patch on his right shoulder with the eagle facing rearward: eagles guarding his front and back. He called it double protection. If Top was the first generation of parachute infantry some twenty odd years before, then we were the second generation. On the rare two or three days per month that we spent in base camp, Top made a point of getting to know us. On several occasions, he pulled up a sandbag and shared some combat lore with us. It was not the bravado stuff, but the credible stuff: the genre of missed shots, miscalculations, and a few outright embarrassing mistakes.

We all experienced a "first contact with the enemy" episode. Quite often, on those occasions, dumb-luck rather than cool tactical efficiency intervened to save our butts. The First Sergeant also stumbled through a firefight or two. On one of our reminiscent sessions, Sergeant Kazmin shared his first chance encounter with an enemy soldier in France. Being a little anxious (possibly nervous) in his attempt to engage a German soldier in Normandy, he inadvertently tugged on the magazine of his Thompson submachine gun. The Thompson does not have a magazine well, and it fires from the open bolt position. If the operator pulls downward on the magazine, the bolt (as it passes forward) can miss extracting a cartridge from the magazine, leaving the firing pin with nothing to fall upon. The result is a misfire; a click rather than a bang. This is what Sergeant Kazmin experienced as he drew down on the German soldier. The "dumb luck" part of the experience was that the German soldier, rather than shoot, skedaddled. The German and Sergeant Kazmin both dumb-lucked out! The sandbag sessions with the First Sergeant always boosted my morale.

So, huddling with the other Tigers in the vestibule of the orderly room tent, I waited for the First Sergeant to assign our specific tasks. What followed wasn't quite what I had expected.

The First Sergeant didn't start by delegating work assignments. Instead, he stated that he had a problem. He wanted to promote all of us, but we were "eleven bushes" and he only had "eleven hotel" slots. In lay terminology, the First Sergeant was referring to our military schooling. Most of us had transferred to Tiger Force from the battalion's line companies. Our military classification was 11B, light infantry. Remember, Tiger Force was formed by combining the battalion's anti-tank and reconnaissance platoons. The promotion slots available to the First Sergeant from the Department of the Army were for personnel with reconnaissance (11F) and heavy weapons, anti-tank (11H) MOSs.

In a Cold War encounter with the Eastern Pact nations, Tiger Force would have operated as a reconnaissance/anti-tank unit. In the jungle highlands and boggy rice fields of Vietnam, the motorized components (designed to operate on a fluid battle field in Europe) didn't support Major Hackworth's "out-guerrilla-the-guerilla" concept. In order to work clandestinely in the opponent's backyard, the Force had parked its gun jeeps and recoilless weapons. The Force had evolved into a light infantry unit and subsequently recruited volunteers with "eleven bush" qualifications. But the available promotions slots available from the DOA were for anti-tank personnel. It was one of those Catch-22 situations!

We understood Top's statement. As a group, we thanked him for considering us, and started to leave when the First Sergeant's "Not so fast!" jerked our chain. He then directed us to meet him at the Supply Room tent after the mess line closed the following morning.

*****

The rest of the day was ours. Back in the states, people would be traveling to see relatives and friends over the Christmas break. Like the folks back home, most of us made our way to the closest "relatives" we had in the area, the comrades in the line companies that we served with before joining Tigers.

I hooked up with John Ruff in Cobra Company and then we journeyed over to Abu Company to hang out awhile with Carl Manners. Our friendships dated back to advanced airborne infantry training and jump school. Then we were four, but Fred Ryan had been killed in June, so now we were three. After some coffee and reminiscing, we parted with the usual wishes for good luck and the understanding that we would rendezvous at the USO show scheduled for the following day.

I diverted from the most direct route back to the Force to check in on Eddie Nunez in B Company area. Eddie had learned that there was a large Catholic community in Kontum City, and he planned to attend their evening Noel service. I accepted his invite to tag

Eddie Nunez,
photo courtesy of Leo Heaney

along. After chow, as twilight started to make its appearance, we headed off in the direction of town. We skirted around the northwestern part of the runway, past the control facility and two light tanks that were part of the ARVN security force protecting the airstrip. I don't recall having specific directions to the Catholic Church. We just seemed to be following small groups of Vietnamese civilians moving on a common heading. The chaplains must have put the word out because other Americans were moving along with us.

As we passed some commercial looking establishments, one in particular caught my attention. Most of it was beneath street level, resembling a mine shaft entrance more so than a residence or store. It had no security gates, just an open doorway into a poorly lit chamber. Within that dark void, vacant faces of several old Vietnamese men stared back at me. "Vacant" isn't an accurate enough description of what grabbed my attention regarding the expressions on those old men. Despondent or hopeless would also serve. A soldier passing by took notice to me staring into that doorless entrance and uttered: "Opium den."

A few blocks later our search was over. The street we were following inclined downhill towards a western style church. A fairly large body of practitioners, mostly Vietnamese civilians with a sprinkling of U.S. military personnel, had assembled around the outdoor service which was already underway. Aware that we were strangers, Eddie and I held back a short distance trying to avoid anything that might be considered socially intrusive. Some time into the ceremony, it occurred to me that I had never attended a religious ceremony where the priests, the ministers, or the congregation didn't look like me. What prompted my thinking was probably what I was observing and hearing. Here were Asian priests dressed in silky chasubles, raising golden chalices, while uttering invocations in Latin. The assembled faithful also responded in classical Church Latin. With nine years of parochial schooling and two years of high school Latin, I felt very much "at home" with that service. Indeed, I felt very comfortable with that night. It was one of those calming experiences that I have come to appreciate more with age.

The rest of the evening was pretty much uneventful until Eddie and I neared the battalion base camp where we observed a spontaneous and atypical fireworks display. Our sister battalion, the 2/502, was bivouacked just west of our Cobra Company. Part of the pyrotechnic paraphernalia (which we all carried) included parachute flares and red-star-cluster signal flares. These devices were intended to be fired vertically, but were now being fired horizontally, canon-like, between the two battalions. That was probably one of the reasons why our stays in the rear areas seldom exceeded three days!

*****

The next morning, after mess, as prescribed, we positioned ourselves outside the Supply Room tent. Also positioned outside the tent were weapons I recognized only from war movies—flame throwers. When Top arrived, he succinctly defined our situation. Flame throwers fell under the classification of heavy infantry weapons. If we qualified with flame throwers, he could consider us heavy weapons certified. Ergo, he could promote us with the existing 11H slots that he had available.

The remainder of the day we spent learning how to charge air tanks, jelly fuel, exchange match cartridges, employ the weapon, and burn stumps. All the while, echoing in the background was music from the USO performance that we were missing. As we were cleaning up after the instruction was completed, I inquired about how the flame thrower was going to be employed. My concern was about its weight. It weighed as much as a fully loaded rucksack. I certainly couldn't foresee someone humping one of them plus their rucksack up some of the mountains that we had climbed in the highlands. The First Sergeant's reply was something to the effect that if one was needed, it would be flown or dropped in to us.

That night, the fireworks displays commenced again. The next day, we were airlifted back to the field and started a new operation.

Brief Summary of Operation Pickett[1]

Timeframe: 6 December 1966-19 January 1967
Base camp: Kontum City near air strip
Area of Operations: Started near the Cambodian border, after Christmas truce, moved to an area north and east of Kontum City
Enemy Situation: 1st and 10th NVA Divisions supposedly in AO
Mission: Search and destroy. Executed in three phases: movement to Kontum from Tuy Hoa, search and destroy operations near border, then shift to AO north and east of Kontum City
Other Considerations: Concurrent with tactical operations, the brigade conducted airborne refresher training at base camp for proficiency jump in area near Kontum City.
After Action Assessment: Intelligence indicated that several of the enemy regiments had recently moved across the border into Cambodia. 62 enemy confirmed KIA.[2]

****

[1]Combat After Action Report—Lessons Learned, HQ, Operation Pickett, 1st Bde, 101st Airborne Division, 17 March 1967.
[2]List of Allied Military Operations in Vietnam 1966, en, Wikipedia.org.

Chapter 18
The Water Buffalo, Murphy's Law
January 1-18, 1967

"...a little child shall lead them." --Isaiah 11:6

"When trouble comes, it comes not in single spies but in battalions."
--Alexander Pope

Enemy activity in Kontum Province at the start of 1967 was abnormally light when compared to what the NVA had thrown against us in that same province seven months earlier. Back then they had forced the evacuation of the Special Forces outpost at Toumorong, assaulted our supporting artillery firebase, attacked each of our line companies, pinned down elements of our sister battalion (the 2/502), and inflicted heavy casualties on Tiger Force. Now the NVA were as rare as hen's teeth! When an encounter did occur, it was usually a chance meeting with a brief exchange of fire power. Fortunately, those types of encounters usually ended in our favor. Generally two or three enemy were killed, intelligence material and weapons were gathered, and a search and destroy mission continued.

Some members of the Force speculated that the drought of enemy activity was a reflection of their reluctance to engage American troops, us in particular. This slightly egotistical premise might have had some basis in fact. One of our tactical strengths was our ability to concentrate fire power. More than likely, however, the enemy was avoiding contact in order to position himself for future operations. Within the next twelve months, the Second Battle of Dak To, the Battle of Khe Shan, and the Tet Offensive of 1968 would all erupt. See Summary Brief at end of this chapter.

In the absence of heavy contact with the enemy, the most recently arrived personnel had time to become accustomed to the way the Force operated, and gain experience in specific tactical positions. In the mountainous jungle terrain of the Central Highlands, the FEBA (Forward Edge of the Battle Area) was usually just forward of the point man's flash suppressor, a device to help obscure the location of the shooter. The terms "point man" and "slack man" carried implied combat dignity. Although most of us walked these positions during our tenure on the line, certain individuals were selected time and again to handle the responsibility. Working with the new Tigers, some obvious point-slack man partnerships were developing. Ernie Moreland and Robin Varney, along with Jim Ward and Dallas Rogers, had adapted rapidly to the point team positions. They gave the old reliables (like Charley Hartz and Bobby Jacobs, and Jim Raysor and Joe Hennessey) time to exercise their team leadership roles.

Even though contact with the NVA was light, there were some contentious moments, not specifically related to interactions with the enemy. One afternoon, a few days into the operation, we entered into a farmstead with a few thatched roof structures. A vast expanse of dry rice paddies, speckled with islands of vegetation and small groups of water buffalos, lay off to our left. I hadn't given much notice to the mammoth buffalo about twenty yards away until it started pawing the ground with its hooves. It earned my undivided attention when it put its head down and charged towards me. The animal drew up about four feet from me, just on the other side of a small sapling about two inches in diameter. When the buffalo moved to its right, I moved to my right. When it went left, I moved left. Several times we may-poled around the sapling, and ultimately we froze transfixed on each other. The looming, blue-grey critter, dripping fluid from its nostrils, apparently hadn't considered that it could just bowl over the sapling to get at me. And, I wasn't inclined to dispatch the buffalo;

neither was the rest of the squad. Killing what more than likely was some farmer's draft animal wouldn't endear us to the local residents. The proverbial Mexican standoff had evolved.

While I was examining my options for vacating the temporary protection provided by the sapling, a solution to my situation presented itself—one without having to shoot the water buffalo. From one of the nearby hooches, a small lanky Vietnamese child of maybe seven or eight years emerged. In route to us, he picked up a branch, casually approached the beast, swatted the giant, lumbering beast on the nose and buttocks, and drove it back into the paddy. Then the little Vietnamese David discarded his "olive branch" and continued on down the trail along the paddies and out of sight, never uttering a word.

As the buffalo lumbered off into the paddy, I rejoined the rest of my squad. They had been standing by, ready to intercede with force if things went south. A few chuckles and smiles greeted me. The rough American paratrooper image that I so carefully groomed and guarded since joining the Army had just been slightly emulsified by a small child with a tree branch. I had just experienced one of life's lessons on establishing win-win situations.

*****

We had patrolled for another week when we were suddenly withdrawn from the field. I say "suddenly" because the operation was only in its second week, whereas a normal field deployment lasted about twenty-five to twenty-seven days. The extraction of the Force went off without any interruption from the enemy. However, as we left the PZ, the Huey that I was riding in separated from the rest of the formation. Mission diversions were common, and I had run into this type before. We were being sent to provide security for a signal unit that had to dismantle a "two-niner-two" radio-relay position. These were antennas that allowed troops to communicate over mountains, similar to today's cell phone towers.

I knew the refreshments and steak would probably be gone before we got in, but at least I figured I had a full night's uninterrupted sleep waiting for me. I was wrong.

It took about four hours to get the signal gear packed. The evening was nearing the dark side of twilight as the choppers dropped us off at the Kontum airstrip. The two tanks that the ARVNs had deployed for perimeter security were gone. In their place were newly constructed, four foot high PLF platforms. I hadn't seen PLF platforms since jump school, nearly a year ago. Something was up, and it didn't take a mental giant to figure it out. About then I really dismissed my hopes about a full night's sleep.

The mortar platoon sergeant was in charge of our refresher training. He was a veteran of the Korean Conflict with a master parachutist's badge. The training session wasn't as long or as bad as I had imagined. We each demonstrated a few landing falls to the satisfaction of the platoon sergeant, and then he sent us off to the bivouac area. There, unexpectedly, the first Tigers in from the field had saved pop and steak for us. The barbeque was the typical fifty-five gallon fuel drum, cut in half lengthwise, with a wire grill supporting the meat. As we ate, other platoon members (who had arrived earlier and had already dined) provided us with an informal accounting of the upcoming agenda. Sometime in late morning we would draw parachutes, board C-130s and make a dawn proficiency jump at combat altitude with full field gear.

I remember sleeping soundly that night. However, the luxury of sleep without guard duty came to an end sometime near "o'dark thirty" when Sergeant Kratzberg delivered the customary fall-in call. Since the company bivouac area was adjacent to the airfield, we moseyed straight from our pup tents to the taxi-way. We picked up our T-10 main and reserve parachutes from riggers who were dispersing them from a two and a half ton truck. Everything seemed very laid back and informal. Everyone seemed to know exactly what to do. I felt like I had been doing this all of my life, yet in reality, this was only my sixth jump--my first one since jump school. The old timers refer to the sixth jump as your "cherry jump." In stateside garrison units, the "cherry jump" is usually preceded with a barrage of practical jokes on the yet uninitiated, novice jumpers. Naturally, I remained hush on this issue. I didn't need someone handing me my unhooked static line as I was about to exit the aircraft. So, I readied my gear, "chuted-up," and quietly sat, waiting for the Air Force transports.

It was still dark when the first C-130 arrived. The aircraft pivoted on its left gear and dropped the rear ramp for us to board. As I was getting into line, Sergeant Kratzberg asked me if I was really going to jump with the reserve that I had already strapped into position. I recognized a "loaded" question when I heard one, so I glanced down at my chest. Sure enough, there in yellow letters, almost invisible in the pre-dawn light, were the words "no jump" stenciled on my reserve pack. Sergeant Kratzberg never admitted switching reserves on me, but I've never been one who believed in the randomness of coincidences. Like, in the poor light conditions, the sergeant just *happened* to notice that someone had handed me--a rookie paratrooper on his cherry jump--a mock-up practice reserve chute which usually had styrofoam packing material inserted to give it bulk, but no actual reserve parachute! At any rate, the obvious was clear. I had to hustle over to the rigger's truck and exchange my training-aid reserve for one that might actually deploy if I needed it. I made it to the deuce and a half, exchanged my reserve, gave the riggers a look which implied that a comment wouldn't be necessary or welcomed, then turned and headed back to the aircraft. About that moment, I started to feel that the U.S. Air Force was in on the joke also, because the plane was already slowly taxing away. I barely made the tail ramp and was helped onboard by a few of the troops. No one said anything and I appreciated it. I just wanted to get that "cherry jump" over with. What else could fate hold for me?

Sergeant Kratzberg had saved a seat between himself and Dennis Crowley. He gave no evidence that he had anything to do with the parachute switch, and I maintained reticence. A quick assessment of the situation refocused my thoughts. We were in the rear of the aircraft near the right door. This meant that we would be some of the first to exit, and I felt this was a good omen. In the formal briefing that we had on the airstrip, someone mentioned that the DZ (drop zone) was only "eleven seconds" long. Each of the two jump sticks contained forty-three men, in line and hooked up to a cable and ready to jump. I did the math: about four men per second had to exit from each door. The troops up front near the pilot's cabin faced the possibility of a tree landing (or worse) if they missed the eleven-second window. (Ultimately, two of the 320th artillery personnel jumping with us ran out of DZ and came down in the local community, one through the roof of a hooch.) Unless the pilots issued a premature green light, I should easily find myself landing on a nice, flat, dry rice paddy. Soon the aircraft banked a few times, leveled off, and the jumpmaster started the countdown commands. Right about there, things started to go south.

In a normal jump, the web paratroop seats are raised and folded out of the way to clear the aisles and facilitate exiting the aircraft. This Air Force crew probably never conducted a parachute jump before; they had all the seats pinned and wired down. This meant that instead of the normal inboard and outboard formations, everyone was jammed into the middle of the aisle, cramped between the still lowered seats--a manageable but unwelcome situation.

As we were hooking up and checking equipment, the left door opened and slid out of the way. The right door should have followed suit, but didn't. The crew chief and the jumpmaster both were working on it, to no avail. About that time, it occurred to me that this exercise was probably more practice for the air crews than for us. Then the green light lit. The jumpmaster gave the go-nod to the left stick. In a mad dash, half the aircraft emptied. Those of us in the right stick looked to the jumpmaster for instructions. He gave us an improvised unhook gesture and indicated that we should u-turn around him and re-hook up for a left door exit. Here, the real fun started.

Because the jump seats were not folded up and out of the way, we were forced very near to the already open door. Since our static lines were unhooked and in our hands, we had to carefully but hurriedly maneuver around the seats close to the door. Naturally, in concord with the way my mind works, the premonition of being sucked out of the aircraft as I slithered past the open door had etched itself firmly into my neural pathways. About that moment, the pilots banked to the left for their go round. The floor suddenly turned into an inclined plane, sloping towards the open door! Having been raised in the anthracite region of Pennsylvania, a coal chute analogy flashed through my mind. To say that I, or rather all of us, hastened towards the nose of the aircraft would be an understatement. Soon we were all in the left aisle, hooking up on the inboard cable. However, now I was about the fortieth man from the door and the drop zone was still only eleven seconds long. There could be no room for hesitation or my "cherry jump" could turn into a tree-landing-and-extricating exercise. The plane leveled off. The green jump light illuminated. The race to "un-ass" the aircraft started.

I hadn't shuffled five steps when I slammed into the back of the trooper in front of me. It was Crowley. The man in front of him had snagged something on the seats and had been tossed forward onto his knees. I saw that about a yard of fabric was spilling out of his main chute pack. In what appeared to be one movement, Crowley quickly lifted the man to his feet, shoved the nylon back into the parachute pack, and pushed the man forward, continuing the race to evacuate the aircraft. I was right behind them with the last three or four troopers following me. I literally ran out the door.

Then I caught my helmet. I should say "the helmet without a chin strap that the First Sergeant had loaned me." I had improvised a strap from a camouflaged handkerchief. Not one of my cleverest moves. As my parachute deployed, the risers ripped the poorly secured helmet forward off my head. Fortunately, my hands "reflexed" upward when I felt the helmet coming off, and it landed right between them. I pulled the helmet into my chest against the reserve chute and waited for the fluttering sounds and tug which confirmed that my main chute had deployed. I checked my canopy to make sure there were no lines across it. Everything seemed fine. I put the helmet back on and tried to better adjust the handkerchief, hoping the landing wouldn't involve my head! I glanced at the C-130 from which we had just deployed. It was moving away fast. I had never seen C-130 from this perspective before. Soon, I became aware that Crowley was hailing me.

At first, I couldn't make out what he was saying. I figured it was some expression of elation, so I shouted something back and waved. But he continued to shout. He was below me and gesturing towards something beneath me. Finally, my mental faculties (which must have been absorbed in soaking up the ambiance of the event) discerned

Dennis Crowley,
photo courtesy of Jim Raysor

the word "tree." A quick glance earthward confirmed that my luck hadn't changed. A single leafless, scraggly tree, jutting upward from a paddy dike was excellently positioned to snag me. I quickly pulled in a riser to slip away from the tree. This maneuver spared me from the immediate tree threat, but I had created another problem for myself. I just increased my rate of acceleration towards the ground which was only the height of a tree away. With contact imminent, I mentally prepared for a hard landing. I got ready for the air to be knocked out of me, as had happened on some of those cold winter days at jump school. Had I had more experience, I would have focused on the fact that combat simulated jumps are conducted at significantly lower altitudes than stateside training jumps. I should have scoped out my intended landing area, noticed the tree earlier, and steered away from it while I still had altitude. Instead, I had bathed in the aesthetics of the moment and the penalty for this breech of concentration was about to be exacted.

One would think that the Fates would have been satisfied with the quantity of stress that they had already successfully administered, but they weren't quite finished with me. They elected to exercise yet another option and squelched my aspiration of landing on a nice piece of flat ground. My feet, which I had to pull up to avoid snagging them in the upper branches of the tree, touched down not in the rice paddy, but on a dike in the rice paddy. Momentum flipped me forward and vectored me towards the ground. Normally impact is absorbed along the feet, legs, buttocks and back. But the dike had set me up like a judo throw. I thought that if I were lucky, I might be able to quickly twist around to get the back side of my arm and shoulder to make contact before my head. Considering the events that had already transpired that morning, Lady Luck coming up on my side isn't something I would have wagered upon. The problem was, at that place and moment my skill assets were pretty much depleted. Luck was all I had left, that and hot air. And hot air did it.

Instead of crashing into the ground like the proverbial sack of potatoes, I nestled on in like a ball of feathers. I had no idea how buoyant warm air could be. I had completed jump school during winter. Therefore my total knowledge of parachutes involved cold air with concomitant hard landings. In Vietnam, even in the early morning hours, the air had enough buoyancy to drop me down easy. I quickly got out of my chute, secured my rifle and put on my rucksack. Part of the combat jump exercise was to leave the chutes and bags on the drop zone. I made my way to the rallying point to regroup with the rest of the unit. My cherry jump was history.

*****

For sometime afterwards we tried to analyze the purpose of the practice jump. The requirement to jump at least once every three months had been rescinded during our combat tenure. The terrain and the missions we faced were more suited to insertions by helicopters rather than parachute. One of our conclusions for the proficiency jump was that we were prepping for a traditional airborne deployment as part of a larger military operation, perhaps involving the Marines up north--maybe taking Haiphong in preparation for a final push on Hanoi. This reasoning demonstrated our misunderstanding of Cold War politics.

The official military statement from higher up cited that the purpose for conducting the proficiency jump was to promote esprit des corps. The senior military staff was correct on that assessment. I recalled that as I crossed the drop zone to the rallying point I had felt more than just a normal feeling of accomplishment. The Tigers that had formed around Lieutenant Carey, waiting for the last of us to report in, were more than fellow soldiers… more like a fellowship of sorts.

Summary Brief of Operation Pickett, Phase II[1]

Timeframe: 1–18 January 1967
Base camp: Kontum
Area of Operations: Dak Akoi Valley, northwest of Kontum
Enemy Situation: The primary NVA threat in AO was the 304th NVA Division. Prisoner of War interrogations revealed that four battalions from the 11th Regiment and 66th Regiment of the 304th had moved out of the AO during December, heading southeasterly to points unknown. The remainder of the 304th as well as a Main Force VC battalion and other local VC units were believed to still be operational in the AO.
Mission: The 1/327th was to conduct Search and Destroy operations on multiple axes within the AO.
Non-tactical Considerations: The battalion rotated forces from the field to the Kontum base camp in order to participate in proficiency parachute jumps on the 6th, 7th, and 18th of January. Later at an award ceremony on 20 January, among other 327th soldiers honored, SSG John T. Flynn of Tiger Force received the Vietnamese Cross of Gallantry with bronze star from Lieutenant General Vinh Loc, Vietnamese II Corps Commander.[2]
After Action Assessment: Evidence on the ground supported the POW statements that the 304th was moving out of the AO. Numerous abandoned hut complexes and several caches were discovered. Eighty-seven weapons, eighty-eight mortar rounds, and eighteen plus tons of rice and other food items were captured or destroyed. Enemy resistance was light and mostly VC, not NVA. Thirty-four enemy were killed in action and two POWs taken.

****

[1] A. White (Cpt. Inf.) and Naughton, Stephen L. (1Lt. Inf.), Unit History, 1st Battalion (Airborne), 327th Infantry, 1st Brigade, 101st Airborne Division, APO San Francisco, California, 96347, 1 January 1967 – 3 July 1967, reproduced at National Archives, Chapter 1, pages 1-7.
[2] Ibid, p. 7.

Chapter 19
The Flash, the Cook, and the Chemist
Late January-Early February, 1967

"From 1965 to 1967, the 1st brigade operated independently as sort of a fire brigade and earned the reputation as being called the 'Nomads of Vietnam,'" said Capt. Jim Page, division historian. "They literally fought in every area of Vietnam from the [demilitarized zone] up north all the way down to the central highlands." --Mary L. Gonzalez [1]

After the last units completed their proficiency jumps, the brigade withdrew from Kontum Province. Between January 21 and 26 the brigade returned to its base camp at Phan Rang for the first time since it had departed that location in 1965.

For most of us, Phan Rang was the place we passed through after leaving Camp Alpha in Saigon. Camp Alpha was the army's administration facility at Saigon that processed most in-coming personnel to that region. Initially, we spent a week in Phan Rang getting acclimatized at the brigade's Proficiency School, "P-Training." Phan Rang was the brigade's administrative headquarters where we dropped off our personnel, finance, and medical records. After that, we reported to our respective battalion orderly room tents and awaited transport to our forward areas. As individuals, we might return to Phan Rang when returning from a hospital, or heading for R&R, or processing to another unit, but the battalions didn't. They moved from one field operation to another. For over a year and four days, the line battalions stayed in the field.

*****

In January 1967, we returned to Phan Rang to find that the scarcity of GP medium tents, which had formerly served to delineate the three battalion areas, had been replaced with single storied wooden barracks seated on concrete foundations. Each structure was outfitted with about twenty plus metal beds, each bed with a fabric mattress. For most of the last year, sleeping off the ground (on a real bed and mattress) usually occurred only if we were on R&R or in a hospital. In retrospect, however, the beds and mattresses weren't the real items of importance. Getting a few uninterrupted full nights' sleep without having to pull guard duty, retreat from an advancing puddle, or fend off a leech assault readily made the Phan Rang accommodations more appreciated.

Bobby (Jake) Jacobs and I staked claim to two beds near one of the entranceways. Around the time of the proficiency jump, Jake and Charley Hartz had been selected to attend the MACV Recondo School at Nha Trang. Most troopers in the battalion would have considered attending Recondo School an envious assignment. Jake did not agree.

According to Jake, he and Hartz had reported in at the school shortly before the cadre held the orientation formation. Here an exposition on the school's grueling prospectus was announced to the potential recondos. The agenda was sweetened with the proclamation that the honor graduate would be awarded a coveted KA-BAR combat knife with the trooper's name, "honor graduate," and class number engraved on a small brass placard attached to the scabbard. Attendance at the school was voluntary, and each of the new volunteers standing in the formation was asked to explain his reasons for wanting to undergo recondo training. As the cadre staff maneuvered in front of each trooper, the prospective student acclaimed his personal purpose for being there. Jake said that the responses were ripe with gung ho rhetoric like: "I want to be a better leader, better soldier, acquire new combat skills," etc.-- all except Hartz. When it was Charley Hartz's time to respond why he was attending the school, he simply announced, "I need a knife."

As soon as Jake became aware that attendance was voluntary, he immediately "un-volunteered" himself. After all, he figured if he wanted "grueling," he could just return to the Force (which he did after a few stops at a local bar or two).

When the three week course was over, Hartz joined us while we were still at Phan Rang. Naturally, he had the coveted KA-BAR. On the scabbard was a brass tag with his name and "honor graduate" engraved on it. And typical Hartz, he didn't relegate the blade to trophy status and ship it home. Instead, he used the sturdy blade in the field to clear LZs and in other areas to chip ice to keep beer cold!

Hartz was originally schooled as a chemical warfare specialist. About this time the First Sergeant arranged for Hartz's rank status to change from Specialist 5th class to Sergeant E-5. As a Sergeant E-5, Hartz was now considered a non-commissioned officer, an NCO. The rank insignia for a Sergeant E-5 is the classical three chevrons, whereas the rank insignia for a Specialist 5 is a rocker with an eagle under it. Reluctantly, Jake gave up addressing his good buddy Hartz as a "bird sergeant." Coming from Bobby, Hartz never considered the remark derogatory. God help anybody else that delivered the epithet.

Before we had left Phan Rang, "Sergeant" Hartz introduced us to a tactic he had picked up at Recondo School. It was basically the same response we would employ if caught in a close-in enemy ambush: saturate the enemy positions with heavy automatic weapons fire and try to overwhelm them. If possible, maneuver on their flank. This was just basic ambush survival. The new twist Hartz added was to verbally direct the saturating fire with commands: "fire power up front" or "fire power left or right." Since none of us were mental giants, Sergeant Hartz had us practice the new technique several times. After Jake threatened a mutiny, our old buddy Hartz finally accepted that we probably had the new technique down and suspended further practice. Some of the fellows were a little critical about the effectiveness of verbal commands in a firefight. I reserved comment myself, and it saved me from later having to "eat crow." In about a week, we would be grateful for the ambush survival refresher the "Hartz period of instruction" had provided!

*****

Garrison routine at Phan Rang wasn't all it was cracked up to be. Some of my personal observations about our home base included the following: We slept dry largely because the metal roof wasn't hastily erected out of leaky ponchos. Since the coffee didn't come out of an accessory packet, it actually had an aroma. We were relieved of the regimen of constantly scanning the ground ahead for our next step, although it seemed that none of us were ever capable of breaking the habit completely--perhaps "comfortably" is the better word. And unlike a field operation, where you are stealthy and mobile, in garrison you are a stationary target--open for a rocket or mortar attack. So the announcement that the scheduled activity for the first full day back in garrison was filling sandbags and constructing shelters was not received with much enthusiasm. Likewise, Jake's reaction came as no surprise--he proclaimed that we (he, Bobby Gordon, and me) needed to get out of the forthcoming work detail. Where Jake had incentive, a plan was sure to follow. After quick consideration Jake announced that we three "needed" to report for sick call.

To the reader, this probably sounds like three GIs attempting to shirk a monotonous chore, but it was based a wee bit on paratroop tradition. Jake had been stationed with the "Hundred and First" at Fort Campbell, Kentucky. He, as well as other Tigers like Jim Raysor, often recounted a story regarding a confrontation between General Westmoreland and some of the public officials from the communities neighboring Fort Campbell. The tale concerned "excessive police tactics." According to the story, the commander presented the local community leaders with a win-win plan to reduce tension over the complaints regarding police profiling and rough-housing of members of the military. According

Bobby (Jake) Jacobs,
photo courtesy of Bobby Jacobs

to the lore, the plan involved assigning military police personnel to accompany local police officers. However, the general's offer was delivered with a caveat: For the sake of public safety, if tensions couldn't be resolved, the general would have no choice but to declare certain neighboring commercial districts "off limits" to his troopers. This put pressure on the local police and community leaders to consider the economic impact their strong-arm tactics would produce if compromise wasn't attainable. According to the legend, Westmoreland concluded his proposition to the community officials with a statement to the effect: "When my men work, they work hard. When they fight, they fight hard. And, when they play, they play hard."

The 1st Brigade had been in the field for over a year. We felt this fact qualified for working and fighting hard, and the fighting was over for a few days. But filling sandbags didn't quite fit any of our definitions of "playing hard." Jake's plan to avoid the sandlot was to report for sick call. Since there was no way that we would pass the thermometer test for a fever, Jake's plan was dental—preventive dental actually, because none of us had any current dental issues. If the reader feels that our rush to action hadn't produced an attractive set of options—i.e. fill sandbags or get a tooth filled—the following account certainly won't refute that assessment.

The medic issuing the sick slips didn't question our dental malady, he just handed us the required forms. Signing out at the Orderly Room, however, was a little more unnerving. Behind the office clerk stood the First Sergeant, arms crossed over his chest, intently eyeing the three of us. After his scrutinizing stare dissolved into a subdued grin, we were on our way. Right about the moment we exited the Orderly Room it occurred to us that since we had never been to the brigade dentist before, we didn't know where we were going. For directions we needed to return to either the Orderly Room or the medical platoon. We chose the medics.

The dental compound was a simple layout. The procedure rooms were tents. The waiting room was the open area between the tents. Counting the three of us, there were five "clients" in the waiting area. After a few minutes the dental officer on duty arrived and asked us what was bothering us. Because the three of us had no toothaches, we felt obligated to justify our "sick slips." We explained that since entering the military, we had not received any routine dental examinations. For the better part of the last year on the line, our diet pretty much consisted of canned food. The brigade's return to base camp now offered the opportunity for some dental maintenance if necessary. Fortunately for our case, the dentist entertained an appreciation for those concerned about dental hygiene. He agreed to check us out, and directed me to go hop into the seat in the nearby tent. There is where the day's adventure really turned memorable.

It started with my introduction to the tactical dental chair. There were no moving parts, and the chair was constructed in the reclining position. A person literally had to hop up to get into it. I flopped up into the chair, and thanks largely to gravity, ended up positioned correctly. I was feeling pretty good about how the morning was progressing. All three of us were accomplishing our goal of avoiding a work detail while at the same time achieving some maintenance on our teeth.

After a quick examination of my teeth, the dentist announced that I had two cavities: one upper right and one lower right. He stated that only one could be filled that day, and he asked me to choose. I told him to go for the cavity that looked like it might cause the most trouble in the immediate future. Then the dentist turned towards me with a syringe to administer a numbing agent. I don't know if Novocain is the correct term for the numbing agent dentists used in those days, but I stopped him to ensure that he was planning to fill and not extract my tooth. My civilian dentist only numbed a tooth for extractions, not for drilling. And I wanted to be sure that I was receiving a filling and not losing a tooth. After being reassured, the numbing agent was administered, and I was sent outside to wait for the drug to take effect. While I was waiting, the dentist examined Jake and Gordon and submitted them to the same protocol. After we were all numbed up, the dentist had me return to the chair to complete the filling procedure.

The next episode didn't proceed as I would have suspected. The dentist started drilling, but the Novocain didn't appear to have any effect on me. The discomfort (some would say "pain") was the same that I had always experienced during filling sessions with my civilian dentist back home. Being used to the "numb-less" technique, the slight aching didn't bother me enough to complain about it. I got what I expected from the incident and thanked the dentist as I departed the tent. Passing Jake on his way to take his turn, I alerted him to the possibility that the Novocain wasn't all that it was made out to be.

When Jake was done and joined us again, I learned that my suspicion regarding the Novocain was incorrect. The Novocain was good, the tooth was wrong! When the dentist looked into Jake's mouth, he shockingly proclaimed that he had just filled the wrong tooth on the other trooper. The phrase, "Oh my God!" was involved in the pronouncement. The dentist had forgotten which of my teeth he had "Novocained" and had performed the procedure on the on the non-numbed tooth. According to Jake, the dentist took slight umbrage when, in response to the officer's comment, Jake reacted with a burst of uncontrolled laughter. Had the tables been turned, I would have laughed too. I laugh just about every time I think of it. The mission was accomplished. I'm plus seventy years and I still have that tooth!

*****

The day was still young when we departed the dental complex. Returning too early to the battalion area could qualify us for an afternoon work detail; we needed to kill some time. Eventually, we made our way to an RMK BRJ construction unit. I no longer recall what bit of intelligence information directed us to that location, but the complex had all we needed. I should clarify that statement; it had all Bobby Gordon needed to make him feel at home. The civilian facility served what might be labeled "bar food" along with beer and soda, but most important, it had a quality pool table.

Gordon had previously "talked" a lot of pool. That day he walked the talk. Gordon ran the first three racks. He was on the fourth rack before he relinquished the cue stick. He seemed to have a routine which he performed with every shot. He'd chalk the tip, keeping the chalk cube in his stable hand. Then he'd call the shot by pointing the stick to the intended pocket, stroke the shot, and immediately head around the table to where the cue ball was heading. Gordon had a moniker, "The Flash." When I asked him how it came about, he responded that he was quick—"Quicker than a finstant, which is quicker than an instant, which is super quick!" I had assumed that his handle was modeled after the comic hero, but after watching him run three racks of pool balls, I had to adjust that premise.

A little money changed hands, but not enough that made anyone feel like they had been hustled. The construction workers were good to be around. We departed shaking hands and accepting and extending invitations to meet again, but that was not to be our destiny. Within a few days we were on choppers heading out on a typical search and destroy mission. Unlike the Central Highlands of Kontum Province, the new terrain ranged from semi-arid, to thorny desert, to open woodland.

*****

The new area of operation pretty much paralleled the coastline inland from Phan Rang south to Phan Thiet. The timeframe was late January-early February 1967. We hadn't been operational but a few days when we were redeployed to a small rustic airfield on the edge of a community called Bao Loc. There were other line companies about, but I couldn't say the whole battalion was present. A few Cessna OV-1 birddogs and Hueys were tied down on the periphery of the strip. We parked ourselves between the aircraft and the cyclone fence that cordoned off the field.

No one seemed to know why we were there, or when we would pull out. Jake, Bobby Gordon, and I made a short reconnaissance trip into the nearby suburbs. The town was clean, with well appointed homes, manicured shrubs, and paved streets. The commercial strip enterprises that typically surfaced around military bases were absent.

When we returned to the airstrip, we faced the prospect of some less than appealing mess tent chow. Here's where Jake made us an offer that we couldn't resist, or at least we wanted to see. Jake offered to cook supper if we could acquire some specific items of culinary stock from friends in the mess tent. He also requested a helmet. (The only headgear Tigers used in the field were soft reconnaissance caps.) Gordon went right to work on the acquisition tasks. In short order, he returned with eggs, potatoes, ground meat, and a "borrowed" helmet. And Jake went to work.

What followed was a combat cuisine masterpiece! Gastronomes, accustomed to sampling gourmet specialties, admittedly we weren't. And ten months of dining on primarily canned C-ration entrees may have slightly biased our analysis of

Jake's meal. We all enjoyed the food immensely, particularly since Jake had cooked everything in a helmet--like he had some innate scholarship in that area. Eventually, one of us sprang the inevitable question about how he knew how to cook in a helmet, or for that matter, how he knew how to cook at all. Was his mother a mess sergeant? The truth was even stranger for us to imagine. Jake's primary MOS was a cook.

Jake, reading the expressions on our faces, began explaining his transition from cook to infantryman. Army cooks at Fort Campbell (the stateside home of the 101st) worked some pretty long, odd hours, so their workloads were adjusted to where they usually enjoyed extended off periods, which Jake sometimes enjoyed more than one might consider prudent. On the last occasion, Jake reported directly from "weekend holiday" to the mess hall and proceeded to throw up all over the chow line. The First Sergeant--not at all happy with Jake's mess line incident--threatened to send him to an infantry assignment in Vietnam. Jake questioned the First Sergeant's ability to send him to the infantry considering that his primary MOS was a cook. There was no need for Jake to continue the story; the First Sergeant obviously won that argument.

So, the highly respected point team of Jacobs and Hartz consisted of a former cook and chemical warfare specialist!

*****

We spent two nights on that airstrip before resuming operations. The Tet holiday of 1967 was approaching. From 8-12 February, we were instructed that our patrolling was to be defensive in nature. We would not engage the enemy unless they fired on us first.

Brief Summary of Operation Farragut I and II[2]

Special Note: Operation Farragut starts on 27 January but is interrupted on 31 January by the imposition of Operations Gatling I,

and Gatling II. Farragut is recommenced following Gatling II on 17 February.
Timeframe: 27–31 January 1967
Base camp: Phan Rang
Area of Operations: 25 kilometers, northwest of Phan Rang
Enemy Situation: A Local Force VC Province and District Headquarters plus four independent VC platoons and support troops are believed to be operating within the AO. Enemy strength could vary between 300 to 500 personnel.
Mission: Search and Destroy
Limiting Considerations: Time in AO; change in tasks diverted attention away from Operation Farragut to Operation Gatling
After Action Assessment: Enemy resistance was light and all VC; no NVA involvement. Two enemy confirmed killed; one probable. Two weapons (Mausers) captured. Tiger Force employed as a surveillance and reconnaissance screen to the southwest.[3]

****

[1] Mary L. Gonzalez "101st Combat Record in Vietnam 'unmatched'." The Fort Campbell Courier. N.p., 21 Jan. 2010. Web. 22 Nov. 2016. http://fortcampbellcourier.com/news/commentary/article_bcd86ea2-06b8-11df-a6f1-001cc4c03286.html.

[2] Jerry A. White (Cpt. Inf.) and Naughton, Stephen L., (1Lt. Inf.), Unit History, 1st Battalion (Airborne), 327th Infantry, 1st Brigade, 101st Airborne Division, APO San Francisco, California, 96347, 1 January 1967 – 3 July 1967. Reproduced at National Archives. Chapter 3, pages 22 & 23.

[3] Ibid, p. 22.

Chapter 20
Fire Power Up Front
Early February 1967

"Do you walk well over uneven terrain?" --Army test question[1]

On the 6th of February, we were following an azimuth straight up an ugly-assed hill! Sergeant Thomas Rosales was in charge of Bravo Force. After leaving the choppers we had dissolved into heavy brush, avoided trails, and moved cross country into our new AO. If we moved stealthily enough, we would be able to slip clandestinely into our opponent's backyard without him knowing we were there. We weren't quiet enough, however.

The hill we were negotiating was as steep as any we had experienced previously in the Central Highlands. I employ the word "hill" here in the Pacific Northwest context. In the eastern U.S. it would be considered a mountain. Frequently we violated basic mountaineering protocol and used shrubbery to pull ourselves upward. If the vegetation snapped or uprooted, the man affected generally cascaded backwards onto the man behind him. Usually no serious injury resulted from a slip, but gaps in movement occurred. The point element had to pause often and hold fast until the rest of the Force caught up.

As we neared the crest of the hill, word was passed up again for the point to halt until everyone could catch up. My team was the lead element. Smitty and Gordon were point and slack. They sat down in a little gully about five meters in front of me to wait for the word to move out again. Neal Bateman,[2] who was carrying the sniper's weapon, sat down beside me to my right. Behind me was Duke Caulder with the machine gun. The crest of the hill was only about forty meters above us, but we were unaware that a well-defined trail ran along the top of the ridge. The trail lay under triple canopy vegetation, rendering it completely hidden from any aerial flyovers. At least three VC moving on the trail probably heard our English and took concealed positions about twenty meters uphill from where Smitty and Gordon had kicked back to rest awhile. It wasn't that we were unreasonably loud. The verbal directive to hold up was barely above a whisper. But in the woods, unless masked by water and wind sounds, human voices are distinctly recognizable.

I hadn't seen Bateman for some time. He had been shot earlier in the upper arm and had some hospital time. During our temporary rest break, I asked about his wound. He rolled up his shirt sleeve to reveal the scar. The bullet had grazed through the outside portion of his deltoid muscle leaving a star-shaped scar. I couldn't help but thinking that if you have to take a bullet, that area of the body was a better place than most. About that moment, we all almost took a bullet.

The firing erupted from the foliage on the other side of the gulley above Smitty and Gordon. A round tore off a portion of Bateman's boot heal. I never saw the enemy, just heard the report of their weapons and saw some branches moving. Someone yelled "Fire power up front!" Smitty, Gordon, and I unloaded a fusillade at the area from where we thought the shots had originated. Duke Caulder had maneuvered his M-60 about five meters uphill to my left and unleashed his ready belt into the suspected enemy position. Smitty, Gordon, Bateman and I sprang forward and started closing in on the VC position. Duke positioned himself further uphill to the left in order to give us supporting fire if we needed it. We didn't.

At the spot where we had concentrated our fire, we found one enemy KIA in khakis with web gear, grenades, canteen and an M-1 carbine. There were two blood trails. The trail to the right led to a second enemy KIA. This individual also had an M-1 carbine and similar gear and dress. The other blood trail leading uphill was much lighter, so it was likely that individual was not seriously wounded. Following the uphill blood spattering we hit the well-used trail that wasn't on the maps. Blood trickled off down the trail to the right, towards our intended direction of travel. Our opponents would certainly soon be made aware that we were stalking in their backyard. We had lost our element of surprise.

We established security on the trail and waited for Sergeant Rosales and the rest of Bravo Force to join us. Sergeant Rosales was an experienced infantry man, and he knew we had just lucked out. To be caught on the downhill side of at least three positioned enemy with automatic weapons, and not get hit when they sprang their ambush, was one piece of luck. To hit three of them without having seen any one of them was definitely fortuitous--okay, lucky!

One of my most striking memories of that engagement did not involve the firefight itself, but the calming period afterwards. Following some moments of reflection, one of the more recent members to the Force, Bobby Gordon, announced that we could have been killed back there! Duke Caulder, a long time veteran of the Force and a man of few words, subtly made eye contact with the rest of us. His facial expression seemed to be making an inquiry regarding Gordon's planet of origin.

I kinda' understood Bobby's epiphany. For most of Gordon's short tenure with the Force, we generally did the surprising and the ambushing. The other guys were usually the surprised "ambushees." Reality had just introduced Gordon to the haunting principle of uncertainty --"shit happens."[3] Training, experience, grit, gumption, luck, etc.--all help to mitigate uncertainty, and yet, an individual can do everything by the book and still take a bullet. Those who are worth their salt understand reality and move on regardless. For the old timers, Captain Agerton's words from Tuy Hoa cemented our spirit. No matter how large the enemy unit, we would find a way to deal with it. In three days, defense of the captain's legacy would be summoned again.

Brief Summary of Operation

A brief summary of Operations Gatling I and Gatling II follows next chapter.

****

[1] Question on Army's standard battery of placement tests administered to recruits at the start of basic training. Anyone not inclined towards an infantry regimen should think hard about responding positively to these types of questions!
[2] Neal Bateman was killed on 15 May 1967 at Tiger Valley.
[3] *Forrest Gump*, Director Robert Zemeckis, stated by Tom Hanks, 1994, Film.

Chapter 21
Doc and Jake
January 31 – February 15, 1967

"Dear Bob,...Needless to say, I was surprised to hear that you had been hit. Good pointmen are hard to find and more difficult to lose. Your performance with the Tigers was one of the finest. I didn't write to bullshit you, but it doesn't take long for a leader to realize who to depend upon for a good job." –Lt. Carey, handwritten letter, April 6, 1966

Doc Nelson was in charge of the battalion's medical platoon which supplied the medical personnel to the line units. He was quite a bit older than most of us and held the rank of Specialist Seventh Class, or SP7, equivalent to platoon sergeant in the infantry. Before the operation to the Phan Thiet area got underway, Doc approached the Force with a request. He had yet to qualify for a CMB. We understood what he was suggesting. He needed "combat experience" in order to qualify for the coveted Combat Medics Badge. Jim Raysor's response to Doc Nelson's request to join us on the upcoming operation went something like: "No problem. If you want to get shot at, come out with Tigers." Doc Nelson did just that. Not only did he get his combat experience, he saved Bobby Jacob's life in the process.

*****

After the hillside firefight on the 6th of February, we married up with the remainder of the Force. Alpha and Bravo Forces reshuffled some of the personnel. We picked up Doc Nelson and Bobby Jacobs. Charley Hartz wasn't present. More than likely he was on R&R or dealing with a bout of malaria. I seldom had the opportunity to patrol alongside Jacobs. Usually, if Jake's team had the point duties, my team had the rear security responsibilities, and *vice versa*. The current mission was no exception: Jake had point and I had rear security. Sergeant Rosales, the CP element, and the machine-gun section traveled between us.

A four-day Tet truce was in effect. The Vietnamese New Year, called Tet, is the most important celebration in Vietnamese culture.[1] But the Tet ceasefire of 1967 was no planned holiday for us. We continued patrolling, but in reconnaissance mode only. Our instructions were to go combative only if our opponents fired first.

*****

On the morning of the ninth of February[2] we were following a well-used trail through a forested area where the sun's rays managed little penetration. The trees were broad-leafed and very tall. The high, dense canopy denied sunlight to most of the lower shrubbery, so at ground level the vegetation was fairly sparse, almost park-like. Eventually the trail split. The main segment led off to the left. A lesser segment branched off to the right along a clear, cool stream which passed between some highly eroded banks. The CP group and the MG crew parked themselves where the trail split, near the only open area in the vicinity. Jake's team was sent to reconnoiter to the left, and my team to the right.

About eighty meters down the stream we encountered a cave--not a natural cave, but man-made, cut straight into the left stream bank. The entranceway was big enough to enter standing upright. Once inside, the cave expanded into two large chambers. The first was stuffed with food items, mainly baskets of rice. A portal from the first chamber led off to the left and into the second large storage area. This room housed about fifty ceramic storage vessels each about five feet high. An odor that I have never come to appreciate emanated from these vessels--rice wine! Obviously, our opponents had some festivities planned to close out their Tet holiday.

Once outside the cave, we moved above the bank, and I beheld a sight that rekindled memories of Dak To. About a hundred meters in front of us, completely nestled under the triple canopied umbrella, was a military complex of thatched roofed structures.

The compound could easily accommodate several hundred individuals. The good news was the absence of activity within the compound. We observed no signs of occupation--no smoke, no moving shadows, no tonal language. I started to breathe easier, sensing that the prospective tenants hadn't arrived yet, and that we might be able to avoid detection until the battalion was alerted. With the truce still in effect, we couldn't initiate offensive actions, but we could observe where necessary.

The shooting started as we were backing off the bank. A few shots, followed by a long burst, resonated on our left. The CP group was behind us, so the firing had to involve Jake's recon team and, considering the size of the complex we just discovered, Jake's team could be in dire straits. We dashed back through the CP element, turned right and headed off in the direction Jake had taken. We passed Doc Nelson who was hurrying in the same direction, which telegraphed that we had a "man down" situation. About thirty meters ahead of Doc, at a point where the trail snaked over a small mound, we came upon Jake. He lay face down, stretched out, with his arm and weapon pointing down the trail. The bolt of his weapon was locked to the rear which meant that he had fully expended his magazine. So the burst we heard was Jake returning fire.

Jake wasn't moving; I couldn't tell his condition. I overcame the impulse to stop and administer first aid. The person best suited for that task was huffing up behind me. What the rest of us needed to do at that time was to create a security envelope around Doc Nelson and his patient.

If my memory serves me correctly, Gordon, Smitty, Marvin Sontag, and I took up positions overlooking the barrack complex. Again, there appeared to be no one moving around in the compound. That observation didn't give us reassurance to breathe easier. If our opponents weren't there, where were they?

Sergeant Rosales and the CP group had also sprung into action. We had barely taken up our defensive positions when an artillery smoke round popped above the small rise about a hundred meters to our left. The artillery FO was preparing to bring in HE (high explosive rounds) if things went south. Almost right on top of that we heard the rhythmic "wap-wap" of a D-model Huey settling down near the CP group, then taking off almost immediately. Jake was being evacuated. When the period of quiet after the storm arrived, I left the security element and went back to update Sergeant Rosales on the situation. In turn, Doc Nelson briefed me on Jake. A bullet had hit him on the inside of his upper left thigh, but the bleeding had been stopped, so he should be okay. Doc Nelson added that Jake was conscious and his chief concern was the condition of his balls! More concisely, he wanted to be assured that they were still attached. Doc reassured him that they were still in working order.

Three months later, while on extension leave, Hartz and I went to see Jake in Connecticut. Jake filled us in on aspects of the story that Doc Nelson humbly kept to himself. According to Jake, when the triage team at the hospital received him from the medevac chopper, one of the doctors commented on the professionalism of the medic that had tended to Jake in the field. The wound was too high up the thigh for a tourniquet. The next best option available for us grunts would have been to apply direct pressure to the wounded area, which was unlikely to have stopped the major arterial bleeding. Without Doc Nelson, Jake would have probably bled to death—Doc Nelson had clamped off the hemorrhaging blood vessels with hemostats! Jake also related that he had made eye contact with the VC before they fired on him. As Jake fell forward, he slipped the selector switch on his weapon to fully automatic and unloaded the magazine in the direction of the enemy. He told Hartz and me that he didn't want to go down without a fight.

*****

As far as we were concerned, the holiday truce had been cancelled by lack of adherence on behalf of our opponents. Jake's burst as he fell forward had wounded one of the enemy. There was a small blob of coagulating blood at the place on the trail where the attackers had initially fired. The trail led off towards the barrack complex. After Bravo Force regrouped, we also headed off in that direction. We moved with authority down the trail and passed through the left side of the compound. Unlike base camps that we had encountered in previous parts of the country, this area was missing the typical defensive positions, i.e. spider holes and trenches, which normally edged NVA bivouac areas in the highlands. These thatched roofed structures, aligned in perfect rows, offered comfortable places to stretch hammocks. Except for the construction materials, the whole setup looked like similar barrack areas back in the States. Along with the food and rice wine storage cave, the compound seemed designed more for relaxing and not for repelling a ground attack. This was not residential in any shape or form--no corrals, no animal pens, and no animals of any kind. The whole complex was a military compound designed for troop R&R during the forthcoming holiday.

We were directed to leave the compound area and follow the shooters. We were aware that the element of surprise rested with the enemy, an enemy that may be much larger than us. As we departed the complex, we set fire to the thatch roofs of four or five hooches closest to the trail. This wasn't solely a vindictive act. Global positioning satellites hadn't yet made their appearance above the battlefield. Should we require TAC air support in a hurry, the rising column of smoke above the triple canopy would help vector the aircraft to our vicinity. Fortunately, we wouldn't need TAC air.

Brief Summary of Operations Gatling I and Gatling II[3]

Timeframe: 31 January–15 February 1967
Base camp: Initially Phan Rang, later Phan Thiet

Area of Operations: Gatling I (31 Jan –3 Feb), mountainous area 80 kilometers west of Phan Rang near Bao Loc; Gatling II (6 Feb–15 Feb), mountainous area 20 kilometers south of Gatling I AP

Enemy Situation: Gatling I--Up to four VC companies suspected of providing security for an alleged secret meeting of key VC military personnel in the AO; Gatling II--reliable sources reported the presence of enemy units in the AO

Mission: Gatling I – Search and Destroy, disrupt meeting and take prisoners; Gatling II – Search and Destroy

Non-tactical Considerations: 3-5 February, the 1/327th stood down at Bao Loc before commencing Gatling II. Tet '67 cease fire in effect from 8–12 Feb

After Action Assessment: No meeting or fortified area was discovered. Light contact with small VC elements occurred, but no significant action developed. Some hut complexes and caches were located but nothing of real consequence. Six VC were killed, 5 others probably wounded, and 3 POWs taken. Five weapons captured, along with 57 tons of rice. No NVA encountered in zone. On 15 February, the 1/327th withdrew to Phan Thiet for a two day stand-down to prepare to recommence Operation Farragut.

****

[1] Tet is the Vietnamese New Year marking the arrival of spring based on the Lunar calendar. The name Tet is a shortened version of Tet Nguyen Dan, Sino-Vietnamese for Feast of the very First Morning. Wikipedia: *https://en.wikipedia.org/wiki/Tết*

[2] Western Union Telegram, Major General Kenneth G. Wickham, Adjutant General, To Mr. and Mrs. Frederick Jacobs, announcing that their son Robert had been wounded on 9 Feb. Dated 17 Feb 1967. Courtesy copy from Bobby Jacobs.

[3] Jerry A. White (Cpt. Inf.) and Naughton, Stephen L. (1Lt. Inf.), *Unit History, 1st Battalion (Airborne), 327th Infantry, 1st Brigade, 101st Airborne Division, APO San Francisco, California, 96347, 1 January 1967–3 July 1967.* Reproduced at National Archives. Chapter 2, pages 13–16.

Chapter 22
Eight Canteens, The Path Not Taken
February 17 – March 6, 1967

"At Phan Thiet when they bury the dead
They place the casket with stone at head
Then heap earth over lid and sides
A mound of ground, a spot of Time" --Leo Heaney[1]

The enemy remained elusive, as they would for most of the operation. Battalion had extracted us for a brief two-day stand-down in Phan Thiet. The town had a feeling of quaintness about it--a seaside community void of the normal hustle, bustle, and strange aromas typical of many Vietnamese cities.

Our first view of the town came from the helicopters that extracted us, and transported us, to our new temporary base camp. On our approach, the sea was on our right, and a sandy expanse of mounds to our left. My sharpest memory of the town is the mounds. These were not the circular dome-shaped mounds characteristic of termites, but elongated, and capsule-shaped.

The mounds turned out to be grave sites. Each grave had an identity plaque or stone imbedded in the front of the mound, and generally encased on the plaque was a picture of the deceased. The mounds were fairly high above ground level. From casual observation, it wasn't obvious whether the deceased or their coffins were actually interred into the ground, or if soil was heaped over the corpse or coffin at ground level. Perhaps it was both? The graveyard was vast, so the custom had been around awhile.

*****

We bivouacked at the Phan Thiet base camp for two nights and then returned to the field. After insertion, the operation pretty much followed a standard pattern. Normally, during daylight hours we operated in five to seven-man recon teams. Then, later in the day, we reunited with the CP group and set up a defensive perimeter.

Contact with the enemy was established on the 18th. One of our light recon teams was closing on our adversaries when an explosive device was detonated. Three of the five-man team members were wounded; PFC John Thomas Odom fatally. Awarded posthumously, the Silver Star citation states:

> *"For Gallantry in Action: PFC Tommy Odom, HHC, 1/327th, 101st ABN, was accompanying a team from the reconnaissance platoon on a patrol in the vicinity of Phan Thiet, RVN. While his unit was moving down the trail, a mine was command detonated. PFC Odom, the radio telephone operator, was mortally wounded along with two men who were seriously wounded. Immediately after the detonation of the mine, Viet Cong snipers began firing intensely on the two remaining members of the squad. PFC Odom realized that if the snipers continued to keep the two men pinned down, the entire squad would be annihilated. Even though mortally wounded and in extreme pain, he began placing effective suppressive fire on the enemy, giving the two pinned down men the cover fire they needed to maneuver on the insurgents. Sustaining his fire, he radioed to another element for assistance. PFC Odom was solely responsible for saving the patrol from annihilation. His unimpeachable valor in close combat is in keeping with the highest traditions of military service and cast great credit on himself, his unit, and the United States Army."*[2]

Some teams were diverted to assist with the casualties; our team was not. Instead, we were directed to continue along a designated route which led us deeper into an unimaginable desert-like region. Rice paddies, bamboo jungles, and triple canopy forests which had typified our former lush conception of Vietnam were replaced by a dry sandy expanse. It was not the bright, sandy, open expanse which one would conjure up from television documentaries of White Sands and Death Valley, but dull grayish tracks of parched soil, desiccated brush, snarly briars, tuffs of brown weeds, and dry rocky stream beds. We quickly realized that water was strategic and shade a luxury, therefore caution needed to be exercised around each. A viper can leave a person just as dead as an adversary with an AK.

Before long the Battalion S4 was "helio-porting" water to us, sometimes in traditional jerry cans or sometimes in "elephant rubbers." Water was bundled in clear, layered latex casings about six inches in diameter and three feet long, resembling elephant-sized condoms. They were delivered from a moving helicopter and tended to bounce along the ground on impact like a fish on a deck. As the operation progressed, most of us were collecting canteens from anyone leaving the field. Eventually, I was carrying eight.

The following chart outlines how much personal equipment I carried each day. I estimate it was a total of about 80 pounds.

Hand-carry
—Rifle with one magazine in the weapon

Necklace
—2 metal dog tags taped together (to avoid noise) and a P-38 (can opener) on a piece of nylon parachute cord

On pistol or web belt
—Two 5-magazine ammo pouches, 1 on each hip
—3 grenades. I didn't carry the extra 4th grenade on the right hand pouch. When we paused, and I rested my weapon beside me, it would interfere with the grenade, eventually breaking off the grenade handle.
—Knife
—Compass (or in my pocket)
—Field dressing (for immediate first aid)

Rucksack-Main
- —15 C-ration meals (3 cans each)
- —2 LRRP meals
- —Poncho liner and poncho stuffed on top of cans to smother all noise
- —7 canteens of water (1 quart each)

Rucksack-3 pockets
- —Few smoke grenades
- —1 white phosphorous grenade
- —Heat tablets
- —Fabricated stove made out of a can
- —Accessory packs that came with the C-ration meals: salt, pepper, Chicklets gum, toothpicks, matches, toilet paper
- —Camouflage stick (face paint)
- —Insect repellent
- —Blood expander
- —Morphine syrettes
- —Toothpaste and toothbrush
- —Flashlight

Rucksack-outside
- —1 canteen of water (#8)

Besides personal items, each soldier also needed to carry some portion of the squad's equipment:

- About 100 rounds of machine-gun ammo
- 200 rounds of M-16 ammo (10 boxes of 20)
- 1-2 entrenching tools
- 1 claymore mine
- 1 LAW (anti-tank weapon)
- 3 maps
- Radio
- Radio batteries

In this desert environment we experienced our next casualty when one of the other recon teams encountered a mine. From the sound of the explosion, that team was off our ten o'clock position, about a kilometer away. Radio traffic confirmed that a Tiger had stepped on a mine. Naturally, we wondered who was injured and how badly. Most often, the kind of mine we encountered was the bounding type, which usually produced fatalities. Soon, from the direction of the explosion, a single Huey came scurrying along about fifteen feet off the ground. As it passed to our left we spied Taupam sitting upright on the web seating and giving us a "thumbs up" gesture. We couldn't help but notice that one of his boots was missing. We returned the "thumbs up" gesture, but internally, our emotions were mixed. The wound was not fatal, but likely life altering. We learned that the mine Taupam encountered was of the "toe-popper" variety, designed to produce non-lethal casualties.

Taupam was a Native American whose complete name I don't believe I ever knew. He seemed to prefer just "Taupam." We had patrolled together several times, and he was of the mold that sought out the dangerous positions. If he wasn't on point it was because his team had rear security duty.

On a two-day stand-down, he and I shared the same defensive position guarding an airstrip that was vacant of aircraft. So one can imagine how significant it was on the enemy's hit list. While the senior NCOs sought shade to play poker, Taupam produced a large, double edged knife and proceeded to practice throwing it into a nearby tree. His skill at knife-throwing had two salient features that were easily noticeable. He almost always hit the center of the tree trunk, and he sank the blade deep into the bark. These were no pansy-assed, little mumblety-peg throws. When I unwittingly commented that his skill probably came naturally for him since he was Native American, he replied that it wasn't so. He said that mastery took a long time and a great deal of practice. He further commented that what drove him to diligently work on the skill of knife-throwing was to satisfy the stereotypical assumptions that some people nurtured about Native Americans, i.e. like they must be good with a bow and a knife. I don't consider myself a gambler, but I would wager that Taupam was also pretty good with a bow.

Since guarding that airstrip posed nothing of immediate tactical strain, I borrowed a bayonet from Joe Evans and had Taupam give me some pointers. I never attained, even closely, the accuracy that Taupam could achieve, but I could sink the bayonet pretty deep into the trunk of the tree, if and when I hit it. Fortunately for me, it never came to pass that I would need to rely on stopping an enemy by throwing a knife.

As the helicopter carrying Taupam to the hospital drifted off, one of those vacant feelings that humans sometimes entertain crept over us for a moment, and then we turned back to the mission.

*****

The arid, desert-like terrain, which greeted us at the start of the operation, had gradually evolved into wooded hills with open areas and bushy vegetation. However, running water was still a rare commodity. A few days later, our patrol encountered its first uniformed opponent.

The incident occurred as we were moving down a dry stream bed and noticed movement to our right. A VC had just emerged from a bushy area on a small trail and turned towards us. He was in khakis, wearing no head gear, toting a slew of canteens, but carrying no weapon. I say "VC" because it is unlikely that an NVA would have set out on a water run without a weapon when U.S. troops were operating in the area.

Upon looking up and realizing that we were Americans, he immediately dashed back around some bushes and retreated off in the direction from which he came. Smitty and Gordon were on point, but neither they nor I had a really clean shot through the undergrowth, so we held fire. We gave chase as fast as we deemed prudent. After a few minutes, we figured that this specific VC must have already rejoined his comrades, alerted them of our presence, and secured his weapon. We slowed down and proceeded at a more cautious pace. There were only five of us, and the element of surprise was lost. We were moving towards an enemy that was expecting us.

The path the VC had taken led us uphill through a shadowy wooded area. It was not unlike moving through a tunnel towards a bright entrance. Smitty and Gordon paused in the shaded area without moving out into the light. As I closed on them, they expressed concern that something didn't feel right. My assessment of the situation also left me with an eerie, almost a palpable sensation. The small trail we were following married up with a wider trail. The new trail, switching back in front of us, was a perfect place for an ambush. The layout offered no cover or concealment to anyone caught on or near the trail. A few enemy with automatic weapons, secluded on the wooded hillside off a hundred meters or so to the right, could wreak havoc over the entire length of the trail in either direction. To further restrict any escape route, the areas bordering the trail were choked with briars, confining movement to the trail itself. The trail in front of us was a perfect killing zone.

Certain paths through life are better left not taken, and we felt that this path was one of them. If some clever devil ever concocts a fool-proof remedy for surviving ambushes, I would imagine that not getting caught in an enemy's killing zone would rank high on his survival check list.

At any rate, the point team felt wary about continuing out on the wide trail after the fellow with the canteens, and I agreed with them. So we backed up into the shadowy area and radioed the SALUTE[3] report (sighting and circumstances) to SSG Kratzberg, the Bravo Force leader. Sergeant Kratzberg was a veteran of the Korean War, and he understood gut instincts. He directed us to return to our original route and task of "re-conning" for base camps and possible POW or hospital compounds. He concluded with something of a caveat about not wanting to have to scramble out and rescue our young asses. His distinctive chuckle resonated in my handset as the transmission ended. We turned ninety degrees and re-established our original search pattern.

As the operation progressed, an overwhelming number of indicators led us to believe that the VC/NVA were avoiding contact, abandoning their base camps and withdrawing from the AO. Wherever destiny was leading them, it seemed that we would not be part of it.

Brief Summary of Operations Farragut IV & V which recommenced after Operation Gatling ended[4]

Timeframe: 17 February–6 March 1967
Base camps: Phan Thiet and Song Mao
Area of Operations for Farragut IV (17 Feb–6 Mar): started in the wide, extremely dry sandy expanses 30–40 kilometers, northwest of Phan Thiet and moved to the mountains north of Song Mao
Enemy Situation, Farragut IV: Within the general AO, there was reported to be an unidentified base camp, a PW camp, and a hospital facility. Local Force VC units included the 482nd Battalion and the 440th and 405th Companies. Troop strength was estimated to be between 550 and 600.
Other Considerations: On the 27th of Feb, Companies B, C and Tiger Force extracted to Song Mao for two-day stand-down. All elements stood down at Song Mao, the new forward base camp, on the 7th and 8th of March before initiating Farragut V.
After Action Assessment: See Operation Summary following Chapter 23

****

[1] Leo Heaney, "The Mounds of Phan Thiet," unpublished, 1967.
[2] Mark Sullivan, Citation accompanying Silver Star, database page for John Thomas Odom, The Virtual Wall, John Odom, PFC, Army, Alexander City AL, 18 Feb 67, 15E059, updated 10 Jan 2005.
[3] SALUTE: Size, Activity, Location, Uniform, Time, and Equipment.
[4] Jerry A. White (Cpt. Inf.) and Naughton, Stephen L. (1Lt. Inf.), Unit History, *1st Battalion (Airborne), 327th Infantry, 1st Brigade, 101st Airborne Division,*

APO San Francisco, California, 96347, 1 January 1967 – 3 July 1967.
Reproduced at National Archives. Chapter 3, pages 24-30.

Chapter 23
A Night Visitor, Waterfalls, The Monk
March 9 – 22, 1967

*"With a mind alive with a fire inside,
The monk spoke of the then and the now"* --Leo Heaney[1]

Darkness made the situation confusing. Some men in positions near the trail stated hearing rasping noises. Others reported something brushing by them on a dash through the perimeter. The absence of rifle fire and explosions removed the immediate threat of an enemy ground attack. My position was located about ten meters from the commotion, so my experience was pretty much all audible. Following the thrashing sounds, I picked up several forms of invective--some outright curses, others directed more in the format of questions. "What the fuck?" was the most recognizable. Smitty was just beginning to respond to the disruption when something leapt over him. Eventually word got around that we had experienced a visitation from a species of our namesake--a tiger. With the first light of morning, we checked out the tracks the big cat had left on the trail.

The tiger episode began soon after the Force had established its nightly defensive perimeter tangential to a trail. The trail passed in front of some of our defensive positions, affording a few of our teams the opportunity to intercept enemy traffic that might come along the trail. These men were in, by virtue of circumstance, a *de facto* night ambush position. A trip flare was strung across the trail, just a little left from where Smitty and his teammates established their position.

The tiger had approached the perimeter from our left, traveling down the trail until it became startled. It then darted through a few of the forward positions before exiting into the brush further on down the hillside to the right.

We didn't believe the trip flare was an issue until we examined the tiger's tracks at daybreak. The big cat had left an easily identifiable path straight down the trail right up to the still intact, taut trip flare wire. The tracks picked up again directly on the other side of the wire. The wire was set about a foot off the ground, and the pin was usually adjusted so the flare trips easily. The cat had either stepped or leaped over the wire! The consensus was that the cat had to have sensed the presence of the line. We found it difficult to believe that the tiger had accidentally lucked out and just stepped over the wire with all four paws without one of them snagging the wire and tripping the flare.

*****

The relatively low turnout of enemy participation didn't necessarily result in boredom. Mother Nature rose to the occasion a few times during the remainder of the operation. About this time, two members of the Force 'created' some excitement by waterfall glissading sans the customary snow and soft landing area! These athletic events weren't planned, nor were they contemporary. About a week separated the two feats of hydro-gymnastics. I retell these episodes lightheartedly because neither accident resulted in life threatening injuries or long-term physical damage, but both individuals did require an extraction for treatment of their injuries.

The accidents occurred while we had been operating in terrain where streams had become more prevalent. On both occasions, an experienced member of the Force ventured off in ankle deep water to the edge of a precipice to peer down over cascading water dropping onto boulders about fifteen to twenty feet below. This momentary visual communion with nature preceded the sounds of rucksack, weapon, and body bouncing off boulders. Of course, there also was the customary "oh shit" (or close equivalent) scream included somewhere within the sequence of audible clashes. Those of us witnessing each event didn't want to believe that we had just watched one of our comrades being swept over a waterfall. It seemed like a slight-of-hand trick played by nature. One moment they were there in front of us, and the next they vanished from sight. I think for a moment that I was suspended in a state of visual denial. I didn't want to believe what my senses insisted that I had just observed. And, the event repeated itself within a week. I witnessed it twice!

I had dismissed the first fall as clumsiness and poor judgment. However the second occurrence demanded further scrutiny. In each case, the Tigers involved were in great shape and more agile than I--and I couldn't imagine myself being swept over the edge by shallow, ankle deep water. So, after the second plunge, a better understanding of what caused the accident was demanded. Another Tiger and I cautiously inched our way out to the edge of the waterfall and peered down at the medic and other teammates tending to the injured man about twenty feet beneath below us.

The stream we were standing in was only about nine or ten feet wide and not more than seven or eight inches deep, rising about half way up the back of our jungle boots. Our boots, aligned with the flow of the water, were providing good, solid traction. It was when I pivoted to return upstream that my balance was compromised. The foot still in the water, and now turned sideways to the current, was experiencing more lateral pressure. The foot out of the water, and stepping forward, no longer provided traction. The effect was somewhat like a "shoestring tackle" where a player's leg is pulled out from under him. Fortunately I was able to quickly scramble forward and re-establish my balance. An individual, not anticipating a problem from the seemingly innocuous-looking little stream, could easily be surprised. And there was nothing to grab onto if they fell in the stream near the edge. Airborne! This was another entry for our "Lessons Learned" journal.

As for our injured Tigers, both had faced the same diagnosis and remedy, each suffering a leg injury. Fractures were an obvious concern; torn ligaments and tendons were certainly a possibility. Other than bruises, there were no major breaks in the skin.

We were in a vast expanse of gently rolling terrain covered in a sea of deciduous vegetation. The trees weren't very tall, but they were pressed fairly close together. Beneath the trees there was very little ground level vegetation to obstruct movement; however, clearing a landing area for a Huey would require axes and chainsaws. Our machetes worked well on bamboo and vines, but they were no match for hardwood trees.

Richard Ammons looking over Ken Kratzberg's shoulder,
photo courtesy of Ken Kratzberg

Since the wounds were not life-threatening, whoever took the medical call in battalion headquarters suggested the following: immobilizing and protecting the limb as much as possible, administering a shot of morphine to the injured trooper, and limping him to an area that would support a helicopter evacuation. It worked. On both occasions, assisted by fellow Tigers and using their weapons as canes, Linneville and Ammons had humped out of the forest to an LZ. Neither had sustained a fractured bone and both returned to the field after a week or two recovery.

*****

Over the next few days we operated in our usual small recon teams. One morning we entered an area that looked like an abandoned campsite. The point team stopped just inside an area sprinkled with the sorriest looking punji stakes I had ever seen in Vietnam. Unlike the lean, long, resilient bamboo stakes of the Central Highlands and the Laotian border areas, these imposters had the appearance of a diminutive tongue suppressor with a dull, isometric point. Gordon pulled one out of the ground and stabbed his boot with it--the stake snapped in two! Also present were a variety of deadfall traps and punji pits all of which were constructed in the same shabby manner.

Another irregularity was the location of the stakes. In the Central Highlands and the border areas, the NVA used punji stakes to hinder access to specific areas like base camps, trails, or landing zones. These stakes were just there, obstructing access to nothing. We concluded that these stakes, deadfalls, and pits were VC/NVA training aids: "dummy" devices employed by our opponents to prevent injury to their recruits while teaching employment techniques and strategies.

*****

Most of our patrolling revealed vacated facilities. Occasionally, however, some of our patrols crossed paths with a few of the enemy's stay-behind elements. One such encounter happened within ear shot of our patrol. A few VC had brought one of our other teams under fire, so a few patrols nearest to the skirmish were diverted to render assistance. Naturally we proceeded with caution. Sometimes the enemy's main target was not the force actually engaged, but the relief element coming to assist. The team that Jim Ward was walking point for arrived on scene quickly and eliminated the threat. The enemy had committed a common error. They were so intently focused on "poppin-caps"[2] at Americans that they failed to establish rear security. They never saw what hit them.

That night, when the Force regrouped and formed its customary defensive posture, I sought Ward out and handed him the can of fruit cocktail I had been carrying as part of our customary ante. Of the twelve C-ration meals, only four contained canned fruit, and only one of the fruit items was the coveted fruit cocktail. Since the time that Captain Agerton had been shot, Jim and I had a running wager on which of us would get the first VC/NVA at the start of each operation. By this particular operation, the big Texan had me by about four cans of fruit and counting! An argument could be advanced that we had somewhat equated or reduced an enemy's life to a can of fruit. Rather than debate that analogy, I offer for consideration that our mission was to out-guerrilla the guerrilla and remove him from the battle area. The exchange of a can of fruit was a confirmation that we were, at least at a personal level, achieving that task. Furthermore, in my entire eighteen months on the line, tramping through the I Corps and II Corps areas, not one armed VC or NVA ever approached me, dropped their weapon, and surrendered.

*****

Before the operation closed down, our team was assigned to check out a small community prior to establishing a night ambush position on the trail leading into that hamlet. The most prominent physical feature of the little community was a Buddhist temple which funneled access into the village proper. The other obvious feature was the demeanor of the local residents: they smiled, nodded courteously, and seemed to welcome our presence.

The trail passed through the temple courtyard. A masonry wall about three feet high surrounded the little plaza. The area was sharp and clean. A solitary young monk greeted us and motioned for us to rest. We nodded back and fanned out along the wall and prepared to have lunch. The monk stayed with us, a situation which lowered the possibility of an attack.

Not long after we had settled into our lunch routine, the monk produced a book--a Latin primer. Some of the Tigers were Catholic and had altar boy experience. I had managed to survive two years of high school Latin: ninth grade in parochial school and tenth grade in public school. Back in my day, in my school, Latin was an academic requirement, though not exactly a course that I welcomed with unmitigated enthusiasm!

In South Vietnam, about eighty-five percent of the population practiced Buddhism, with Roman Catholics forming the next largest religious group. I imagine that the young Buddhist monk was trying to understand his Catholic counterparts better. Since we had time to spare before striking off to our ambush site, we helped the monk with Latin pronunciation and meaning. Most of us were probably lucky if we remembered that the verb usually came at the end of a Latin sentence. Or that "v," "c," and "ae" were pronounced differently in church Latin versus classic Latin. But we were what the monk had to work with at the time, and he seemed to appreciate our attempts to assist him. As evening approached, we started to give our "goodbyes" to the monk and the several adults and children who had gathered around the courtyard since our arrival.

Santana (Sam) Carnero,
photo courtesy of Sam Carnero

At this point, a few of us realized we had some issues that needed to be addressed.

Our mission was to establish a night ambush roughly three hundred meters up trail from the temple complex. In an L-shaped ambush, the MG is usually positioned where it can rake the trail. Sergeant Santana ("Sam") Carnero's machine-gun team was attached to us. Sam was a highly respected member of the Force, as well as an accomplished foot soldier, and he often walked point during the Tua Hoa operations. Since Dak To, Sam Carnero, Jim Raysor, Joe Hennessey and I had covered each other's back on numerous occasions. Except for an occasional R&R or episode of malaria, we were pretty much each other's shadows. Now, Sam was the leader of the machine-gun squad.

Normally we established night ambushes in areas where enemy traffic was highly expected. However, while patrolling the surrounding areas over the past few days, our team had uncovered virtually no evidence to support a significant or recent enemy presence in the vicinity: no sniping, no casual contact, no camps, no defensive positions, no cooking smells, no booby traps, none of the customary fresh trail signatures, etc. We felt that a night ambush had exceptionally low odds of successfully netting any enemy. Conversely, the chance of civilians entering our killing zone was higher than normal. This little *Brigadoon* enclave, tucked away in the foothills, seemed to have been sheltered from much of the realities of the war. If this were the case, then there was a good chance that some of the local residents might not strictly adhere to the rural curfew laws.

Our instincts compelled us to remind the monk of the national curfew, and the dangers his parishioners might encounter, if they used the trails after dark. With gestures and a few jargon terms, like "via," "kah ka dow," and "number ten,"[3] we endeavored to convey to the monk that trails needed to be avoided at night; particularly *that* trail, *that* night. He nodded that he understood, and we departed the courtyard.

We understood that we were taking a chance by letting the monk know that we would be in the area that night. Opposition to Saigon's policies at the start of the conflict was largely orchestrated by Buddhist monks. Some even resorted to self immolation in order to draw attention to their objections. The young monk, we figured, probably shared some sympathy for the causes of our opponents. Even so, our instincts left us feeling that he and his people were okay; we went with our instincts.

Our next task was to set up a place where we could complete our ambush mission, while not causing harm to the local civilian population. Naturally, in case our assessment of the monk proved to be a misjudgment, protecting our own butts was also on our minds.

We found some uneven terrain that offered cover. We established our ambush, registered an artillery concentration, readied a few parachute flares, and set in for the night. Our plan was not to engage travelers using the trail, unless we could positively confirm that they were carrying weapons. If we had to abandon our present position, we would regroup about two hundred meters up trail, moving further away from the village. If we suffered a casualty, we would defend in place.

The night passed without incident. At first light we packed up and headed off to rejoin the Force. The operation closed with a motor march back to Phan Rang.

Brief Summary of Operations Farragut V[4]

Timeframe: 9–22 March 1967
Base camps: Phan Thiet and Song Mao
Area of Operations for Farragut V (9 Mar–22 Mar): started in dense, mountainous terrain northeast of Song Mao, southeast of Phan Rang

Enemy Situation, Farragut V: In the area south of Phan Rang, three Local Force VC companies were rumored to be located--the 270th, the 102nd, and the 105th. In the mountainous region a VC headquarters, two PW camps and a hospital were believed to be located along with a base camp of two NVA companies and one Local VC company. Captured documents later confirmed that two of the Local VC companies were staffed by NVA cadres.

Mission: Search and Destroy

Other Considerations: On the 27th of Feb, Companies B, C and Tiger Force extracted to Song Mao for two-day stand-down. All elements stood down at Song Mao, the new forward base camp, on the 7th and 8th of March before initiating Farragut V. About two weeks later, on 22 March, all elements motor marched to Phan Rang base area on Highway 407.

After Action Assessment: There was a noted absence of any large scale enemy activity during the resumption of Operation Farragut. Light contact characterized encounters with enemy troops. Numerous abandoned hut complexes, most with defensive positions and food stores, were discovered in zone. Enemy activity was primarily limited to snipping activity, land mines, and surprise encounters. NVA were encountered during the final phases of Operation Farragut. Enemy loses included: 10 NVA killed, 15 VC killed, 2 NVA POWs, 18 weapons captured.

****

[1] Leo J. Heaney, *The Tao of Gao*. Occasionally I composed and sent little poems home, which my mother kept because mothers do those things. These little ditties later served as mnemonic keys which helped me recall my feelings at the time.

[2] Slang term for shooting a weapon.

[3] Connotes way, death or killing, and very bad.

[4] Jerry A. White (Cpt. Inf.) and Naughton, Stephen L. (1Lt. Inf.), *Unit History, 1st Battalion (Airborne), 327th Infantry, 1st Brigade, 101st Airborne Division, APO San Francisco, California, 96347, 1 January 1967–3 July 1967.* Reproduced at National Archives. Chapter 3, pages 24-30.

Chapter 24

Blood and Water
Khanh Duong: March 28 – April 29, 1967

"God gave Noah the rainbow sign, no more water, the fire next time!"
—James Baldwin

At Khanh Duong, fire came first, water followed.

At o'dark thirty hours[1], on the 28th of March, the 1/327th departed Phan Rang in a motor march heading northeast towards Nha Trang. For the forthcoming operation I was assigned to Charley Hartz's team. I hadn't seen Hartz much over the previous two months, which wasn't all that odd, considering that most of our missions were conducted in detached recon or combat patrols.

That morning we were traveling in the lead deuce and a half of the convoy heading up Highway 1. Panoramas of the South China Sea appeared and disappeared on our right, interspersed with coastal hills and rocky outcrops. The battalion's Convoy Control Officer's jeep preceded our truck in the order of march. Since most of the highway was paved, land mines probably weren't going to be an issue. However, the threat of a command detonated device still remained. The beds of our trucks were covered with sand bags to mitigate the effects of mines and other small explosive devices. Against a converted 175mm artillery round, the sandbags wouldn't do us much good.

Decapitating wires strung across the narrow portions of the road were a remote possibility, particularly once we left the main highway and turned inland. In order to defend against threat, those of us standing near the cab of the vehicle leaned forward on our weapons keeping the barrels positioned where they would intercept any wire strung across the roadway. Naturally, we would be jerked backwards into the bed of the vehicle, but that thump would be kinder on our bodies than the intended alternative. Of course, we could just nestle down into the truck's cargo area and avoid the decapitating wire threat altogether, but the scenery was magnificent, the weather was dry, and after all, it was a road trip!

Not long after passing Nha Trang, we arrived at a place called Ninh Hoa and bivouacked there for the night. The next day we continued northwest to Khanh Duong, the battalion's next base camp area.

The new location reminded me very much of the terrain where Captain Agerton had been wounded. We were setting up in the open, just downhill from a dense wooded area which provided excellent concealment for any lurking opponents. After completing our customary two-man prone shelters, we set about helping with the other customary tasks involved with establishing a new base camp. When additional muscle was needed, we assisted raising the larger company tents. Initially we dug slit-trench latrines which eventually evolved into an outhouse once lumber was procured. Grenade sumps were also a common feature in the company area. These pits were generally a three feet square excavation about two feet deep. These were not elaborate, just deep enough to store items like claymores, grenades, C4, and blasting caps beneath ground level. Digging the sump hole was usually a team effort: a couple fellows would take turns with the entrenching tool. However, at Khanh Duong, the effort was different. Gary Kornatowski, after a falling out with the First Sergeant, won the sole honor of digging the sump himself. I'm not sure if I ever knew the specific reason that Kornatowski landed the sump-digging detail, but acrimony he didn't hide. If the First Sergeant wanted a grenade sump, Gary was going to give him a big, deep one! When it was completed, it looked more like a grave than a traditional grenade sump—a grave large enough to bury a water buffalo! Fortunately, by the time everything was finished, the situation had turned humorous. The sump issue would resurface again before we departed this AO.

A few hours into our routine, a truck-mounted quad-50 rolled into position about twenty meters to our left and pointed its guns up toward the wood line. During World War II, the quad-50s were deployed as anti-aircraft systems, but the advent of jets ushered in more sophisticated weaponry for that role. I wasn't even aware that the quads were still in the Army's inventory. After a second "Fire in the hole" proclamation, the quad proceeded to rake the edge of the woods with an awesome display of fire power. If any of our opponents nurtured intentions of harassing us from the wood line, they would have an additional distraction to contend with--one that would certainly draw their attention away from us.

*****

The operation out of Khanh Duong served as a pivotal point in my memories of Vietnam. When the battalion departed Khanh Duong, two major changes occurred: one involved the theater of operations and the other concerned the rotation of leadership personnel.

In early May, the 1/327th departed the II Corps area and went north to the I Corps area. At this time, some of the Force's most experienced leaders were rotating to other assignments. Sergeant Charlie Evans finished his last mission in March. Sergeant Santana (Sam) Carnero was also on the super short list, and would soon leave the line. Lieutenant Kube, who joined the Force after Captain Tom Agerton had been shot, was promoted to captain and reassigned to another unit. Lieutenant John Carey was about to complete his tour of duty. And Lieutenant Gary Forbes was moving into the sole leadership position of the Force. Likewise, Kratzberg, Hartz, Raysor, Hennessey, and I (to name a few) were also finishing our first year with the battalion.

*****

The most poignant memory of the Khanh Duong operation was the loss of a Tiger that was not a result of enemy contact. PFC Sterling Hendricks died instantly when his weapon discharged as he was negotiating some uneven terrain. We constructed a poncho litter and a few of us carried his body and equipment back to the LZ that we had used the previous evening for a normal resupply delivery.

Waiting on the LZ for the chopper to extract the body was a period of mental reflection. For us, the war had paused. For Sterling it had ended. Had we felt that words might mollify reality, we would have exercised more. As it was, most of us chose a waiting-in-silent-contemplation option. Fortunately, the chopper arrived, picked up our loss, and left us to catch up with the rest of the Force which had continued on with the mission.

*****

Khanh Duong had some bright spots. Perhaps "illuminating" would be a more precise term, if the psyche of some of the Force personnel was the subject of inquiry.

On one of our insertions, the helicopters couldn't find an open spot to set down. Ultimately, a single boulder jutting out from the face of a hill was selected to serve as the landing spot. The boulder posed some distinct insertion challenges. One, the boulder, although large, wasn't flat and it was rounded and sloped downhill. So if someone lost their footing getting off the chopper, they were in for a significant fall. Two, since the boulder was situated not at the top of the hill, but protruded from the hillside like a nose on a face, the pilots were forced to hover the chopper above the rock in order to avoid striking the hill side with their blades as the rotor tilted forward. Personnel, once on the ground, also had to be especially aware of the blades.

We leapt from the skids a few feet above the rounded surface. Hartz and several members of the first team on the rock had grounded their gear and took up positions to assist the Tigers with heavy equipment, particularly the machine gunners and RTOs. Since only one ship at a time could drop its load on the boulder, the overall insertion time was much longer than normal. Once a team hit the ground, they moved out immediately to afford room for the next chopper to offload. By the time we were all on the ground and underway, the enemy was waiting for us.

At this point, some additional information is necessary to help clarify portions of the following narration. The previous operations out of Phan Thiet convinced most of us that a direct relationship existed between the carrying of extra canteens and personal creature comfort. Before Phan Thiet, I got along adequately with three canteens because water was abundant in the highlands. As I mentioned previously, the desert-like nature of Phan Thiet pushed my creature comfort index up to eight canteens. I stuffed seven of them in my rucksack. The eighth I carried in the conventional manner, in a canvas canteen cover attached to the outside of my ruck. I saturated the cover with water so evaporation could keep the canteen and water cool. Those who didn't care if the sun warmed their water hooked their plastic canteens directly to the rucksack frame. On sunny days, the water in these externally mounted, uncovered canteens became quite hot. These simple, mundane acts, like so many other daily activities, usually pass into mental oblivion unless they are attached to other loci in our minds, as is the following case.

Once everyone was on the ground, Hartz established the order of march and we moved out. Since I was not part of the point element, I was relatively free to scan the scenery. The trail that we were using was firm and well established, the kind that hikers prefer. The vegetation was sparse on the hillsides, consisting primarily of stunted brush among boulders. A few hundred meters to the left of our heading was a string of trees suggesting a stream course. Our trail stayed pretty much parallel with that tree line. Because of the openness of the terrain, we were maintaining a greater-than-normal interval between men. The area reminded me of the granite-infested hills that I roamed over throughout most of my elementary years in Pennsylvania ...nostalgia?...yes!

We hadn't progressed very far up the trail when we crossed a false summit where the terrain leveled off for about fifty meters and then began to rise again. About a hundred meters up the hill, a Montagnard lodge dominated the vista. Just to the left of the lodge, barely discernible lying between two boulders, peering over his gun sight, was one of our opponents.

Nostalgic time was over, and reality time rushed back. The situation did not afford the traditional "breathe, relax, aim, and squeeze" type shot. It was point and shoot quickly. My intent was to zing as many rounds as possible near his head, hopefully to distract his concentration and sight picture. He got a round off, jumped up, then exited for the tree line to his right.

Hartz and the point element immediately swept forward. Bob Stanczyk was in front of me. He was lying face down. It was then that I realized that he had been hit. I got to him, saw the blood on his upper arm, cut open the sleeve, and issued a sigh of relief. Bob had the classic "million-dollar" wound: not life threatening, but guaranteeing a few weeks in a clean bed and non-C-ration food, and maybe even a trip stateside. The muscle seemed to be the only tissue damaged. The bleeding was minimal. I got out his aid dressing and bandaged the wound. I told him to take it easy, that there was nothing to worry about. His retort startled me. He told me not to lie to him. He said that he could feel warm blood flowing down his back! He believed he was seriously wounded and that he was probably bleeding to death!

Army first aid procedure directs that a wounded individual be checked for multiple wounds. I had screwed up. I saw the upper arm bleeding, so I went for it. Since I thought that the enemy had only gotten off one shot, I hadn't checked for additional wounds. I eased my hand between Bob's rucksack and his back, and sure enough, his shirt was warm and soaking wet. I started self castigation, wondering how much blood I had allowed to gush forth while I attended the non-life threatening arm wound! Then, out of somewhere, logic clicked in. I realized that although Bob's shirt was warm and soaking wet, the fluid the shirt was soaking up didn't have the "feel" of blood. I checked again. The fluid was warm, but it didn't have the stickiness or smell of blood. Then I spied the canteen on Bob's rucksack with the bullet hole. The round that nicked his arm continued on and passed through the canteen that was mounted behind his shoulder. When he fell forward in a prone position, the warm water seeped out and down his back. I took that moment to apprise my friend that he stood a better chance of drowning than bleeding to death!

And, it did turn out to be a "million-dollar" wound. Stanczyk was a short-timer, so the First Sergeant found him a job at base camp to recuperate and wait out his DEROS date.

*****

The operation may have started dry, but it ended wet. Upon returning to base camp, we found the grenade sump (which Kornatowski had dug when we had first arrived in the area) filled with rainwater to ground level. It looked like a puddle, an impression not lost to others. While we were tending to the re-establishment of our former sleeping accommodations, one of the company personnel on his way to his squad tent (encumbered with fresh sheets, blankets, and a pillow), disappeared into the presumptive looking puddle --"*Kersplash*"! Those of us in the immediate vicinity helped him regain firm ground, his bedding and composure. In "the Nam," never ignoring where you are about to place your feet is a healthy concept to adopt. Lord knows, all of us with time on the line suffered through a few puddle episodes!

Later that evening, a few of us gathered around the sump puddle, perched our butts on some sandbags, and pondered the battalion's imminent move north to the I Corps area. We had been instructed to double up on ammo. Our basic load for the M-16 was eleven magazines: five in each ammo pouch and one in the weapon. We were also issued a few M-72 anti-tank weapons. The I Corps was the military region closest to DMZ where the NVA were thick. In military slang, the I Corps was described as the area where "...even the chickens carried hand guns and the cows had RPGs."

The customary post-operation ration of iced beer and soda was provided. We sat there in our makeshift docket as twilight faded into darkness and an almost full moon cast its reflection on the sump puddle around which we were arranged. Not unlike campers around a fire, some primordial fascination with light locked our focus on the lunar image captured in the puddle, a reflection that appeared vividly solid. While half listening to the conversations emanating around me, the surreal concreteness of the captured moon in the puddle provoked a question. I wondered if it was possible for an individual to contact the water's surface just right and springboard to the other side of the sump. Ditching airplanes can sometimes skim off water for a ways, and just about all of us had skipped rocks across ponds as kids. My koan[2] was answered shortly thereafter. Just about the moment we called it a night and started to break for our sleeping positions, Hartz sprang up, dashed forward, and crashed into the puddle --"*Kersplash*"again!

After the initial proclamations of disbelief, introduced with phrases like "what the f*+&@," accompanied by some chuckling, we helped our comrade onto dry land and awaited an explanation. Now, this is the psychic part of this water event: I already sensed how Hartz was going to explain his impulsive dash. We all remained quiet and just waited for Hartz to react to our silent interrogation. His response was something on the order of: "... if I had hit it just right...!" I would like to believe that it was one of those "great minds think alike" moments! But considering the scene, that assessment wouldn't hold water.

Hartz and I were on our way to an enduring friendship. Obviously circumstance played a part in the formation of this fellowship, but the most compelling rationale was that we obviously thought alike—well, nearly.

Charley and I had slightly different ways of responding to enemy engagements. He preferred overwhelming the enemy with fully automatic fire. I usually resorted to a directed semi-automatic response. We both had the same amount of ammo, just packed differently. Hartz carried twenty-one fully loaded magazines: ten in his ammo pouches, ten in a fabric bandoleer, and one in the weapon. On the other hand, I carried eleven loaded magazines and enough boxed ammo in my rucksack to reload ten. Hartz commented that during a heavy firefight I might not have time to reload my expended magazines. I justified my point of view by telling him that by the time I went through eleven magazines, he'd probably already be shot, so I would just use his remaining magazines!

The next day we readied for the excursion to the I Corps. Hartz was carrying twenty-one fully loaded magazines; I had my eleven ready, plus ten. Not quite alike, but close enough.

Brief Summary of Operation Summerall[3]

Timeframe: 28 March–29 April 1967
Base camp: Khanh Duong
Area of Operations: Khanh Duong is about 45^+ kilometers NW of Nha Trang.
Mission: Search and Destroy
Other Considerations: Departed Phan Rang on the morning of the 28th of March. Motor convoyed through Cam Ranh Bay, to Nha Trang, to Ninh Hoa. Bivouacked one night at Ninh Hoa. Proceeded the next day to Khanh Duong and established a forward base camp. Operation Summerall kicked off on 3 April.
Change of Mission/Change of Status: In late April, 1st Bde of 101 Div became OPCON to Task Force Oregon. Movement from Khanh Duong starts on 1 May and is completed by 8 May. Most of the battalion motor marched from Khanh Duong to Nha Trang then

moved by LST up the coast to Duc Pho. An advanced element was airlifted on CH-47 Chinook aircraft directly to Duc Pho. The base camp was dubbed Carentan, reminiscent of the WWII battle site in Normandy.

****

[1] Departed early, before sunlight. The more contemporary term "zero dark thirty" is synonymous.
[2] A Buddhist riddle to develop intuitive thinking.
[3] Jerry A. White (Cpt. Inf.) Naughton, Stephen L. (1Lt. Inf.), *Unit History, 1st Battalion (Airborne), 327th Infantry, 1st Brigade, 101st Airborne Division, APO San Francisco, California, 96347, 1 January 1967–3 July 1967*. Reproduced at National Archives. Chapter 3, page 30.

Chapter 25
Black 'n Blue and Purple
Early May 1967

Task Organization Update:
In February of 1967, General Westmoreland realized that a seventh Army division was needed to counter the enemy build up in the I Corps military region. To meet the immediate requirements to position another division sized combat unit in country, on the 20th of April, Task Force Oregon was created. Major General William B. Rossoni organized this force, by placing under its operational control: the 196th (Light) Infantry Brigade, the 3rd Brigade of the 25th Infantry, and the 1st Brigade of the 101st Airborne. By September, after additional reshuffling of units, Task Force Oregon transitioned into the Americal Division. In late November, the 1st Brigade of the 101st Airborne was released from operational control of the Americal Division and returned to the II Corps military region. The remainder of the 101st Airborne Division arrived in country in December. –Unit history, 17th Cavalry[1]

During its two and a half year tenure as an independent, separate unit, "...the first brigade traveled 2,500 miles and engaged in operations in 3 of the 4 established tactical zones. The men of the Brigade killed six thousand enemy troops, captured enough weapons to arm eight enemy battalions, and took two thousand tons of rice. Medical attention was given to 25,000 friendly Vietnamese and 15,000 were relocated as refugees by the brigade." --Unit history, 1/327th Infantry[2]

Most of the battalion made the journey north to I Corps on naval LST transport. I was assigned to SSG Kratzberg's force which provided security for the battalion's advanced party. We missed out on the sea voyage; our form of transport was a CH47 Chinook helicopter transport. We hadn't been given much information about where we were headed or what type of enemy activity to expect, if any.

We set down in an open sandy area. To our right was the sea, as well as quite a bit of air activity, so we landed west of some fairly active airfield. We assumed a normal tactical dispersion and headed off to find an area where we could set up for the night. En route we encountered a lightly equipped Marine patrol. The Marines were armed with M-14s, two magazines of ammo (one in the weapon's well and the other taped to the stock), no ammo pouches, and one canteen of water on their pistol belts. I hadn't noticed any field dressings or grenades. This suggested that we were in a relatively secured area. Regardless, once in our night location, we established our customary defensive perimeter, and linked up with the elements of the battalion which arrived the following day.

The base camp that we established at Duc Pho was one of several we would work from over the next several months. Others included Chu Lai, Da Nang, Phu Bai, and Hue. As customary, we went straight to work on the usual tasks that accompanied relocation to a new base.

By evening, with the preliminary tasks completed, a few of the lads decided to try to find a Marine enlisted men's club rumored to be nearby. Two of the team members, Hartz and Raysor, had a long history together. They grew up about seven miles apart. They played against each other in high school football. They both served in Sergeant Rose's team in Tuy Hoa. I had elected out of the entertainment excursion, preferring a full night's uninterrupted sleep....I didn't get it!

"Wake up...fall in...platoon formation!"

I didn't know whether to take a weapon or not. I decided against it and headed towards an area illuminated by vehicle headlamps. I joined the Tiger formation in front of the Headquarters Company Commandant's tent. The vehicles providing the light were not Army. One was a small truck and the other resembled an oversized variation of a jeep. A Marine bird colonel seemed to be having a rather intense conversation with our HHC commander, Captain Helms. It wasn't really much of a conversation since the colonel seemed to be doing most of the talking. "Diatribe" is probably a more accurate description. Captain Helms was a paratrooper from the Korean War era. I assumed, because he was notably older than most of the captains we had experience with, that he probably was a former NCO before acquiring his commission. When the verbiage ended, both officers and a small gaggle of other tagalongs headed over towards our formation.

Accompanying the officers were a few Marine enlisted men, most of them looking a little bedraggled with bruised faces. Some even displayed what appeared to be blood spots on their uniforms. One large Marine in particular grabbed my attention, and not only because of his bulk. He also sported a bruised and puffy face, with one eye severely swollen and barely open. As this procession passed before us with each Marine intently scrutinizing our faces, it became apparent that we were actually a platoon-sized "line up." After a few of our men were identified, the group moved back to the lighted area around the vehicles. It didn't take a mental giant to figure out the genesis of our nocturnal assemblage. An interservice altercation probably developed during our lads' quest to quench their thirst and quell their restless spirits.

The specifics on the evening's adventure came later from various accounts, no two identical. A composite version of the sojourn to the drinking establishment indicates that events proceeded in the following manner. The Marine club was easy to find and everything started off cordially. As time progressed, however, interservice rivalry intensified until one individual, a large Marine (the one with the puffed up eye), boisterously manifested that he had never seen anyone from the Army whose ass he couldn't kick. With that proclamation, Sergeant Charles E. Hartz II figured it was time to introduce himself to the myopic Marine. The arrogant Marine's second mistake was to lead with his face. That's how the fight began. Now, Marines have a renowned reputation for supporting their own, and since most of the uniforms in the club were Marine, our guys soon needed a diversion to affect their escape. Raysor, whom I have always suspected provided the distraction, has remained silent about any complicity regarding the club's thatched roof catching fire and the subsequent conflagration.

Jim Raysor, photo courtesy of Leo Heaney

Those of us who had not joined in the club adventure stood silently in platoon formation as the drama continued. When the Marine colonel finished seething, he demanded that Captain Helms take disciplinary actions against the perpetrators. Captain Helms affirmed that he would indeed take action. Salutes were exchanged and the Marine vehicles departed leaving us standing in the faint glow emanating from the lantern in the officers' tent.

Perhaps the most memorable focal point of the whole episode was Captain Helm's question and response after the colonel left. He asked Hartz if he was indeed responsible for the events described by the Marines. Hartz averred that he was. The captain paused for a second, and as he turned to enter his tent he replied: "Well done, Sergeant Hartz."

The next day, four days before the entire brigade had yet to arrive on station, and a week before the new operation was scheduled to commence, the Force was on choppers heading west by north. *Out of sight, out of mind.*

*****

The insertion LZs were on the high ground so we started off with a downhill hike. The weather was as fine as any trekker could wish for--bright, cool and no rain. Hartz was with SFC Rosales's force, about a kilometer or two off to our right. SSG Kratzberg was further to the right and slightly ahead of all of us. I was with SSG Harold Trout's force. About lunch time, we met up with Sergeant Rosales's unit at a small hooch complex. Two women occupied the little farmstead. One was about twenty years old, while the other was probably her grandmother. Noticeably absent were children and adult males.

Both women appeared very nervous with our presence. They avoided direct eye contact, resorting to an occasional glance our way. Eventually, the older woman approached us with a note. In legible cursive English, this message from the local VC contingent, in short, acknowledged that although we were adversaries, they asked that we respect their women and not rape them. With a nod of affirmation, we returned the note to the women. Shortly thereafter, Sergeant Rosales moved off with his element, and Sergeant Trout led us towards a small hill about half a kilometer from the farm. By now the enemy was surely aware of our presence in the area, so our goal was to find a defensible piece of terrain which we could use for a night location. The little knoll we were heading for looked like it would fit the bill. In reality, none of us would be spending the night there.

The odd thing about the blast is that I don't recall the noise that must have accompanied the spraying debris. I was pummeled with sand and gravel, but no shrapnel. Sergeant Trout was between me and the blast, and he absorbed any metal fragments heading my way. When the dust settled, of the eleven Tigers present, Ernie Moreland, Joe Evans, and I were the only ones not wounded. Some men were hit in the front, some in the back, and others in the side. My first thought was a mortar or RPG, but when no secondary attack followed, my assessment shifted to a bounding mine.

Although a booby trap was also a possibility, that alternative didn't seem likely. We had followed a well-defined trail to a clearing of compacted soil near the top of the hill. The explosion appeared to have originated in an open area off the uphill side of the path. Booby traps are generally encountered on the trails and seldom hit more than three individuals.

The next few minutes was an example of handling chaos by the numbers. Joe and Ernie were helping with the wounded near them. They already had battalion on the radio and were requesting medevac assistance. When battalion asked our location, since I was the only person who had a map and wasn't bleeding, Joe passed me the handset. I forwarded the coordinates of our location. The individual on the S3 side of the communications rather blatantly came back with something on the order of: "What the hell are you doing in a purple area?" His response verified my hypothesis regarding a mine being the source of the explosion. I returned, "I have no purple on my map...over." The individual started to reply, but paused for something. The push-to-talk button on his handset was still depressed, so the heated exchange between individuals in the background was transmitted before he continued with his message. Suddenly the tenor of his voice had changed; he told us a chopper was on its way.

Except for the critically wounded, everyone had a job to do. Joe and Ernie were tending to the situation to my left. Sergeants Trout and Watson appeared to have suffered mostly leg wounds. Barnes was hit in the chest, Dallas Rogers the abdomen. Others in the area further to the left seemed to have received the lightest wounds. The most seriously wounded were those to my front where the blast apparently originated.

At the time, Joe Evans was the only man in the Force that I knew who carried a bayonet. Putting a bayonet stud on a weapon with a plastic stock never seemed all that logical to me. One good vertical butt stroke and your M-16 might just convert into a pistol.

Most of us left the bayonets with the supply sergeant. But the radio conversation with battalion had indirectly confirmed that I needed a broad, blunt blade to probe for mines. The color purple on military maps and overlays is reserved for manmade obstructions, i.e. mine fields. The S3's map placed us in a purple area, which meant that we had entered into an active or abandoned mine field. There are established protocols regarding the transfer of mine field data and responsibilities between incoming and outgoing units. The 1/327th had not laid the field, but it had knowledge of the field's location. On the battalion S3's operations map, the coordinates that I reported placed us inside an area outlined with a purple grease pencil. Somewhere between that map at the battalion TOC and the boot that triggered the mine, the system had failed. The word didn't get to the troops that needed it, and as a consequence, we discovered the presence of the mine field the hard way.

With Joe's bayonet I started probing my way towards Smitty and George Hatten. George had immediately stood back up after the blast, his weapon ready. We had directed him to sit back down. Both he and Smitty had been wounded on their back sides, indicating that the mine had popped up behind them. The typical bounding mine is ejected from its base plate and explodes about chest high. Both men suffered numerous wounds, including fragments striking the backs of their heads.

We had trained in the States on how to probe for mines. In training, the mines were buried in soft Georgia sand. The hard packed soil I was working in that day was not easily penetrated by the bayonet. The field had been subjected to the effects of weather and sun, and it was like trying to stab a brick. Wind and water erosion tended to expose the three prongs and upper detonator portions typical of bounding mines. As I continued my probing routine, I meticulously scanned for any of those little "metallic sprouts." I didn't spot any, which I felt was a good sign, indicating that the departing unit had made an effort to clear up most of their mines. Obviously they had missed at least one, and uncertainty dictated that we continue checking for any others.

Smitty was face down, but alert. He had several wounds but most seemed to be intramuscular and not life threatening. I asked him if he was in a lot of pain and he acknowledged that he was. As I broke the seal on a morphine tube, I noticed the wound behind his right ear. Blood had scaled over a piece of metal lodged in the large muscle just behind the ear. Morphine isn't to be administered to someone with a head wound. I don't recall Smitty's verbatim response when I reminded him of that first aid caveat. Contextually it ranged beyond "shit" and "damn."

As I continued on my hands and knees towards George, my probing effort pretty much transformed into a visual scanning exercise; the soil was too compacted for any cautious employment of the bayonet. When George had sat down, he then lay back and died. His head wounds were fatal. Clearly visible were two quarter sized holes in the back of his skull, almost contiguous, resembling a number eight. It is difficult to contemplate his attempt to stand up and respond to an enemy threat after suffering those two wounds…ingrained tenacity, I suppose.

In typical medevac fashion, the chopper pilots were knocking at the door before everyone was bandaged. We briefed the pilots on the situation and the possibility that the LZ area was not safe to put the skids down or even be around should another mine detonate. They volunteered to hover the aircraft a foot off the ground while we loaded our wounded, dead, and gear. Each time we inserted an individual or pack, the floor of the chopper listed in our direction, but the pilots quickly stabilized the aircraft, again and again. The whole time period between explosion to dustoff probably didn't exceed twenty minutes.

As the "wop-wop-wop" of the rotor blades gradually diminished, Joe Evans, Ernie Moreland, and I had a moment to appreciate the stillness, the absence of hustle. Reality returned with the crackle of squelch in Joe's handset. Joe informed us that Sergeant Kratzberg had turned his force around and was on his way to us and we should sit tight. Then Joe asked Ernie and me if we understood the second part of the sergeant's transmission. According to Joe, Sergeant Kratzberg wanted to know if the lion was okay. I told Joe to reply that the lion was fine. Hartz, Kratzberg, and I had completed our first year in country and were taking leave together, starting the next morning. In order not to violate radio protocol by using a proper name, Sergeant Kratzberg substituted "lion." My name, Leo, in Latin means lion.

Brief Summary of Operation Malheur[3]

Timeframe: 11 May–2 August 1967
                (Phase I: 11 May–8 June, Phase II: 8 June–2 August)
Base camp: Duc Pho
Area of Operations: North, northwest and southwest of Duc Pho, Quang Ngai Province
Enemy Situation: 2d VC Regiment in base area directly west of Duc Pho.[4]
Mission: Search and Destroy: "To find, fix and destroy VC/NVA forces and to neutralize VC/NVA base camps in the areas west and northwest of DUC PHO. The mission was later expanded to include areas southwest of DUC PHO as well."[5]
Other Considerations: Operation Malheur II morphs into Operation Hood River, 1/327th is initially the reserve battalion for that operation on 2 August.
After Action Assessment: 1/327 statistics compiled in Chapter 26

****

[1] ftrp17cav196.com/tforegon.htm.
[2] 327infantry.org/regiment_history/Vietnam.
[3] Combat After Action Report: Operation Malheur, 1st Bde. 101st Abn Div, AD#386041, Department of Defense, Ltr 3 Oct 67, *Unit History, 1st Battalion (Airborne), 327th Infantry, 1st Brigade, 101st Airborne Division, Declassified from Confidential,* Scribd.com, pages 1-71.
[4] Ibid., p. 8.
[5] Ibid., p. 7.

Chapter 26

Tiger Valley
May 15, 1967

*"...But since it falls unto my lot,
That I should rise and you should not,
I gently rise and softly call
Good night and joy be with you all"*
– The Parting Glass, An Irish farewell toast.

According to Task Force Oregon's After Action Report on Operation Malheur, the engagement that Tiger Force members dubbed "Tiger Valley" started: *"On 15 May one platoon of the 1st Battalion (Airborne), 327th Infantry contacted an estimated VC battalion size force with automatic weapons and mortars in fortified positions. Continuous artillery and tactical air strikes were called in against the enemy positions and mortars. Upon the insertion of a reinforcing company, 1 UH-1D helicopter sustained a direct mortar round and was destroyed. Results of the contact were 3 US KHA (Killed in Hostile Action)*, 34 US WIA, 1 UH-1D destroyed, 7 UH-1D damaged, 5 UH-1B damaged and 20 VC KIA (Confirmed)." The reinforcing units here were 3d and weapons platoons of B (Bravo) Company.* --1/327 Unit history[1]

The engagement as reported by the supporting helicopter unit: *"The 14th CAB (Combat Aviation Battalion)* ORL states that while in support of Operation Malheur I aircraft of the 176th Avn Co were called upon to extract casualties for the 1st Brigade, 101st Airborne. The initial pick up ship, on landing, was hit by a mortar round and totally destroyed. In the subsequent action to extract wounded, a total of 11 UH-D's and 7 UH-1C/B's from the 176th and 161st Aviation Companies were committed. Eight of the slicks and all gunships were hit by intense ground fire. Five crewmembers were WIA. With the exception of the first ship, all reached secure areas before being forced to land. Five required extraction by CH-47. A total of 22 U.S. wounded were evacuated in the operation. Total casualties in the 14th Battalion this day were 19 aircraft hit and 7 crewmembers WIA. This was by far the worst day ever suffered by the Battalion."* --14th CAB Unit history[2]

Tiger Valley was preceded the day before by a similar event labeled "Mother's Day Hill." This battle primarily involved A (Abu) Company of the 1/327th. Abu Company contacted an enemy force of unknown size in well-fortified defensive positions. Friendly casualties were 8 KHA (Killed in Hostile Action)* and 36 WHA (Wounded in Hostile Action).[3]

These two actions amounted to the enemy's stiffest resistance during the operation. Following these attacks, confrontations were limited to much smaller unit-sized engagements which characterized the remainder of Operation Malheur I combat actions. The After Action Report lists the following daily engagement between enemy forces and the 1/327th Battalion for the period 11 through 20 May: 11 May – ten contacts, 12 May – eight contacts, 13 May – twelve contacts (one a company-sized engagement), 14 May – eight contacts (one "Mother's Day Hill"), 15 May – six contacts (one "Tiger Valley"), 16 May – eight contacts, 17 May – one contact, 18 May – three contacts, 19 May – one contact, 20 May – two contacts.

*****

Staff Sergeant Ken Kratzberg, Sergeant Charles E. Hartz, and I had left the field on 7 May to begin our thirty day extension leaves. We went to Phan Rang to draw a partial pay from brigade finance, then hopped an AF MAC flight to the states. After about a week together in Pennsylvania, Kratzberg grabbed another MAC flight and continued on to Germany. Hartz and I drove north to Connecticut to pick up Bobby Jacobs, then on to the Montreal Exposition in Canada. A few days before we were to head back to Nam, Hartz came down with fever, chills, and headaches--a recurring bout of malaria. The military medical facility at Valley Forge was near Hartz's home, so I drove him there for treatment.

While waiting in the hospital's admittance area, I recognized a soldier I knew from basic infantry training. He had been wounded in Vietnam and was rehabilitating at the hospital. We updated each other, and when he learned that Hartz and I were from the One Hundred and First, he told us of a paratrooper in his ward who was also from the One-O-One. He asked if some of the tall yarns the trooper had spun could possibly be true, i.e. that our units usually spent twenty-five to twenty-seven days in the field at a time, averaging one cooked meal and shower per month? (I didn't mention the Tuy Hoa operations where the Force was out ninety-four days with only one scuttle day to the rear.) I asked my friend from basic infantry days to take us to his ward so we could make the acquaintance of the paratrooper in question. It turned out that we already knew the individual. Perched on a bed, sporting blue hospital garb and a camouflaged Tiger hat, sat Thomas Birsson, formerly one of Sergeant Carnero's machine gunners, and soon to acquaint us with the events of 15 May.

*****

From reports, narratives, and later conversations with Force personnel, a synopsis of events involving Tiger Force during the initial phase of Operation Malheur follows.

The search and destroy mission was designed to remove hardcore local contingents of the 2nd VC Regiment, and later the 1st VC Regiment, from an area where the indigenous population was not overwhelmingly committed to the government of South Vietnam. The AO included the Song Ve and Song Tra Cau Valleys which were only ten kilometers west of major coastal urban centers. Both valleys were a major food source for the local VC forces.[4] The operation commenced with an airmobile assault on 11 May. All three battalions of the 101st were committed. On the 13th, 14th, and 15th the enemy conducted large scale assaults against the $1/327^{th}$. After May 15 (Tiger Valley), contacts decreased in size and frequency as the enemy broke up into smaller units and withdrew to the west and north.

On the morning of the 15th, the Force had been directed to move from its defensive base and position itself where it could be deployed quickly to support other battalion units. Before long, the Force was given an *about face* command and told to reoccupy its original base. By this time, however, enemy personnel had moved into the former defense base and were manning the positions originally prepared by the Tigers. Initial contact occurred around 9:30 a.m. and lasted until 7:30 p.m. that night. During the protracted engagement, Lonnie Butts, Neil Bateman, and Steve Jarras were killed and approximately twenty-five other Tigers wounded.

Because of the intensity of enemy fire throughout the day, evacuating wounded was difficult. Sergeant Rosales recalled that SSG Tyrone Watson told him Apodaca was hit. Lt. Forbes told Tyrone to get him across the creek where a chopper could land. Tyrone personally picked Pete up, cradled him in his arms, and carried him 500-600 meters across the creek to wait for a chopper. This was no easy task. Apodaca was the size of an NFL receiver. Pete was the fourth fatality from Tiger Valley; he made the chopper, but died on 31 May from complications of his wounds.[5]

Among the other casualties was Lieutenant Gary Forbes, the Force commanding officer, who was seriously wounded and would not return to command. Tony Langley, RTO for the 320th Artillery FO team, was reported critically wounded and probably paralyzed. Another Tiger was revived at the Graves Registration Point after someone noticed he was still breathing. It was rumored that Malcolm Budd was winged in the butt. Jim Potts stopped a mortar fragment with his forehead. The Force medical personnel were operating in the *"above and beyond"* mode. Medics Lonnie Butts and Arthur L'Hommedieu were awarded the Distinguished Service Cross and the Silver Star respectively for tending to wounded troops while under intense fire. As noted, Lonnie's was issued posthumously.

The Distinguished Service Cross was awarded to Tiger Force medic Lonnie Butts "...*for extraordinary heroism in connection with military operations involving conflict with an armed hostile force in the Republic of Vietnam: Specialist Five Butts distinguished himself by exceptionally valorous actions on 15 May 1967 while serving as senior medical aidman during a search and destroy mission near Duc Pho. When the lead element of his unit became pinned down by machine gun fire, Specialist Butts executed a flanking movement on the hostile emplacement and silenced the two Viet Cong who were manning it. He continued forward, moving from one emplacement to another and drove the enemy back with hand grenades and machine gun fire. One insurgent threw a grenade between Specialist Butts and his platoon sergeant. Taking no heed of his own safety, he threw himself between the sergeant and the grenade, catching most of the shrapnel in his legs. Although he was seriously wounded, Specialist Butts went to the assistance of another casualty and treated his wounds. During the remainder of the firefight, he refused medical attention until all of the other wounded men were treated. Specialist Butts was mortally wounded as he moved toward a helicopter for evacuation. Specialist Five Butts' extraordinary heroism and devotion to duty, at the cost of his life, were in keeping with the highest traditions of military service and reflect great credit upon himself, his unit, and the United States Army."*[6]

*****

When the battle was over, the remnant of the Force was removed from the field to regroup at Carentan base camp near Duc Pho. Late that afternoon, in the battalion "pub" (a GP medium tent), SFC Rosales and Ernie Moreland took stock of the situation. The original complement of forty-one men was reduced to thirteen. If Hartz and I had been there, the beer would have been on us, but as it was, Tom Rosales and Ernie Moreland were drinking by themselves.

In later inquiries about the contact on the 15th, Ernie Moreland's name surfaced several times from veterans of the engagement. Single-handedly he did quite a job of keeping the enemy at bay. Richard Ammons and Jim Raysor told me that Ernie Moreland had time and again maneuvered about the battle area, effectively placing suppressive fire on enemy positions, buying time for many of our troops to move to safety. In Ammons's and Raysor's eyes, quite a few Tigers owed Ernie more than a beer and a handshake.

Operation Malheur (Phase I)

Timeframe: 11 May– 3June 1967
Base camp: Duc Pho
Area of Operations: West and northwest of Duc Pho, Quang Ngai Province in Base Area 124, (Song Ve and Son Tra Cau Valleys)
Enemy Situation: 2d VC Regiment in base area directly west of Duc Pho. Later elements of the 1st VC Regiment were encountered in zone also.
Mission: Search and Destroy: "To find, fix and destroy VC/NVA forces and to neutralize VC/NVA base camps in the areas west and northwest of DUC PHO. The mission was later expanded to include areas southwest of DUC PHO as well."[7]
Other Considerations: Operation Malheur I set up Malheur II which began on 8 June and ran through 2 August. Following the reduction of enemy resistance in the valleys, Phase II was to eliminate the food sources for these valleys provided the local VC forces. The OPLAN included removing the indigenous population and livestock to relocation centers, employing defoliants, and establishing "free-fire zones.[8]
After Action Assessment: Phase I daily contacts cited in chapter above. "Operation MALHEUR was characterized by small unit contacts. Initially the enemy defended his position in platoon and larger size force. Contacts with large forces, however, gradually declined as did the enemy's will to stand and fight. Soon contact with a squad size enemy force became rare and the Brigade made most contact with groups of two or three men who attempted to withdraw

on contact." During the ten day period, 1/327 permanently removed 91 enemy from the battlefield with 5 additional probable KIAs with 53 individuals of military age detained as possible POWs and turned over to South Vietnamese authorities.[9]

****

* Parentheses and description added for clarification.
[1] Combat After Action Report: Operation Malheur, 1st Bde. 101st Abn Div, AD#386041, Department of Defense, Ltr 3 Oct 67, *Unit History, 1st Battalion (Airborne), 327th Infantry, 1st Brigade, 101st Airborne Division, Declassified from Confidential,* Scribd.com, pages 21 & 22.
[2] Unit History Information for 176th, 14th CAB, 178 ASHC, 1 BDE 101 ABN, for date 670515.
[3] Combat, op. cit., p. 21.
[4] Don Kochi, *Screaming Eagles and the Battle for Mother's Day Hill.* 327infantry.org. p. 5
[5] Conversation with Tom Rosales, 6/26/17, Deadwood, S.D. Tiger Reunion.
[6] General Orders Number 4149, Award of the Distinguished Service Cross, posthumously, 15 August 1967.
[7] Ibid., p. 16.
[8] Kochi, op.cit., p. 5
[9] Combat, op. cit., extrapolated from data on p. 18.

Chapter 27
An Indifferent Allegiance?
June 1967

"He becometh a foe who seeketh to control others by force."
—the Mahabharata

"Both the Song Ve and Song Tra Cau Valleys featured a hostile local populace and a deeply embedded VC infrastructure....Both valleys, a major food source for the local Viet Cong forces, had several of its rice fields under defoliation consideration once the indigenous population was evacuated and resettled at the nearby detainee and relocation center during Phase II. The gradual absences of local inhabitants also had the additional effect of permitting large four by six mile area swathes declared as free-fire zones throughout the lower valley regions."--Don Kochi[1]

Hartz and I converged on Phan Rang near the middle of June. We reported to the 1/327th rear detachment and were told that they would probably have a flight forward in a day or two. Having time to kill, we hitched a ride on a deuce and a half and made our way to town. If any members of the Force were passing through, returning from leave, R&R, or a hospital, the odds of finding them downtown were far better than assuming that they might be lingering around the battalion rear area waiting to be selected for a work detail.

Since Hartz and I were both sergeants now,[2] we didn't need a pass to go off base into the local community. However, there was a slight issue with the local community that hadn't existed prior to our going on leave. The Vietnamese commercial businesses just off the Air Force side of the base had been recently designated "off limits." As fate would have it, this bit of information was presented to us, after the fact, via the local MP constabulary.

The absence of the normal hustle and bustle should have been a clue, but my acumen fell way short that day. While I was waiting outside the local barber shop for Hartz to get a haircut, a pair of MPs drove up and asked to check my ID. In case they questioned my NCO status, I presented my promotion orders that First Sergeant Kazmin had forwarded to me while home on leave. There were no warning signs posted proclaiming the area "off limits," but ignorance of the status change was obviously no excuse. They cited me for being in an off limits area and gave me a lift in their jeep to the city limits. After they disappeared down the main highway, I returned to Hartz and updated him on events. I wasn't even remotely familiar with the nuances of the military legal system; I didn't know what might be involved with receiving an MP citation. Whenever uncertainty arose in areas such as this, I always had Joe Hennessey's reflections on reality to mitigate potential pulses of anxiety: "What are they gonna' do, send us to Vietnam?" Still, I imagined that the First Sergeant would eventually be involved--an event which came to pass sooner than I imagined.

Once I was back in the battalion forward base at Duc Pho, I reported to the company orderly room. While engaged in the customary reunion salutations with the administrative personnel, First Sergeant Kazmin made his appearance. After we also exchanged pleasantries, the First Sergeant followed with an "Oh, by the way" declaration. Top stated that he seemed to recall seeing an MP report from Phan Rang come across his desk which involved me. Bad news certainly travels fast! The First Sergeant continued, asserting that he probably could "lose" said documentation providing I could be on the next chopper to the field. When I inquired when that might be, his reply was: "Ten minutes." He was primed for my protest, motioning to the corner of the tent where a rucksack and weapon were sitting--waiting for me! I recognized that Top had made me an offer that I couldn't refuse...but ten minutes?

I scuffled over to the supply CONEX, located my duffle bag, retrieved my web gear, a bandolier of boxed ammo, compass, poncho, poncho liner, a few extra canteens, and returned to the supply tent and crammed everything into the rucksack which already had about a week's supply of C-rations inside. I pulled the draw string tight, swung the ruck onto my back, and picked up the M-16. As I headed towards the landing pad, I pointed to an incoming chopper, inquiring if that was mine. The First Sergeant grinned and nodded in the affirmative. That grin also confirmed that I was home again among what an anthropologist might refer to as my *fictive kin*.[3]

*****

Enemy Situation

According to the Intelligence portions from Operation Malheur II After Action Reports,[4] our opponents were the 1st and 2nd VC (Main Force) Regiments. Again, I don't recall ever being informed at the time of the operation's name or the numerical IDs of the enemy regiments. Regarding my rank and role in the scheme of things, that knowledge didn't matter.

Throughout May and early June, all of the line battalions of the 1st Brigade had sustained significant and frequent contact with the local VC/NVA units. Intelligence believed that the enemy had broken down into squad-sized or smaller elements and infiltrated out of the AO, primarily to the west and north. However, the frequency of enemy contact that continued into and throughout June suggested that although the enemy may have broken down into smaller sized units, quite a few remained in the two valleys.

During the first part of June, two B-52 strikes on enemy complexes preceded an airmobile assault into the Song Ve Valley. On the 17th and the 20th of June, large numbers of sampans were intercepted carrying civilians out of the area. At least 30 of these civilians were males of military age. All were evacuated to the refugee center at Ngia Hanh. A second refugee center was located at Ba To.

Part of the resource denial plan included moving livestock out of the AO. On 21-22 June, the 1/327 concluded "Operation Roundup," which involved moving 1004 head of cattle and 192 water buffalo to a designated rendezvous point where the local district chief at Ngia Hanh and MACV advisors could take over and move the animals to the refugee center. The herd had originated within the operations areas of the 2/502 and 2/327 and then passed on to our battalion for final delivery to the district authorities.

Another part of the operation was to eventually evacuate all of the people and rice from Song Ve Valley. That endeavor started on 15 June, working from south to north. Later in the operation the valleys were subjected to defoliants (i.e. Agent Orange). The purpose was to destroy crops, and eliminate vegetation for concealment, in order to render the valleys incapable of sustaining a large insurgent force. Major coastal urban centers lay only eight to ten kilometers to the east. The Tet Offensive of 1968, which involved many of the population centers along the coast, was only six months into the future. Hartz and I arrived after the cattle drive, but were present when the modified C-123s passed low overhead spraying defoliant.

Once all of the local population was removed to refugee centers, the tactical plan provided that large swaths of valley floor could be declared "free-fire" zones. The trails at night were already free-fire zones. The enemy moved under cover of darkness, and we regularly ambushed them to deny them access to the trails and thus restricting guerilla movement. From Day One in Vietnam, the rural trails during nighttime were free-fire zones. Civilians were aware that using rural trails at night was forbidden, and they did so at their own peril. We didn't need authorization to engage targets on the trails after dark. Efforts were always made to insure other

American or allied forces, as well as our Air Force gunships, were aware of friendly troop locations to insure we wouldn't endanger each other.

In the Song Ve and Song Tra Cau Valleys, the flaw in implementing the "free-fire zone" concept was that not all of the locals, for whatever reason, chose to accept the government's offer, to relocate out of the combat zone and into the relative safety of the refugee centers. It wasn't until many years later, after I came across some after action reports, that I realized the plan was to remove all of the civilians from the AOs. In late June, when Kratzberg, Hartz and I returned to the field, that effort had obviously been abandoned. We were not instructed to force any civilians to relocate. The battalion's guidelines to us were to assist civilian personnel desiring safe conduct out of the AO. On several occasions we were confronted by civilians waving the yellow Chieu Hoi leaflets. Usually, within minutes of reporting our location and situation, a C&C ship arrived with a battalion staff officer and interpreter. Never did I observe a case where civilians presenting the leaflets were not extracted. Not only did the leaflet warrant them safe passage through the hostile area, it netted them a novel ride in a helicopter.

The rules of engagement, however, were amended with respect to handling males of military age. Because of the high density of enemy militia troops within these two valleys, the handling of unarmed males of military age required more attention. In essence, young males of military age became a special class of non-combatants in the sense that they needed to prove that they were non-combatants. By leaflet and loudspeaker over-flights, young males of military age were informed of the procedures to follow if they were confronted by our patrols. South Vietnam had military conscription. Males of military age should have been able to present ARVN IDs, leave orders, medical disability letters, discharge papers, deferment papers, etc. Anyone without documentation was to be detained for an explanation to the Vietnamese interpreter scout that generally travelled with the CP element. This situation customarily resulted in a helicopter evacuation of these individuals to a refugee center where the Vietnamese authorities handled the situation. If, when confronting a patrol, a male of military age failed to comply with these instructions, and the individual (or individuals) tried to run, deadly force was authorized. The caveat here: any military aged male would be wise not to attempt to flee when directed to stop. If they were innocent, it only would cost them a helicopter ride to the local refugee center.

*****

My helicopter ride that first morning back to the field varied from the usual. The pilots followed a river, keeping barely twenty feet above the water. Normally we flew at a much higher altitude. As we rounded a bend in the channel, we passed about eye level with a woman emerging from a cave entrance dug straight into the river bank. She stepped into the sunlight looking upwards, probably figuring that the source of the rotor noise was above her. When she realized that our aircraft was almost directly off her right shoulder, and that we had obviously spotted her, she dashed back into the cave. Over the next four months while operating in this area, most of our contact with the local residents met with similar reactions. Avoidance seemed to be their coping strategy.

The chopper set down in a parched field tangential to a well-used trail. The trail separated the open space from a lightly wooded area. The Force CP was located in the treed area to the left of the trail. The first familiar person I bumped into was SSG Trout. He seemed to have recovered fully from the wounds he received in early May. Sergeant Trout, normally the leader of one the three sub forces, was acting platoon sergeant, filling in for SFC Rosales. Later, Sergeant Robert Diaz took over the platoon sergeant slot. In late September, Sergeant Diaz would lose a leg to a land mine, and

Sergeant Trout would for awhile again handle the platoon sergeant's role.

The two lieutenants in the CP group seemed pretty engaged with some planning strategies. I figured that one of the officers was the Force leader and the other the artillery FO. Since both were deeply involved in what they were discussing, I felt that introductions would be better held for later. I asked Sergeant Trout where some of the old Tigers might be located. He pointed me down the trail to the place where both the path and the open area doglegged left. There stood the familiar lanky form of Ervin Lee, former resident of Anniston, Alabama. For the past ten months, Lee and I had cut through the same jungles, forded the same rivers, and absorbed the Vietnam experience pretty much from identical perspectives. We even made buck sergeant at the same time.

After the "good to see you again" greetings, I updated him on our leave and told him that Hartz would be checking in within a few days. He told me Kratzberg was already there, along with quite a few of the old timers who had recovered from wounds and returned. As the conversation was drawing down, one of Lee's team members called him over to their position. As I stood there focusing down the trail, two armed opponents (dressed in black, wearing flop hats, packing rucksacks, their weapons at sling arms) emerged onto the trail about 80 meters away. We spotted each other simultaneously.

I initiated the engagement. I employed the modified "quick kill" technique (to point the weapon without using the sights) introduced to us at P-training when we entered country: splash the first round low in front of the target(s) then make your adjustment. Some people relied on tracers to quickly confirm where their barrel was pointed. I used tracers also, but not the first few rounds.[5] If you were to fire quickly at the target and your first round missed high off to the side, unless it's a tracer, you get little or no feedback for your adjustments. The low-in-front shot provides feedback as well as the possibility of striking the target with the ricochet. This was the method of engagement I favored when I had to quickly respond to short-range targets. However the method has a major drawback. The concept wasn't conceived to be employed with a single-shot flintlock.

The two individuals coming at me were walking side-by-side. My first and only round kicked up dust low on their right, exactly where I envisioned it striking. Had it been a normal engagement, my next four or five shots would have been right on target, except for my weapon's failure to eject the expended cartridge casing. This was the typical malfunction of the early versions of the M-16, but it usually occurred after a few magazines had been fired. This jam happened on the first round.

Both of my opponents froze on the trail, yet they made no attempt to un-sling their weapons. They might not have been aware that my weapon had jammed. A person with nerves of steel may have tried to bluff them with a beckoning, confident gesture and body language telegraphing that they better behave or consequences would turn ugly. Unfortunately, I do not possess nor project that demeanor. Since I had no side arm, I settled on the fragmentation grenade option and spiraled an M-26 their direction. Because of the distance, the grenade had no chance of getting to our opponents, but it did cause them to think twice about moving towards me. The grenade also bought me enough time for Lee to arrive at my side. While Lee provided cover, I quickly assembled the sections of my cleaning rod and "ram-rodded" the jammed cartridge from the chamber. Our adversaries elected to exit into the thick vegetation on their right.

A few moments later, Sergeant Trout arrived on scene. Lee and I gave him a quick update on the situation. He then examined my weapon and asked me how I felt about it. I let him know that I

Harold Trout, photo courtesy of Pamela Flores

didn't trust it. It jammed on the first round, and we normally encountered the enemy in small groups. Sergeant Trout understood. About an hour later, as we were forming up to move out, Sergeant Trout presented me with a different rifle in exchange for the one that had jammed. I hadn't heard a resupply chopper, so how he acquired another "sixteen" so quickly, I hadn't a clue.

*****

Reflections on the Area of Operation

The first phase of Operation Malheur ran from early May to early June. During that period, contact between the units of the 1st Brigade and the 1st and 2nd VC Regiments was pretty much a daily affair, initially quite intense. In that first month's action, the 1/327th suffered 32 fatalities, with another 121 troopers wounded in action. The Brigade's total losses for the same period were 71 fatalities and 313 wounded. A year earlier at Dak To, the Brigade (2/327 was not deployed on Operation Hawthorne) sustained a loss of 45 killed and 241 wounded.[6] The 1st and 2nd VC Regiments put up as good a fight as the NVA regulars at Dak To. The NVA units at Dak To sought sanctuary in neighboring Laos and Cambodia. In contrast, the VC in the Song Ve area broke up into less observable smaller units, but remained in the area. We also discovered over the next few months that some of the enemy killed wearing black pajamas or mixed color clothing were actually NVA with their khaki uniforms in their rucksacks.

The civilian population of the Song Ve area, unlike the civilian populations of the Dak To, Phan Thiet or Tuy Hoa, displayed a much different attitude towards our presence. Characteristics that we were used to seeing in the southern Two Corps area, such as children waving to us, young girls smiling demurely, people approaching us with items for sale (like French bread or the ubiquitous orange soda), were almost totally absent in the Song Ve operations area. What we experienced instead was a population bent on avoiding contact with Americans. Like the woman that I observed from the helicopter on my first day back, the residents seemed to have withdrawn into their manmade caves, deep thickets, or some other furtive niche. They apparently considered us agents of the centralized government that was determined to remove them from their traditional homesteads. Whatever their reason, whether it was fear of being forced to relocate to a refugee center or some other emotional or political factor, the civilians pretty much tried to remain "invisible." Winning their hearts and minds was a hard sell. In the six months that I was to serve in the AO, that particular task was only remotely accomplished.

Brief Summary of Operation Malheur (Phase II)[7]

Timeframe: Phase II: 8 June–2 August
Base camp: Initially at Duc Pho but would shift to Chu Lai later in the summer
Area of Operations: North, northwest and southwest of Duc Pho, Quang Ngai Province, Song Ve and Song Tra Cau Valleys
Enemy Situation: Operations after 9 June revealed the presence of elements of both the 1st and 2d VC Regiment in AO.[8]
Mission: In addition to the usual Search and Destroy mission, the Province officials requested that the Brigade assist with the evacuation of the civilian personnel from both valleys in order to deny the VC a source of food and taxation. Nghia Hanh refugee center becomes the main detainee point.[9]
Other Considerations: On 3 July, the 1/327th is withdrawn to Carentan Base in preparation for commitment to Operation Lake from 6–12 July. Operation Malheur II morphs into Operation Hood River. 1/327th is initially the reserve battalion for that operation on 2 August.

****

[1] Don Kochi, Screaming Eagles and the Battle for Mother's Day Hill. 327infantry.org. p.5.

[2] While on leave, the First Sergeant forwarded me a copy of my promotion orders to Sergeant E-5, dtd. 10 May 1967.

[3] An anthropological term referring to perceived kinship ties not founded on blood relationships.

[4] Exhibit 442 For Official Use Only. 1/327th Inf. Reproduced at the National Archives, 72-CID046-27852.

[5] There might be times when you may not want to fire tracers. During the Tuy Hoa River crossing experience, I easily picked out the enemy and friendly machine-gun positions by the color of the tracers.

[6] MACV Command History. Cc SEA/Chronology/MACV/_1966.html.

[7] Combat After Action Report: Operation Malheur, 1st Bde. 101st Abn Div, #386041, Department of Defense, Ltr 3 Oct 67, *Unit History, 1st* Battalion (Airborne), 327th Infantry, 1st Brigade, 101st Airborne Division, Declassified from Confidential, Scribd.com, pages 1-71.

[8] Ibid., p. 15.

[9] Ibid., p. 15.

Chapter 28
Stone Grenades
Early July 1967

Who'd a thunk it?

Recommendation for Award of the Presidential Unit Citation: *"From 11 May 1967 to 25 November 1967, the 1st Brigade, 101st Airborne Division and attached units distinguished themselves in combat by displaying extraordinary heroism in the face of a determined, well armed enemy. While conducting operations MALHEUR, BENTON, and WHEELER, the 1st Brigade daily engaged in bitter conflicts with the enemy. On numerous occasions enemy units of superior size were overwhelmingly defeated by the 1st Brigade. These "Screaming Eagles" pursued the enemy tenaciously, driving him from his traditional sanctuaries thereby robbing him of much needed supplies and arms."*—Frank L Dietrich[1]

In early July, we air assaulted into an operations area southeast of Duc Pho. The unit history refers to this as "Operation Lake." The Force was at full complement with three subunits plus a 320th artillery forward observation team and a Vietnamese interpreter. SSG Haugh led the "one zero" element, Alpha Force. SSG Kratzberg had the "two zero" element, Bravo Force. And SSG Trout had Charlie Force, the "three zero" element.[2] This structure was not "cut in stone," so to speak. Sergeant Kratzberg started off with Bravo Force and finished with Charlie Force. Since many of the Tigers tended to go on R&R or leave with friends (myself included), and casualties from explosive devices often impacted several men from a single force, personnel rosters were reshuffled to keep the sub forces relatively balanced. Hartz and I were assigned to Charlie Force. Whenever SSG Trout was tapped to fill the platoon sergeant position, Hartz (the ranking E-5) assumed the lead of Charlie Force.

The battalion's mission during this short operation was to provide security for engineers working on Route 1, the coastal highway. Two tank platoons were opconned (placed under operational control of the 1/327th commander) to assist the battalion. Also, we had five-inch naval gun support from destroyers, some of which may have actually been World War II vessels inherited by the U.S. Coast Guard and manned by Coast Guard personnel.

For the Force, this short operation was low impact and fairly uneventful. During most of it we occupied key pieces of terrain while the other units cleared towards us. One evening, early in the operation, we set up on a hill overlooking a long stretch of beach. Below us one of the tank platoons seemed to be establishing a defensive position for the night. While settling in we also discovered that the field behind us was a potato patch. Considering that most of our food came from cans or was reconstituted from a powder, fresh baked potatoes quickly became the culinary delight on the menu that evening. Butter would have enhanced the repast, but C-ration cheese spread with a pinch of salt and pepper still managed to carry the ambiance.

Before night had fully descended, on the beach below us, and a little to the right from where the tanks had established their defensive positions, a brilliant flash and din erupted. Topography obstructed our direct view of the location where the explosion occurred. Since the normal weapons' chatter associated with a full scale firefight was not present, we figured that the armor unit had the situation under control. We stood ready to move and assist if needed, but we never received any directions to do so. The next morning, a few of the more inquisitive members of the Force took off to reconnoiter the previous evening's activities down on the beach. Upon their return, we learned that the armor unit had lost one of its tanks.

According to our reconnaissance team, the incident followed a sighting of a few VC. One tank crew darted off in pursuit of the enemy. When the VC reached a dried irrigation ditch, they split right and left around a dirt overpass erected over a section of corrugated pipe. At this point in the dissertation, one of the older, experienced Tigers interjected an inquiry phrased critically: "You're not gonna' tell us that the tank crew drove across the dirt overpass?" The response was: "Yep!" The tank had proceeded across the raised dirt overpass and that's all she wrote. Two booby-trapped 175mm artillery rounds completely ejected the turret from the tank, killing the three men inside of the turret. Only the driver, seated forward of the turret, survived. The turret of a medium tank weighs about eleven tons.

*****

We continued providing security along Route 1 for the remainder of the operation, which lasted about a week. We didn't complete a large amount of combat patrolling; usually we occupied key terrain waiting for an enemy that didn't attack. One afternoon, however, we did experience an attack of sorts.

We had found a good defensive position for a night location, so we set in early. The area was open, with only a small smattering of deciduous trees about twenty to thirty feet tall--not unlike a disused orchard. Since we had sunlight left, I did something I seldom conceded to in the field. I took my boots off to dry my feet. There has to be some corollary to Murphy's Law that specifically relates to removing footgear in a combat environment. Before I could fully appreciate the absence of wet socks, a double "thud-thud" drove us all to prone positions and counting: "One thousand, two thousand...eleven thousand," but no explosions. Chicom grenades have notoriously unreliable fuses. However, if the "thuds" were grenades, they should have detonated by eleven seconds. We replied with two M-26 fragmentation grenades which exploded after "four thousand." Chattering, screeching, branches thrashing, and what an individual might interpret as "monkey cursing" erupted in the leafy canopy above and before us. A troop of grey monkeys apparently took umbrage at our presence in their territory and tossed a few stones our direction. It could have been a lot worse. When I was much younger, at the San Francisco Zoo, a similar situation developed where the objects thrown were not stones, but feces.

According to battalion records, Operation Lake terminated on 12 July and we were extracted back to Duc Pho. After a night at the Carentan base camp, we air assaulted back via helicopters to the Song Ve and Song Tra Cau areas where we re-entered Malheur II.[3]

Brief Summary of Operation Lake

Timeframe: 2–16 July 1967
Base camp: Duc Pho (Carentan) and Chu Lai
AO for Operation Lake: Skirting Route 1 about 15 kilometers southeast of Duc Pho[8]
Enemy Situation: 1st and 2d VC Regiment in AO
Mission: Provide security for engineer work parties along Route 1
Other Considerations: On 3 July, the 1/327th is withdrawn to Carentan Base in preparation for commitment to Operation Lake from 6–12 July. After Operation Lake, the battalion returns to Operation Malheur II which morphs into Operation Hood River. 1/327th is initially the reserve battalion for that operation on 2 August.

****

[1]Letter, Department of the Army, Recommendation for Presidential Unit Citation, Frank L. Dietrich Commanding.
[2]If the Forces's call sign was: "Red Robin," then "Red Robin 10" would identify Alpha Force. The call signs usually changed each operation, but the suffix designators remained same.
[3]Exhibit 442 For Official Use Only. 1/327th Inf. Reproduced at the National Archives, 72-CID046-27852, p.8.

Chapter 29

The C-Ration Ambush
Middle July 1967

> *"Above the Rest and Second to None*
> *If We Can't Do It, It Can't Be Done*
> *Recon, Attack, Ambush and Raid*
> *The Best Outfit in the First Brigade"* --Don Thornton[1]

My team had established a night defensive position overlooking the river, at the most likely place an adversary might try to ford. When I heard my name whispered, my first thought was that my turn for guard duty had arrived. Rank has its privilege, so I had placed myself in the guard sequence near the middle. The hour before dawn was the shift that I preferred least. As I started to respond to my intruder, two issues that my groggy mind hadn't precisely resolved slowly made their way to my forethoughts: how did the middle of the night arrive so soon and why was the lieutenant's RTO delivering the time-for-guard-duty summons? His clairvoyant response quickly resolved my quandary: *Sergeant Doyle's team was in contact and needed immediate backup, ASAP.*[2]

I started circulating the warning order for the team to get ready to move, then made my way to the CP location for specifics. Fortunately my team was mostly composed of experienced Tigers. In less than two minutes they could stuff their ponchos and liners into their rucks, don their web gear, secure their weapons, and make ready to move. There would be no foot dragging; being summoned for a night move signaled that something was up.

I was not aware that Sergeant Doyle's team had been directed to set up a "stay behind" ambush at a place where we had been resupplied earlier. A few days prior, my team had worked the area after an air strike. We were pretty familiar with the trails running throughout the zone where Doyle's team was located. Usually abandoned resupply sumps were an irresistible temptation for our adversaries to rummage. This one proved no exception. Doyle's team was about four kilometers away and in contact at the time. Our team's mission was to close the distance as quickly as possible and reinforce Doyle's lightly manned element. To expedite our night movement, battalion had initiated an illumination mission utilizing helicopters to drop parachute flares.

As we were setting out, SSG George Jorkowski volunteered to join us. George not only added an additional rifle to the team, but our friendship also went back a long way. We took R&R together. His tactical expertise far surpassed mine. If the team needed fire support, "Big Ski" would be the man to direct it. This wasn't the first time that Ski volunteered to accompany an away team. He seemed to sense when an extra pair of eyes and ears might come in handy.

Night ops were testy for several reasons. One, before GPS navigation, distances were easily misestimated in the dark. Another complication was bumping into a friendly patrol. Civilians were also a concern. In this particular area, for whatever the reason, many civilians tended to use the trails at night, ignoring the nationwide rural curfew. Often these individuals were carrying farm implements which could easily be mistaken for weapons, especially on a moonless night. Normally the Force maneuvered at night without illumination. However, battalion had laid in illumination support to expedite our sprint to reinforce Doyle's team. The mission evolved in a manner that I hadn't anticipated.

The illumination support was being provided by helicopters dropping parachute flares laterally to our line of movement. With usually two or three flares drifting in the air at one time, the lighted area progressed with us continuously. My past experiences with illumination were confined almost entirely with defensive postures, where we remained stationary in prepared positions. Flares were delivered by artillery or mortars to the area in front of our positions, lighting up the panorama before us. This night, en route to Doyle's ambush, we were "in" the panorama! When a flare neared its burn out point, the helicopter crew dropped another. As the wind carried the parachute flares in one direction, on the ground, shadows circled objects in the opposite direction: multiple flares, multiple shadows. The terrain was alive with moving shadows!

We were returning on the trail we had used the day before. It transected a large, dry rice paddy network. Actually, the trail itself was nothing more than a wide paddy dike running down the length of the valley. The main river was a couple hundred meters to our left. Not quite as far to our right, a woodline framed the dry paddies. The illumination support, designed to facilitate our race to Doyle's team, deprived us of any chance of remaining clandestine. We had sacrificed the element of surprise for speed.

I had envisioned an attack coming from the tree line on the right, so Ski's declaration to "Run!" caught me somewhat flat-footed because Ski was behind me! Actually, he was pushing me away from the trail off into the dry paddy. After covering a grenade-throw distance without experiencing any hostile action, we stopped, affording me the opportunity for the inevitable question: "What are we running from?" Ski's response was also a query: "Didn't you see it?!" "See what?" The genesis of Ski's frenetic dash away from the trail was a bounding mine which popped up behind me, in front of him. The reason we were having any conversation at all was because the mine had failed to detonate.

Since the entire Force, minus Doyle's contingent, had passed over that trail in the previous day's movement from the resupply point to the night position on the river, the mine was probably just recently deployed. The illumination mission had compromised our intentions and the local adversaries took advantage of the situation and "seeded" a mine on our route. There probably weren't any more mines, yet prudence dictated avoiding the trail for the last kilometer to Doyle's ambush site. The paddies were dry, so travel really wasn't impeded. It also affirmed for me that the illumination wasn't necessary. We continued on, keeping the trail about ten meters off to our right. About twenty minutes later, we closed on the ambush site.

I slipped in beside Doyle. The rest of the team positioned themselves about the small hill overlooking the kill zone. Night hadn't given way fully to morning yet, but discernible were several bodies sprawled to the left of the C-ration bait trove. Beside the tree behind the C-ration cartons leaned two carbines.

Sharing some of his coffee, Doyle filled me in on the details. The VC, in their scavenging, first triggered an M-26 grenade which had been rigged into a B-3 can. In spite of suffering casualties, the enemy returned to their rummaging. Doyle's men proceeded to up the ante and threw a few grenades into the mix. According to Doyle, the VC never seemed to comprehend that there were Americans present. They appeared to be working under the premise that the ration dump was well booby-trapped. Upping the ante again, Doyle's men command detonated three claymore mines. After that, all enemy activity ceased. The VC lay where they fell, their weapons propped against the tree.

*****

The remainder of the Force joined us shortly after daybreak. For the better part of the next two weeks our patrols remained in close proximity to the river, fording the water course several times, working both sides of the river. About this stage in the overall operation (which had started in mid June), a few prominent features regarding the local area and enemy began to solidify.

One, the river had "moods." The first time we crossed it, we barely got our knees wet. In contrast, at a subsequent crossing at that same fording point, the water was chest deep. Later, when staging for a movement across the river, battalion warned us to make it quick. Because of heavy rainfall in the highlands, the water level was expected to rise significantly. While the Force was in transit, in less than a ten-minute time span, the current had progressed from gentle to raging. We had barely made the opposite bank when battalion radioed that we should establish a vigil for troops in the water. Three men from one of our line companies crossing upstream of us had been swept away. Shortly after that caveat, we received instructions to conduct an immediate head count because an intermediate unit had recovered four bodies! The extra body turned out to be that of a missing Marine.

Two, encountering civilians in the area was rare, but it wasn't because the civilians had accepted the government's invitation to move en masse to relocation centers. The remaining general population was avoiding contact with U.S. personnel. Well-established trails spread out on both sides of the river. Most Vietnamese activity seemed to occur on the side of the river away from us, indicating that a reliable communication network existed. At night we observed civilians on the trails and in hooches. During the day, however, they pretty much vacated these areas for obscure hideaways. Quite often they relocated to excavated earthen chambers in hillsides and river banks. Across the population spectrum there was almost an entire age group not represented: the young adult group, both male and female, between late teen and thirty-something. The AO was not only a "hotbed" of VC activity, but the residents appeared to be more supportive of the "home team" than the national government. The notion surfaced that had the boundary separating North and South Vietnam been established south of Quang Ngai Province, most of the residents would have been okay with that. But how often do bureaucrats, imposing "straight line" boundaries consider cultural preferences?

Three, the enemy came in two distinct "packages." The local VC seemed to feel at home in this valley. On an almost daily basis, one of our teams encountered small numbers of males armed only with weapons, no web gear or extra equipment or ammo. It was almost as if they were leisurely strolling about their estate, idly meandering from Point A to Point B, with no apparent military purpose. More often than not, their jabber gave them away and sealed their fate. Whereas, the itinerate NVA that we occasionally encountered in the zone were customarily festooned with weapon, web gear, rice bandoleer and rucksack within which they had packed their khaki uniform, hammock, and "kitchen sink." On their person was usually found a lighter engraved with a regimental number, plus the ubiquitous photo of the girl back home.

Four, although the South Vietnamese government's aspirations for removing the majority of the human population from the valley was not achieved, the livestock population had definitely dwindled. Also, the defoliants took their toll on the vegetation. The trees had dropped much of their foliage and resembled a bare New England woodland in late autumn awaiting the first snow. The rice paddies were dry. The objective to deny the enemy their customary food base seemed to be moving toward accomplishment. Lending credence to this assessment, the VC in Doyle's ambush, even after suffering casualties, had returned to scrounge through the C-ration cartons a second time.

*****

One morning as we closed down a meeting with the lieutenant, he mentioned that battalion wanted us to destroy the small groupings of water buffalo that were lingering about in the nearby dry paddy. I missed the June cattle drive, but from the complaints associated with it, one could pretty much guarantee there'd be no repeat of that event. The battalion was out of the livestock herding, driving, and cattle punching business at least where water buffaloes were concerned.

Applying deadly force against armed aggressors didn't disturb my personal moral code; shooting peacefully grazing animals that were doing me no harm did. My mental dilemma was further complicated by my social position at that time. Would not having my team fire on the buffalo be considered disobedience to a direct order from a superior officer? The Code of Conduct classes that we attended in basic training clearly stated that no one could order us to violate moral principles. My immediate problem was that my knowledge of the Code was a little vague with respect to water buffalo.

As usual, the team was packed up and ready to go when I joined them. Someone right off asked what today's assignment entailed. I told him that the lieutenant wanted me to check out a hilltop off to our left. Someone else chimed in with something like, "Do you mind if we tag along with you?" My reply likewise was on the order of, "I wouldn't mind at all." In the Force, leadership wasn't as much about ordering as it was about doing. I served with a lot of great mentors since Dak To, both officer and NCO. Sergeant Trout was one of those leaders. His guidance to us young bucks was: "Don't ask or expect the men to do something you wouldn't do yourself." I was also aware that any one of these men was capable of leading the recon team up that hill and back. At that particular moment, I was the team's point of contact, so to speak. In a few months, one of these men would replace me and inherit my call sign.

Soon some of the other teams started firing on the water buffalo near them. Someone in our team asked what the shooting was about. Before I could respond to that question, the lieutenant had come up behind me and asked why my men weren't shooting the water buffalo. John Feeney, who was on my right, responded quite matter-of-factly, "Sir, we don't shoot water buffalo." The lieutenant said nothing, just passed us with the rest of the CP group heading toward the next intended location. We had our mission. We would join them later at the night defensive position, but right then we had a hill to recon.

Brief Summary of the Continuation of Malheur II

Timeframe: Mid July 1967
Base camp: Duc Pho (Carentan)
AO for Operation: Song Ve Valley, Quang Ngai Province
Enemy Situation: 1st and 2d VC Regiment in AO
Mission: Cordon and destroy enemy combatants. Assist with the evacuation of civilian personnel.
Other Considerations: After Operation Lake, the battalion returns to Operation Malheur II which morphs into Operation Hood River. 1/327th is initially the reserve battalion for that operation on 2 August.

****

[1] Don Thornton, stanza from his *"Tiger Force"* ballad, adapted to marching cadence, reflecting Col. Hackworth's premise that the 1st Battalion, 327th Infantry could accomplish any mission, 1966.

[2] According the battalion radio logs, this action began at 22:07 hours on 18 July 1967. Exhibit 442, For Official Use Only. 1/327th Inf. Reproduced at the National Archives, 72-CID046-27852, p.11.

Chapter 30
Night River Crossing and the Old Man
Late July 1967

*"War, a Political Knot that Having Failed to
Give Way to the Tongue,
Is Untied with the Teeth".* –Ambrose Bierce[1]

*"Earth Bares no Balsam for Mistakes
Men Crown the Knave and Scourge the Tool
That did His Will"* --Anonymous[2]

After a helicopter resupply, the Force waited for darkness to settle in and then executed a river crossing the night of 23/24 July[3]. Our team (plus a 2-man machine-gun section) drew the point duty. The water was about waist deep. The far bank at the egress point was about four feet high, and the water dripping off us made the clayish soil slippery. Slightly above the exit point a well-defined trail ran along the bank, parallel to the river. The team split and took up security positions down trail in each direction. The machine-gun section went to the right, the intended route that the Force would assume when the crossing was complete. Once the main Force passed us, our team would fall in behind it and become the rear security for the rest of the night.

The night movement served two purposes. First, the Force would regain the element of surprise, which was difficult to maintain during daytime in fairly open terrain, especially after defoliants had cleared much of the zone. The local civilians and adversaries quickly came to know which side of the river we were working on, thus avoiding that side. Second, we were directed to link up with some Special Forces CIDG troops operating north of us, so we needed to pass over to their side of the river.

Normally when we executed a river crossing, the point element moves straight out onto the intended line of march as it emerges from the stream. For some reason (perhaps a head count issue or a last minute mission change from battalion) things began jamming up. Sergeant Kratzberg's force was clustered just shy of the trail, near the machine-gun position, and it stretched back almost to the CP group. The CP group was gathered near the egress point. About a third of the Force was either in the water or still waiting on the far bank.

About the time Sergeant Kratzberg's force had completed its crossing and was rallying around the top of the bank, our first night wanderer arrived. I was standing on the trail beside the machine-gun position as the dark shape lumbered towards us. In the poor light the shape didn't seem human at first. None of us said anything. We just let it continue to advance. It wasn't until the thing literally bumped into me that I recognized what we had intercepted. An old man, bent forward, was utilizing a stick across his shoulder to counter balance two wicker cages of waterfowl. Out of the dark (a little way behind the old man) two other figures also emerged, hesitated, and then quickly backed off. Trusting the MG team to handle any situation that might go south, I turned my attention to the individual in front of me. For the old man, enlightenment had just arrived and his immediate reaction was a surge of slurred babble, mixed perhaps with high intensity praying.

His assessment must have included the realization that he had just been apprehended on a trail after curfew while transporting food items. His action could be construed as abetting the local VC forces, if not actually relegating him to said status. He was probably also aware that the trails during curfew were true free-fire zones. The machine-gun team could have blown him, and those behind him, away at first sighting. This didn't happen because the team was well trained and disciplined. They held their fire in order to ascertain the presence or absence of a weapon. If there had been a weapon, the old man would most likely already be dead.

The old man's physical presence wasn't the problem. His shrill, klaxon-like bantering was. We needed to calm the old man down before his clamoring could draw the attention of any VC contingent lingering about. He eventually came to realize that my hand motions and shushing sounds meant for him to be quiet. He actually seemed to relax a little. The two other travelers behind the old man also hadn't slipped my mind.

My next task was to get the old man away from the security element and to the CP group where the interpreter would be located. I moved very close to the old man and gestured with what I hoped would be construed as a "follow me" signal. He understood, and off we went past Sergeant Kratzberg's sopping wet team.

As I approached the CP party, I met Sergeant Trout. I briefed him and then moved the old man toward the main body and the interpreter. I left the old man with the CP group and headed back to join my team. My new task was to move the machine gun further down the trail to ease the congestion issue as more men filtered into the tight rally area.

While nearing Sergeant Kratzberg's force, I heard a conversation in tonal Vietnamese start up in the CP area. I figured the old man and the interpreter had just made introductions. It appeared the old man had shifted into panic mode again and renewed the cacophony in high-pitched, tonal Vietnamese. Tactically, the situation was dangerous. We were in an area where we expected to surprise our enemy. But two other individuals had exited down the route in the direction we would be heading, and now we had a human siren beaconing our location. As I made eye contact with Sergeant Kratzberg, a shot rang out and the sergeant's facial expression transmitted: "Damn!" I'm sure my face mirrored the same reaction. The old man's hysterical bantering had immediately ceased. Someone at the CP location, seeking an immediate solution to restore noise discipline, leapt to the extreme option and purchased silence with a bullet.

Subsequent conversations with veteran members of the Force agreed there were other less drastic options available. But we also understood that roughly two-thirds of the men (including most of the CP party) were volunteers who had filled the ranks after the fifteenth of May. Since they had started working in this area, grenade attacks on their positions at night were a common experience. It was no surprise that someone felt that the old man's bellowing might solicit a grenade attack--a consensus which was valid. Considering the old man had violated the national curfew as well as transported food items after dark, he was listed on the battalion radio logs as an "unarmed VC."[4] The Army conducted an intense investigation on this incident. The Army, the Department of Defense, and the administration elected not to pursue judicial actions against any member of the Force. Mitigating factors that may have guided the Army's decision not to prosecute:

One: The VC were well represented in the area and active on both sides of the river. Small arms contact with enemy elements was frequent. At night, grenade attacks on U.S. positions were common. A few nights prior to the river crossing episode, the Force had suffered four casualties from grenade attacks on its perimeter. Four nights after executing the river crossing, four more casualties were sustained by another night grenade attack, two of which were fatalities. Losing eight men out of approximately thirty-five translates into a loss of about twenty-five percent in combat strength in roughly a week. The area was not a sleepy farming community.

Two: The old man placed himself in the killing zone. He made the choice to ignore the nationwide prohibition regarding using trails during curfew in order to transport food items, one of the principal reasons the government had imposed such restrictions in the first place. Also, consider the location: the Song Ve Valley, where for the preceding two months the government and the military undertook extraordinary measures aimed at removing sources of sustenance for the enemy from this valley. Measures included a massive cattle drive, spraying of crop killing defoliants, transporting stored rice reserves to the relocation centers, slaughtering residual cattle and water buffalo that avoided incorporation in the original livestock movement, and attempting to implement the evacuation of the entire civilian population from the area. The old man knew what was taking place within the AO.

Three--and most important: The old man's verbal outbursts posed a danger to the entire Force. By this stage of the operation, the VC had been restricted to operating mostly at night. The intensity of his clamoring, if allowed to continue, would easily have summoned enemy attention to the crossing site and jeopardized many of the men.

*****

There's nothing like the report of a weapon at night to get things organized and moving along. Special Forces CIDG troops from the Minh Long and Ba To camps were supporting the Brigade. We had forded at a place where the river flowed south to north. And once on the other side, we then turned north to follow the river. Three days later we hooked up with a crusty old E-7 and his platoon of CIDG troops. Since Minh Long was nearer to us than Ba To, I assumed his detachment was from the closest base camp. At the time, however, confirming that bit of supposition hadn't occurred to me. Knowing which camp the CIDG troops came from had no bearing on our mission.

We spent a few hours with the Special Forces sergeant before getting ready to head off into our night locations and subsequent recon sectors. Earlier, while sharing coffee, the sergeant asked if a few of our men could be informally attached to his unit to help him with his radio watch. His concern wasn't fatigue, but suspicion. He expressed doubts about the loyalties of a few of his men. I hadn't realized that unlike the CIDG troops that we had worked with in the highlands, these fellows weren't Montagnards. I trusted the Montagnards at Dak To, literally, with my life.

We moved out, leaving three of our men to reinforce the sergeant. They weren't enough. Around midnight, radio traffic signaled trouble--a grenade attack. Three Americans in the CP area were critically wounded, two fatally; both were Tigers. Sergeant Domingo Munos died at the scene; Sp4 Clarence Brooks died a few days later.

Brief Summary of Completion of Malheur II

Timeframe: End of July 1967
Base camp: Duc Pho (Carentan)
AO for Operation: The Song Ve Valley
Enemy Situation: 1st and 2d VC Regiment in AO
Mission: Cordon and destroy enemy combatants. Assist with the evacuation of civilian personnel.
Other Considerations: Operation Malheur II morphs into Operation Hood River. 1/327th is initially the reserve battalion for that operation on 2 August. We stay in the field and continue business as usual until we are extracted to the rear area on 10 August.

****

[1] Ambrose Bierce, The Devil's Dictionary.
[2] Anonymous, The Fool's Prayer.
[3] According to the battalion radio logs, Exhibit 438, Original Confidential downgraded to For Official Use Only. 1/327th Inf. Reproduced at the National Archives, 72-CID046-27852, 23:45 – 02:01 hours 23/24 July respectively.
[4] Ibid., footnote 3.

Chapter 31
Free-Fire Zone?
May through November 1967

'All seems infected to the infected spy,
As all looks yellow to the jaundiced eye'. –Alexander Pope[1]

Division Level: *Task Force Oregon OPORD -- "The remaining two battalions continued their search for the 2d VC Regiment and <u>evacuated</u> the population of the SONG NE(sic) Valley to NGHIA HANH, once again at the request of Province officials."* --After Action Report[2]

Battalion Level: *1/327th Infantry Battalion Unit History -- "The 'Above The Rest Battalion' attempted to compete its mission of <u>evacuating all people</u> and rice from the northern portion of the SONG VE Valley in preparation for a stand down the following day.* –327th History[3]

Company Level: *Sergeant from A Company, 1/327th -- ".... once the indigenous population was <u>evacuated</u> and resettled at the nearby detainee and relocation center during Phase II. The gradual absences of local inhabitants also had the additional effect of permitting large four by six mile area swathes declared as <u>free-fire zones</u> throughout the lower valley regions."* --Don Kochi[4]

Almost forty years after the fact, an examination of the event at the river crossing resurfaced in a book.[5] Since this is the timeframe in which the incident occurred, this chapter is the appropriate place to address circumstances pertinent to its resurfacing.

In 2006, following a series of newspaper accounts published three years earlier, a book was released where the whole Force was typecast a "rogue unit" and its members as "rampaging GIs."[6] An Army CID investigative report, compiled in the early 1970s, served as the basis for expanded allegations. Although these allegations never led to charges being levied against any individual, some were repeated again in 2017 in a much lauded TV documentary.[7]

So how did Tiger Force, one of the most highly decorated combat units in the Vietnam conflict, end up being typecast as a "rogue unit" of "rampaging GIs?" Before I attempt to tackle that question, I need to provide some general background information regarding news coverage of the conflict in Vietnam. After I had left Vietnam and was in college back in the states, I began to question the way information regarding the Vietnam War was being presented to the American public. The following example can help illustrate my apprehensions regarding this issue.

In 1973, while attending a counter-intelligence lecture at Fort Huachuca, my concerns—about the manner in which some news was presented in the media—were rekindled. The speaker presented a video along with still photographs that I and many Americans had first viewed on national news during the Tet Offensive of 1968.[8] At the lecture, I came to realize that I (like most television viewers) had been duped, and our opinions swayed, by the selective manner in which the story was presented. A critical part in understanding the whole story was omitted from the video and newspaper accounts. Again, in a recent documentary prepared for television, the same video was presented in the same fashion, with the same omissions.

The video in question is the black-and-white presentation that ran across most of the news networks in January of 1968 depicting the execution of a VC captive. In the video a South Vietnamese general places a revolver beside the head of a disarmed VC in civilian attire and pulls the trigger. My reaction, like many other military personnel, was betrayal. We brought our ideals about the worth and rights of individual human beings to Vietnam, as a counter balance to the state-dominated philosophies of the gulag builders, and the-end-justifies-the-means proponents. Because of the general's apparent impetuous reaction, our democracy, if not our social fiber, was certainly called into question for supporting the country that the general represented.

For five years, from 1968 to 1973, whenever the video or photograph resurfaced (which was quite frequently), I empathized with the slain VC and considered his slayer the villain. But, after the counter-intelligence lecture at Fort Huachuca, my opinion changed. My initial reaction, like many others, resulted from what was presented in the video and press-released photographs. What had been omitted from the visual presentations submitted in 1968, and again in the more recent documentary, was an exposé of the VC's action immediately before he was summarily executed.

The VC was a captain in charge of a political death squad sent into the local community with a list of names of people that needed to be eliminated. The captain had been apprehended at the mass killing site where he had supervised the slaying of seven local police officials and as many of the officers' family members as could be found: thirty-four in total, mostly women and children. The method of execution was throat slashing. When captured, the VC captain didn't deny his deed, he bragged about it. His flippant boasting might have arisen from the amount of military police present in the video. He may have assumed that he was on his way to a POW compound where he would sit out the rest of the war and eventually be released. The Vietnamese general was the counter-intelligence supervisor for that district; the seven slain police officers were the general's men. He knew their families well.

The Geneva and Hague Conventions that establish and recognize the rights of non-uniformed combatants also allow for summary executions. In my revised reassessment of the video, the general administered justice according to convention. In this case, the press didn't lie; it just chose not to tell the whole truth. Because of the way that the story was presented, the villain was perceived as a martyr. That perception will continue to be propagated every time that video is presented without an accompanying clarifying statement. Thanks to the internet, cross-checking news accounts is an easier task than it was before the digital age, providing an individual is acquainted with and can recognize selective reporting techniques.

An additional note here, the journalist, Eddie Adams, who received a Pulitzer for his original photos of the event, commented that he regretted releasing the material after he saw how it was handled by the press. According to Eddie Adams:

> *"Two people died in that photograph: the recipient of the bullet and General Nguyen Ngoc Loan. The general killed the Viet Cong; I killed the general with my camera. Still photographs are the most powerful weapons in the world. People believe them; but photographs do lie, even without manipulation. They are only half-truths...What the photograph didn't say was, 'What would you do if you were the general at that time and place on that hot day, and you caught the so-called bad guy after he blew away one, two or three American people?' This picture really messed up his life. He never blamed me. He told me if I hadn't taken the picture, someone else would have, but I've felt bad for him and his family for a long time...I sent flowers when I heard that he had died and wrote, "I'm sorry. There are tears in my eyes."*[9]

Followup: Eddie Adams provided the following postscript about the general. "What happened to General Nguyen Ngoc Loan after the war? Sadly, the photograph's legacy would haunt Loan for the rest of his life. A few months after the execution picture was taken, Loan was seriously wounded by machine-gun fire that led to the amputation of his leg. Following the war he was reviled wherever he went. After an Australian hospital refused to treat him, he was transferred to the United

States, where he was met with a massive (though unsuccessful) campaign to deport him."

"He opened a pizza restaurant in the Washington, D.C. suburb of Burke, Virginia at Rolling Valley Mall called "Les Trois Continents." In 1991 he was forced into retirement when he was recognized and his identity publicly disclosed. Photographer Eddie Adams recalled that on his last visit to the pizza parlor, he had seen written on a toilet wall, "We know who you are, fucker." Nguyen Ngoc Loan died of cancer on 14 July 1998, aged 67, in Burke, Virginia."[10]

The visual photographs and videos taken out of context and presented with no background information projected the slain VC as the "victim." The public was not made aware that the VC had just helped orchestrate, in an extremely gruesome manner, the deaths of thirty-four civilians, the majority of which were women and children. The background information was available but not included with the 1968 release. Nor was it incorporated when the video was included in the latest documentary. Why not? Can a story be complete if half of it is untold?

*****

Thirty-some years after Ft Huachuca, I was introduced to the accusations levied against the Force when some of the Tigers whom I had maintained communication with over the years contacted me about a book and newspaper articles. I looked up the newspaper articles on the web, and checked out the book from the local library.

The account of the old man's death near the river was presented as a brutal murder of a poor carpenter traveling home through a tranquil farming community that was not in the least bit a hotbed of rebellious activity. The tactical aspects surrounding the incident were disregarded, or perhaps never really understood or even researched. Their sources displayed little knowledge of the actual situation as it unfolded. Their version of the story had the old man crossing the river and the setting occurring in the Central Highlands.

Actually, the Force had crossed the river (not the old man) and the event occurred within ten kilometers from the sea, on the coastal plain. Also, there was no inquiry regarding the reason the old man's intended direction was towards the VC-controlled foothills, and not the residential areas to the east. Or, why he chose the dark of night to undertake the movement of a few bamboo baskets of waterfowl. Or, that his actions were jeopardizing our troops.

I started attending the Force's reunions regularly. I took notes, vetted stories presented in the book, and started researching military records regarding the operations in the Quang Ngai area in 1967. I don't think that I was really planning on this narrative so much; the process just evolved over the years.

What happened between May and November 1967, specific to Quang Ngai Province, that hadn't existed before or after those dates?

According to the media reports, during that period, several U.S. combat units (Tiger Force one of them), were alleged to have fired upon civilian non-combatants in the Quang Ngai region. One of the principal explanations cited for firing on civilians was that some ground commanders took the "free-fire zone" directive literally. If the "free-fire zone" directive was not to be employed as it is literally interpreted, then what was the correct non-literal interpretation that should have been followed? How was a viable target designated and identified, and what parameters had to be met before weapons were set "free" on it?

Additional speculation suggested that civilian casualties were incorporated into the battlefield death counts, in order to foster the impression that the war was being won through attrition. In simpler terminology, the accusation was that the military wasn't opposed to incorporating civilian casualties into the enemy KIA statistics, because it made it appear that the war was progressing as planned. An examination of the "free-fire zone" concept--and the body count statistics--might provide the reasoning behind the allegations regarding the targeting of non-combatants in the Quang Ngai operations.

Free-fire zones: I can cite at least two types of "free-fire zones" that were established during my combat deployment in Vietnam. All of our operations areas (maybe all of Vietnam) were "free-fire zones" with respect to methods of engaging insurgents and guerillas. All **armed** opponents (whether uniformed or not) were viable targets for the employment of deadly force. The presence of a weapon was the qualifying prerequisite for freely firing on an adversary. The *weapon* was the qualifier. This parameter existed at all times unless specific directions were issued not to engage the enemy unless fired upon first. These latter situations usually pertained to religious cease-fires, lasting for a designated period of time, normally three or four days.

A second established "free-fire zone" involved the **use of rural trails at night**. Because the insurgents infiltrated during the hours of darkness, we ambushed the trail networks at night. To protect civilians and ourselves, the government of Saigon placed nationwide restrictions on the use of rural trails after dark. Civilians caught after curfew could face arrest for violating the law. They could be imprisoned under the suspicion of aiding the enemy. They could get caught up in one of our ambushes. They could run into a four-legged tiger or other similar creatures of the dark. This was a land without street lights. Losing trail privileges at night seemed to have had little effect on the civilians, except those assisting the other side's effort.

Until I started researching OPLANs and After Action Reports in preparation for this narrative, I wasn't even aware of any attempts to designate a third type of "free-fire zones" unique to the Quang Ngai Province. The Task Force Oregon OPLAN and the 1/327th After Action Report address the "free-fire zones," saying that the purpose of removing the local residents was to enable the ability to create the "free-fire zones." However, unlike the other two zones that I mentioned above, where a **weapon** or a **trail-user after curfew** was the qualifier for employing deadly force, the new concept offered no definitive description of just what constituted a viable target within the designated zones, once they were established after the evacuation of civilians.

The original military plans envisioned all designated free-fire zones vacated of non-combatants. All of the civilians were to have been evacuated to relocation centers along with their rice and livestock. The plans called for the establishment of the "free-fire zones" only after evacuation was complete. The plan was predicated on the assumption that if all of the civilian non-combatants were removed to refugee centers, ergo, only combatants would be left and could be freely fired upon. American troops are criticized for endangering civilians by taking the "free-fire zones" literally? It seems that the adverb "literally" isn't the point of focus here. The term "free-fire zone" is the phrase under scrutiny. Obviously not all of the civilians were evacuated from the areas in question, which was a prerequisite for establishing the zones in the original plans. The self-imposed criteria for establishing a "free-fire zone" wasn't met. I am uncertain what effect this ambiguity might have caused, because I witnessed no firing on groups of civilians. It is not beyond comprehension that some American GIs interpreted the presence of civilians in the evacuated areas in the same light as civilians on the trails at nighttime. They were both in violation of the government's directives, and therefore they qualified as viable targets.

Another management nightmare existed regarding this specific concept of "free-fire zones." How does an individual infantryman, or a civilian, know if he is in a "free-fire zone?" The entire AO was *not* classified as a "free-fire zone." According to the OPLAN, free-fire zones were intended to be smaller tracts of land, roughly four by six miles in dimension, where inhabitants and livestock were totally evacuated. These tracts may, or may not, be adjacent to one another. There were no street posts or chalk lines delineating the battle zones. Consider the following incident described by Steve Merrill.

Steve Merrill, photo courtesy of Steve Merrill

"It was around midday. We were in the open on that flat area where hooches are built. A Huey came in with rockets and miniguns firing at us. We all scattered, and that was when Pappy went one way and I another. I had the radio and he had the handset. The handset went MIA. I can't remember who had the 60, and I didn't see it happen, but I heard he stood his ground and pointed the 60 at the chopper. The pilot broke off....I had no idea we were in a free-fire zone until we got back to HQ. That's when I learned a nearby river was the boundary, and we were on the wrong side."[11]

I had experienced a similar situation when a Huey door gunner started shooting at us. Not being aware of these free-fire zones, I thought the door gunner had just mistaken us for the enemy. We fired a burst of red tracers well in front of the ship, hoping the pilot would know we were friendlies. He banked away from us.

Hartz, Kratzberg, and I returned to the field in late June. Richard Ammons also returned about that time. The Second Phase of Operation Malheur was already about three weeks underway. No one appraised us about any "free-fire zone" concept. As I stated above, I didn't discover that the concept even existed until I started research for this narrative. We continued the war where we had left off. Armed adversaries were our targets. We detained military aged males without papers until battalion picked them up. We assisted and protected civilians waving the yellow Chieu Hoi free conduct passes, until battalion could arrange for their extraction. Other civilians not indicating that they were interested in the government's offer to be relocated outside of the combat area, we bypassed. We received no instructions to use force to remove the civilians. If directions to the contrary were issued at the onset of the operation three weeks earlier, we were not made aware of them.

Casualty reporting: The following summary is drawn from the battalion radio logs covering May through October 1967, the period that I was in the I Corps area. The brigade left the I Corps in November 1967. The statistics are compiled by month for Tiger Force only. The number to the left of the slash reflects the combined count of NVA and VC killed in action (Note: 20 of the May enemy KIA count occurred at Tiger Valley, and the October KIA count included three fresh graves). The number to the right of the slash represents the combined count of individuals that the Force evacuated from the field, i.e. enemy WIAs, POWs, detainees, and evacuees. Assuming that I didn't count a finger twice or forget a thumb, these are the stats from the battalion radio logs.

May: 39/66, June: 10/140, July: 25/63,
August: 21/21, September: 20/1, October: 36/15

Note, these stats are totals recorded for the **entire** Force by month, not one team. The numbers are consistent with what we were observing on the ground. Nowhere do the registered entries support the accusation in the book and the documentary that a team killed at least one hundred and twenty civilians in a one-month period. That number would average to thirty civilians a week. While I was with the Force (late June until mid-October), a team might net three to five enemy a week, and put a lot of wear on their foot gear achieving that average. It should also be noted that if civilians were being targeted across the zone in order to reflect a higher body count, not reporting the one hundred and twenty claimed casualties doesn't support that original postulate (need for a high body count).

*****

The lack of government action pursuant to the Army's CID report was questioned by journalists.[6] Individuals had been interviewed (including me in 1973), and allegations were compiled over four and a half years by CID investigators. But no action was ever taken or charges levied. Unfortunately, repercussions still followed some members of the Force for years.

Sergeant Trout's military career was put on hold, even though he did not pull the trigger on the old man. His "flagging" (barred from favorable personnel actions) imposed punishment without establishing guilt. The second time Sergeant Trout was passed over for promotion he acquired a military lawyer to commence action for a court martial. This might sound counter-intuitive, but Sergeant Trout's attorney wanted to exercise his right to an Article 32 investigation. The investigation precedes a court martial and ascertains whether a crime is committed and if a trial is necessary. It does not establish guilt or innocence, but it does weigh the credibility of the allegations—in this case the CID report. Unlike the CID investigation, the defense is entitled to discovery and can present testimony and evidence—the other side of the story. The investigator determines whether there is probable cause to recommend a general court martial. Trout wanted to either convene a court martial or remove the flag that prevented his promotion.

Actions by the Staff Judge Advocate General Core weighed the strength and merit of the CID report. An Army Lieutenant Colonel from the Judge Advocate General Corps conducted the investigation of Sergeant Trout. Any commissioned officer can be assigned to an Article 32 investigation. A junior lieutenant might be assigned to investigate a fender bender involving negligent driving in a motor pool. The fact that a JAG experienced attorney with the rank of LTC had been assigned indicated the Army was giving special attention to the issue.

The investigation took three months and concluded favorably for Trout. Court martial proceedings were deemed inappropriate and suspended, and the flag was removed from his personnel records. Within a month he was promoted to E-8, and eventually to Sergeant Major E-9, the highest pay grade of the enlisted ranks. He retired in 1985.

The administration and the Department of Defense, like the Army, elected not to follow up the accusations with criminal charges. What had initially been reported as a whole "rogue" unit of "rampaging GIs" was ultimately reduced to allegations involving eighteen soldiers. And once those allegations reached the light of day, and were subjected to closer scrutiny, they lost much of their credibility.

So, for the record, during the operations in Quang Ngai Province, during the period from late June to mid-October 1967, I never witnessed any member of the Force mutilating a body. I never observed anyone displaying a necklace of ears, or any detached ears for that matter. I never saw or participated in either direct or indiscriminate firing into residential areas where women and children might be caught up in the line of fire. None of my team set fire to any residential structure. No member of my team dropped grenades into bunkers where there were women and children. I had not seen, heard, or participated in the rape or murder of any Vietnamese woman. No one in my team tortured or killed any prisoners or detainees. No officer (battalion or company level) or non-commissioned officer ordered me to fire on non-combatants. During that entire period, we operated under the same rules of engagement that we had from the start of my combat tour in Vietnam. The only addition to our original rules of engagement concerned the handling of males of military age in order to check identity papers or lack of same, in which case they were detained and evacuated. My team employed deadly force only if a male of military age refused directions and tried to run. Trails at night time remained a true "free-fire" zone. The establishment of a "free-fire" zone" during daylight was never conveyed to me at any time. When my team encountered civilians waving yellow safe-conduct passes, we assisted with their extraction from the conflict zone to the relocation centers. Other civilians not indicating that they wanted to opt for safe-conduct to the relocation center, we bypassed.

This is the Force that Richard and I served with; we weren't aware of the alter-Force until we read about it. I left the line in mid-October. Richard was shot through the wrist in early November. Prior to that, he had been wounded by mortar fragments to the chest and grenade fragments to the back at Tiger Valley on fifteen May. At one of the recent reunions, Richard jokingly "complained" to Jim Raysor that if he hadn't let Jim talk him into volunteering for Tiger Force, he probably never would have been wounded. Raysor responded that, "If you had gone to any other assignment, you would have been killed…I saved your life."

Of the forty-nine men that started the operation in late June, by mid October only sixteen were still left. From the list of alleged participants, five of the named individuals had been killed in action before October. At least two others, prominent in the allegations, had died before the book was published. And what of the other thirty-one Tigers not cited in the investigation? How did the book impact their lives? The book branded the "whole" unit. If the allegations aren't substantiated, what does publishing half a story really accomplish?

In closing, vanity and pride of fellowship dictate that I include this paragraph at this time. As my tenure with the Force was winding down, and I was starting out on one of my few remaining patrols, we passed by the CP element. The RTO on the battalion push issued a "Congratulations Sergeant Heaney." Salutations of this out-of-the-blue nature sometimes precede a punch line. I gave a quick thought to what I might have overlooked, then responded: "What for?" He replied that battalion had sent down congratulations acknowledging our team for having the highest kill-to-weapons ratio in the battalion. I hadn't even been aware that those statistics were even kept. The punch line, I guess, is that my team, who had removed the most armed enemy combatants from the battle area, was the team that had refused to kill the water buffalo! Here's my pride of fellowship stat: we accomplished this without losing one of our own. We had an attached medic hit in the upper arm, and in another contact our point man suffered a bullet wound to the calf. True, a bullet that hits someone anywhere could just as easily have been fatal except for luck. Yet I would like to think that these guys, over the course of their time on line, had a hand in creating luck--bad for the guerrillas, good for us. And in the process, they saved my butt several times.

****

[1] Alexander Pope. -- Essay on Criticism, Part ii, Line 358 (paraphrased). (1688-1744).
[2] Combat After Action Report: Operation Malheur, 1st Bde. 101st Abn Div, #386041, Department of Defense, Ltr 3 Oct 67, *Unit History, 1st Battalion (Airborne), 327th Infantry, 1st Brigade, 101st Airborne Division, Declassified from Confidential,* Scribd.com, page 3 *(underlining applied by the author).*
[3] Exhibit 442 For Official Use Only. 1/327th Inf. Reproduced at the National Archives, 72-CID046-27852., citing events as of 22/23 June 1967. Page 39. *(underlining applied by the author).*

[4] Don Kochi, *Screaming Eagles and the Battle for Mother's Day Hill.* 327infantry.org. p.5 *(underlining applied by the author).*
[5] Michael D. Sallah and Weiss, Mitch. *"Tiger Force: A True Story of Men and War."* June 13, 2007. Little, Brown, and Company.
[6] Michael D. Sallah and Weiss, Mitch. *"Rogue GIs unleash wave of terror in Central Highlands."* The Blade (Toledo, Ohio), Oct. 19, 2003.
[7] Ken Burns, *"The Vietnam War." Episode Five: This Is What We Do. July 67-Dec 67*, PBS Documentary, Released 2017.
[8] Eddie Adams, credited with the still photographs and an NBC camera crew with the video version of these events.
[9] Eddie Adams, Time Magazine, 1998. Re-quoted in web site: rarehistoricalphotos.com/saigon-exeution-1968/.
[10] Ibid., Eddie Adams.
[11] Steve Merrill, email correspondence, reference Free-Fire Zones, 30 April 2018.

Chapter 32
The Perpetual Can of Fruit
August 2– September 1, 1967

Expiration date: ?

Over the course of our tenure on the line, we heard stories of female auxiliaries to the enemy regiments. I had yet to encounter any women accompanying armed VC. This changed in the Song Ve Valley.

The operation had also changed. The 1st Brigade's 2/502 and 2/327, as part of a larger joint allied operation, had air assaulted into the mountainous region west of Quang Ngai. The other allied units included ARVN, CIDG, Korean marines, plus the U.S. 196th Light Infantry Brigade. Our battalion was the reserve reaction force. Relegation to a reserve position had virtually no effect on our search-and-destroy tasking. We continued patrolling the trail networks that fed into the rice paddy areas near the river.

The Task Force Oregon's After Action Report suggests that the enemy appeared to have had some early warning about the operation. Whatever the case, the enemy seemed to be able to avoid the noose. With all the different nationalities involved in the sharing of tactical information, it might just be a case of "too many cooks!" Also, some of the units were mechanized. Clanking like a tank in mountainous terrain doesn't lend itself to *"out-guerrilla-ing"* the guerrilla.

*****

At platoon level we probably weren't even aware that the battalion was in reserve status, or that a new operation had commenced. One morning, as the whole Force was moving along, the CP element called a halt, probably to handle some radio traffic on the battalion net. This kind of stop normally took ten to twenty minutes. On our left, a large valley tapered off towards some low hills about a kilometer away. To our right lay the river. My team had point, so we moved forward to a position that afforded better observation of the river, leaving the CP element about fifty meters behind us.

The enemy appeared on our left about five hundred meters up the valley. Four individuals emerged from the thicket on the right and were making their way across a narrow point of the clearing. They were dispersed tactically, roughly five meters apart. They moved at normal cadence with no real rush to their pace, which indicated that they hadn't spotted us. Those Tigers with binoculars identified the first and last individuals (dressed in light colored shirts and black pants) as armed. The other two (dressed in traditional black pajamas) were unarmed. Later, when we finally took the pair in black pajamas into custody, we discovered they were women. The two armed men had no web gear, just long weapons balanced on their shoulders like shovels. Perhaps they had assumed that we had vacated the AO, along with the "Five-O-Deuce" and the "Second Batt."

The machine-gun crew nearest to the CP group elevated the gun on a paddy dike and engaged the targets with a few short bursts. Our adversaries responded initially with a quick huddle, which was followed almost immediately by a rapid departure of the two armed males back towards the thicket that they had emerged from originally. The two females remained in the dry paddy. The CP group with the interpreter headed for the two in the paddy. My team was directed to pursue the two armed individuals darting for the thick brush. They had too much of a lead for us to intercept them before they reached the trees and underbrush. Once in the thicket, they could find cover and fire on us as we approached across the clearing. To avoid getting caught in the open, we set a parallel course to theirs so we could gain the thicket below them and then turn left towards their entry point into the heavier growth. Most of my teammates had been in country since December; they were well experienced in firefights. Our opponents (lacking web gear and back-up ammo) would be at a distinct disadvantage in a fire-and-maneuver scenario. So we entered the thicket beneath the point where the males had disappeared. The enemy abandoned the field, and we established security at a point where we could observe and cover the CP element.

About fifty meters out in the paddy the interpreter was questioning the two female VC. I walked over to let the CP group know where our security was established. From the interpreter's shouting and the expressions on the women's faces, the conversation appeared not to be going well for the women. The reason they had stayed behind was also quite obvious: one of them had been hit in the leg. The medic administered first aid. Shortly thereafter, a helicopter arrived and transported them from the AO.

*****

According to battalion records, the battalion moved to a new base camp at Chu Lai on the 10th of August. We were introduced to the new battalion commander, LTC Gerald Morse. First impressions of the new commander seemed good, and they were confirmed and strengthened over the following months.

The next operation would take us to more mountainous terrain northwest of the Song Ve Valley. In retrospect, I assume that intelligence was picking up movement of troops in preparation for what would evolve into some action relative to the Tet Offensive of 1968. Also, indicators of change were taking place in our routine. We were issued M-72 LAWs (Light Anti-tank Weapons). And, we had to practice ladder assents and descents from CH-47 Chinook helicopters. In all of my previous insertions with the CH-47, the helicopter had set down. The ladder insertions that we now practiced were from a high hover with full combat load and rucksack. Two of the principal disadvantages of this particular deployment technique were the protracted exposure time to enemy fire and the noise generated by the helicopter in hover mode. Naturally, part of our instructions specified what to do should we come under fire while attempting an insertion or extraction. If on the ladder, we were directed to interlock our arms around the rungs and hang on for the "ride" because the bird would be exiting the area. If on the ground, vacate the area underneath the chopper unless you want a firsthand experience of what a napalm strike feels like. As one might surmise, insertion by ladder didn't rate all that high on any of our bucket lists.

*****

Operation Benton officially started on the 13th of August. Again, the battalion served as the Immediate Action Force, and joined the other maneuver units on the 15th of August. The AO had higher hills than the previous coastal operations. The open areas were not as extensive as the paddies nearer to the coast. Also, these open areas were usually bordered by taller strands of trees within which most of local residence structures were constructed. However, the local residents still remained elusive. Contact with our armed opponents followed the pattern established after mid May: no large-scale slug fests. Most often we made contact while patrolling, which evolved into a quick firefight, and ended just as abruptly as it had started. No tactical objectives were involved other than removing guerillas from the field.

Within this milieu, the perpetual can of fruit changed hands. It was preceded by an adjustment to our normal patrolling pattern. After a brief contact around dawn, which netted one VC, Jim Ward asked if I would mind switching from slack to point. I couldn't remember a time when he didn't vie for the point position. As we swapped positions, I asked if there was a problem. He responded that his weapon didn't feel right during the morning engagement. He said it seemed sluggish, not firing as fast as normal. Jim had just returned to the field and had been issued one of the new A1 versions of the M-16. The model had corrected numerous faults

Jim Ward, photo courtesy of Leo Heaney

that had been plaguing the original M-16s. One of the corrections was a new buffer assembly to slow the rate of fire. We would soon come to realize that the only advantage the old model had over the newer version was related to opening C-ration cases. The flash suppressor on the old version ideally functioned for snapping the wire banding around the ration cases. The newer model lacked this feature. Eventually, I was issued an A1 version. It never jammed.

In the shaded areas, the undergrowth was almost nonexistent, virtually park-like. We emerged from the tree line into some sparse vegetation on a small slope that merged downward into a dry paddy. We picked up the jabber about the same moment we started into the brushy area. Three VC were moving obliquely away from me about one hundred meters out. The lead and trail individuals were balancing their weapons on their shoulders which was common. Also customary was their attire: light colored shirts tucked into black slacks. The middle individual was dressed in black pajamas and unarmed. They had no web gear. It was like they were just out for a stroll down the middle of an open area, without a care in the world. That idyllic setting soon changed for them.

Before engaging the targets, I quickly scanned for any others that I might not have observed, and then I waved Jim up so we could concentrate our fire simultaneously. Two weapons like two eyes are better than one, particularly if one might jam. We dropped the trailing man first. When the other two turned to ascertain what was happening, we took out the point man. We didn't fire on the unarmed individual, not so much because we had a change of heart, but more so for his sprinting ability. He dashed into the nearest undergrowth.

After securing their weapons and intelligence material, we checked out the area where the third individual had disappeared. We saw spider holes lining both sides of the trail, but on closer inspection the holes turned out to be tunnel entrances. Barely big enough for humans, the tunnels teed off in both directions along the trails and resurfaced again further down the line. Our opponents had spent a great deal of time and energy improving their backyard.

We melted back into the wood line to continue the patrol. Eventually we made our way back to join the main element. As we settled into our typical night defensive ritual, Jim fished about in his rucksack, pulled out a can of fruit, and tossed it to me.

Brief Summary of Operation Hood River[1]

Timeframe: 2–13 August 1967
Base camp: Starts at Duc Pho (Carentan) moves to Chu Lai
AO for Operation: about 20 km west of Quang Ngai
Enemy Situation: 1st and 21st NVA Regiments in AO. ARVN intelligence had reason to believe that the two NVA regiments would link up and attack the town of Quang Ngai before the presidential election in early September.
Mission Summary: This was a joint operation involving the 1st Bde 101st along with a battalion of ROK Marines, 2 ARVN Ranger battalions, 1 ARVN Airborne battalion from Minh Long and a mechanized task force from the 196th Light Infantry Brigade.
After Action Summary: The element of surprise seemed to have been compromised from the start. Contact was extremely light. The NVA regiments were never pinned down and eliminated. The 1/327th was not committed. It conducted limited Search and Destroy missions in its designated assembly zone.
Other Considerations: Operation Malheur II morphed directly into Operation Hood River. The 1st Bde is still OPCON to Task Force

Oregon. The 1/327th is held in reserve for this operation. The battalion remained in the field rather than return to base camp. On 9 August, LTC Gerald Morse assumes command of the 1/327th. On 10 August the battalion moves to its new base camp at Chu Lai: troops by air and support equipment by motor transport.

Brief Summary of Operation Benton[2]

Timeframe: 13 August–1 September 1967
Base camp: Chu Lai
AO for Operation: 40 km west of Chu Lai, I Corps
Enemy Situation: 21st NVA Regiment, 2nd NVA Division and the 72nd Local Force Battalion in AO
Mission Summary: Conducted offensive operations to locate and destroy enemy forces and installations
After Action Summary: Enemy losses were vetted 396 KIA confirmed with an additional 86 probable. Large caches of ammunition were uncovered and many building and fortifications were destroyed.
Other Considerations: The 1/327 isn't committed until the 15th of August. "Some villages were found to be using NVA currency as the principle medium of exchange."[3]

****

[1] Wikipedia.org/Operation Hood River. Incorporates public domain material from the United States Army Center of Military History.
[2] Exhibit 442 For Official Use Only. 1/327th Inf. Reproduced at the National Archives, 72-CID046-27852, pp.15-17.
[3] Operation Benton, Task Force Oregon. Original Source: The Americal Division ORL Oct 67. vhpa.org/KIA/panel/battle/67081300.HTM.

Chapter 33
Tunnel Vision
Late August 1967

If it quacks like a duck...then it probably is a duck.
If a military age male ignores your directions and runs...he's probably a VC. --combat intuitive logic

We drew CP security, so I parked myself in a shady spot and figured on an easy day ahead. Radio traffic earlier reported Sergeant Lee's team in contact and a man down. Some new activity was stirring within the CP element, which caught my attention, and indicated we might be called out to assist Lee if needed. The water was almost hot enough to add a coffee packet when Sergeant Bob Diaz issued the warning order. Actually, it was a "We need to move now!" directive, but not in support of Lee's team as I had originally surmised. Sergeant Diaz stated that the battalion commander's chopper[1] was shot down in the area that our team had just recently been patrolling. Coffee would wait. Jim still didn't feel all that comfortable with his new rifle, so I took point. The danger would be on the trails near the crash site: the enemy would assume that some American ground units would be racing toward the survivors.

Again, chatter gave them away. At the place where the individual in black pajamas had disappeared two days prior, we came upon a cluster of four of our opponents. At this point the trail turned right; our opponents were off my left shoulder on the other side of a hedge-like bush. Their chatter seemed excited, as though they were responding to a humorous punch line. Their attention was focused in the direction we were heading. They probably had a hand in (or witnessed) the downing of the chopper. When one of them sensed our presence and turned to face me, it was already too late for all of them. Two seconds later silence dominated; not chatter, not weapons fire. We stepped around the hedge. Scattered about were four bodies with the weapons they never got to use. As we moved forward to pick up the weapons and intel material, Sergeant Diaz told us to forget it. He reminded us that our immediate mission was to get to the chopper site. I recall muttering under my breath that the weapons probably wouldn't be there when we returned. I was wrong.

As we closed in on the crash site coordinates, battalion came up on our net and instructed us to turn around and quickly get out of the area. The battalion command team and air crew had been picked up, and Tac Air was being directed onto the chopper to destroy anything of use to the enemy.

When we returned to the contact site we found it pretty much as we had left it--except for a missing body. There were three enemy dead, four weapons and a pale blue shirt. The mind is an amazing organ. I probably wouldn't have remembered the color of the shirt except in association with the three blood-stained bullet holes in it. As well as blood, an orange-colored frothy mucus surrounded the middle bullet hole--an indication that a lung had been punctured. About ten feet away was one of those spider holes that dropped into a tunnel.

I had little experience with tunnels, nor was I even in the least bit interested in acquiring any particular intimate knowledge of that subject matter. Yet I knew that if the hole-tunnel complex needed to be checked out, the obligation would be mine. Rank might have certain privileges, but it also comes with liabilities. I borrowed a .45 caliber pistol from someone and removed the red lens from my flashlight. Figuring that some critters other than a wounded VC might also be lingering in the tunnels, I prepped my descent into the hole with a hand grenade. This feat only echoed my inexperience in these matters, because then I had to wait about twenty minutes for the dust to clear!

I use the word "tunnels" to describe these subterranean labyrinths, but human-sized, mole-hole networks would just as accurately fit the billing. Once in, there was no turning around. I mean that literally. About three feet down the spider hole the tunnel ran off to the right and off to the left, which from my perspective appeared to be paralleling the trail. Perhaps a better description would be: "a tunnel system that ran alongside the trails where spider holes provided the entrance and exit points."

The air was acrid and visibility was like a dense fog, limited to a few feet in either direction. I chose to follow the trail segment that branched to the right. There was barely enough room for me to squeeze through, and it soon occurred to me that should the need arise, firing a weapon in that claustrophobic environment might have a lasting, negative impact on my ability to hear! Not being my parents' smartest or bravest son, and not seeing any blood or other evidence that the tunnel had been used recently, I inched my way backwards into the left hand branch and exited up the spider hole.

Upon returning to the CP location, we took up our previous defensive positions. My B3 can of water was still on the cold stove where I had left it earlier. Not every Tiger returned that day. Sergeant Lee's man down was James Messer. Jim Messer was only eighteen and had started his tour of duty just two months earlier. Lee's team had encountered a lone male of military age who tried to evade them. He was the bait. As the team gave chase after him, the VC sprang their ambush. Messer was hit twice, and one of the wounds was mortal; he died almost instantly. After a brief exchange of fire with the enemy, the two comrades carried their friend's body to a Huey for extraction. They returned to Lee's team and the mission continued—short one pair of boots. Radio logs list three VC KIA (Steve Merrill remembers only two enemy killed) and one M-1 carbine captured.[2]

Tommy Kellogg, Steve Merrill, and Jim Messer all volunteered for Tigers about the same time. The three amigos, like may paratroopers, had all been friends in the states. Merrill and Messer knew each other from basic training, and they continued on through Advanced Infantry Training and on to Jump School. There they met Kellogg. Messer convinced Merrill and Kellogg to join the Force. It was probably more than a coincidence that they all ended up in Sergeant Lee's team.

Brief Summary of Operation Benton[3]

Timeframe: 13 August–1 September 1967
Base camp: Chu Lai
AO for Operation: 40 km west of Chu Lai, I Corps
Enemy Situation: 21st NVA Regiment, 2nd NVA Division and the 72nd Local Force Battalion in AO
Mission Summary: Conducted offensive operations to locate and destroy enemy forces and installations
After Action Summary: Enemy losses were vetted 396 KIA confirmed with an additional 86 probable. Large caches of ammunition were uncovered and many building and fortifications were destroyed.
Other Considerations: The 1/327 isn't committed until the 15th of August. "Some villages were found to be using NVA currency as the principle medium of exchange."[4]

****

[1] According the battalion radio logs. Exhibit 438, Original Confidential downgraded to For Official Use Only. $1/327^{th}$ Inf. Reproduced at the National Archives;, 72-CID046-27852, 11:46 hours, 22 August 1967.

[2] Conversation with Steve Merrill (Lee's RTO on the patrol), 25 June 2017, Deadwood, SD.

[3] Exhibit 442 For Official Use Only. $1/327^{th}$ Inf. Reproduced at the National Archives, 72-CID046-27852, pp.15-17.

[4] Operation Benton, Task Force Oregon. Original Source: The Americal Division ORL, Oct 67. vhpa.org/KIA/panel/battle/67081300.HTM.

Chapter 34
Casualties Mounting
September 1967

*"Whether at Naishapur or Babylon,
Whether the Cup with sweet or bitter run,
The Wine of Life keeps oozing drop by drop,
The Leaves of Life keep falling one by one." --Omar Kyayyam[1]*

Phase One

Since May, the 1st Brigade had been working its way through the I Corps from south to north: Duc Pho, Quang Ngai, Chu Lai, and now Tam Ky. Our opponents had pretty much established base camps in the foothills to the west and northwest of the rice producing areas of the coastal plain. The basic objective was to take out as many of them as possible, while denying survivors access to the sustenance that the area customarily provided.

Task Force Oregon was completing its transition into the 23rd Infantry (Americal) Division. Operation Wheeler was a continuation in the pursuit to knock out the 2nd NVA division which was composed of the 3rd and 21st NVA Regiments, and the 1st VC regiment.

The 1st Brigade had been assigned the task of finding and knocking out the headquarters of the 2nd NVA Division. Our two sister battalions were given the assault mission while we were assigned blocking positions to the south in order to pick up stragglers trying to infiltrate out in that direction. Indigenous allied forces were allocated the egress routes to the west. Not long into the operation, intelligence refined its original assessment, and concluded that the enemy headquarters was a further seventeen kilometers to the west of the initial AO. The paradigm shift ushered in Phase 2 of Operation Wheeler which commenced on 26 September.

*****

Obviously, since we were not deployed where the enemy was heavily concentrated, action during Phase 1 was very light. Except for a bounding mine, we almost got away unscathed.

The incident occurred in the early afternoon, in similar terrain to where we lost George Hatten in May. The whole Force was on the move. At the time, I think my unit was designated the "Two Zero" element, Bravo Force. Hartz was Bravo Force leader, and I had his point team. The rest of Tiger Force was behind us. Lately Hartz and I hadn't worked together much because our force was usually divided into two teams when patrolling.

We had just departed an area of fairly good concealment, and were moving into sloping grassland, when word came forward to halt. Sergeant Diaz came up and told us to stay in position while the CP element went to check out a small knoll to our right front. Clearly visible on the small hill were remnants of a triple-concertina wire barrier. Classic mine fields are normally deployed between barbed wire barriers. The evidence suggested that some of our allies, at sometime in the past, had established a defensive position on the hill that the CP group was now aiming to reconnoiter. Experience told us that seldom were all the mines recovered when a unit withdrew. Hartz, pointing to what remained of the wire barrier, reminded Bob Diaz to be careful. Our force moved off the trail and took up outward facing positions as the CP group passed through us and on up the hill. About five minutes later, the explosion preceded the cloud of black smoke. Five Tigers were hit. Bob Diaz lost a leg; Terry Oakden lost his life.

This was also about the time that I had lost track of Jim Raysor. I figured he had finished his extension tour, and I had missed his departure from the field because I was on patrol somewhere. My premises were correct. I was on patrol when his tour came to an end and he abruptly departed the field. However my conclusion was not correct. I had assumed that everything ended well and that he made it home safely--wrong! Some thirty-five years later, at a reunion, Jim provided the part of his exodus agenda that I had missed.

Jim's team had been assigned as a point scout force for one of the inexperienced units of the new division. Raysor's recommendation that an open area be avoided fell on deaf ears. The lieutenant deployed his platoon in spread out, textbook fashion. The enemy couldn't resist such a target-rich environment and poured it on. Jim left cover to assist a wounded soldier. Out in the open, Jim took a round in his back and lost a kidney.

It was also at a reunion that I learned that Jean Soucy had been shot the day before Jim Messer was killed. Jean took a clean shot through the lower arm area. Because of the way the Force operated it was not uncommon to assume that a missing person had either returned to the states or transferred to a different unit. We weren't always aware when members became casualties.

Jean Soucy, photo courtesy of Jean Soucy

Phase Two

With the newer intelligence data, the focus of the operation shifted westerly, placing the center of the AO about 35 kilometers west of Tam Ky, at the confluence of two small rivers, the Song Trang and Song

Khang. Our battalion was again positioned in the southern portion of the AO. This scheme of maneuver seemed to have struck a nerve, so to speak, and enemy contact increased significantly.

Our first fatalities occurred the day after we air assaulted into the fray. My team was one of several directed to assist one of our teams in contact on the far side of the river. Once on the other side, we came upon a medic and one or two other Tigers administering first aid to PFC Cecil Peden who had suffered a serious chest wound. Someone quickly gave us an update. Down the trail lay the bodies of two other Tigers, Robin Varney and Jerry Ingram. We were told that Varney was shot chasing after an apparently wounded NVA. Ingram was killed while trying to assist Varney. I assumed that Peden was hit in the initial exchange that wounded the NVA, but I never followed up confirming that point. There were lessons to be learned here that I already knew:

'The point man doesn't outrun his backup.'
'The slack man needs to stick to his point man.'

Two pair of eyes and two weapons are twice as good as a single set of each. The alternative is piecemeal commitment of assets, which usually gives the advantage to the other guy. Whatever happened was past tense. Our immediate task was to create a security envelope so the medevac could get Peden and the bodies out. We continued along the trail that our adversary had probably used, but we never encountered any blood trail. Once the chopper left, we returned to our original reconnaissance zone.

Two days later, two more dead. The CP group had set up on a knoll with the river to their back and a well-used trail a hundred odd meters inland. Our force had CP security. The initial radio traffic indicated that the shooting was one of our teams engaging a few of the enemy, and would be returning soon with some captured weapons. However, the subsequent firing was a lot closer, and the team on the radio stated that they had casualties. The lieutenant, who was positioned about ten meters behind me, directed my team to go. We didn't need coordinates--the clatter was beacon enough. The artillery FO volunteered to come with us because the radio exchanges between the team under fire and the CP element indicated that they had their hands full: two Tigers were down (both probably KIA) and the team was still under fire.

We stopped at the base of the hill where the trees abruptly gave way to a narrow open area which extended off towards the trail. About eighty meters out in the open space I recognized the lanky silhouette of Sergeant Ervin Lee. We turned around and headed back in the direction from where we had just come. To the questioning stares from Doc Hise and other members of the CP group as we passed by them (this time heading in the opposite direction), I only replied that we couldn't go the original way. The plan was to circle around, pick up the trail and come into the fray from the left flank. Crossing the open area to help Lee would not have relieved the tactical disadvantage, and worse, would just provide more targets for an enemy that had already demonstrated he had shooting skills.

In less than half a minute we made the trail. We turned right upon reaching it, then squatted down to assess the situation and work out our next move. There was a lull in the firing, and that posed a problem. As long as the enemy remained quiet, we had no specific target to engage. We figured that he was probably on the hillside to the left. Lee's men would be downhill and off on our right. The FO asked how he could help. My thought was smoke. I asked the FO if he could lay down a diagonal line of smoke between the high ground on the left and Lee's men on the right. As the FO and I were figuring out the smoke screen mission, Richard Moore jumped into action. We were wrong about the enemy probably being located on the hill to our left; he was a little below us on the right. There, about twenty-five meters down trail, backing out of the bushes on the right, in khaki uniform, adorned with tree branches for camouflage, and armed with an SKS, was one our adversaries. His attention seemed fixated on Lee's position.

Moore came up beside me, and with the muzzle of his weapon alongside my face, he fired at the sniper. A series of mishaps followed. Moore missed the enemy. His weapon jammed. His flash suppressor must have accumulated some dirt which was expelled sideways into my eyes blurring my vision. The ringing in my ears didn't add to the ingratiation process. My vision was affected, but not enough to cause me to miss the enemy at this short range. Unfortunately, he fell into a well-eroded rut which afforded him limited protection. As he was bringing his weapon around again, we finished him with a grenade. I picked up his SKS and jacked the three remaining rounds out of the weapon well. He had no web gear; no backup ammo. He probably was based nearby and not an itinerate NVA. He hadn't planned on an extended fight-- just kill a few Americans and get away. He almost got away with it.

If there were more of our opponents around, they didn't engage us. We cut a path. Actually, it was more like wading through waist deep brush, straight down to Lee's men to assist them with their casualties. The two fatalities were Edward Beck and Kenneth Green. Since dusk was setting in, battalion told us they would send a chopper out at first light and extract the bodies. We carried the bodies back to the night defensive position at the CP area. Once at my defensive position, Doc Hise came over to check out my eyes. Fortunately the normal watering process had removed most of the grit.

I would have to resort to understatements in order to describe the mood at the night location as anything less than somber. No one seemed to have much to say. Eventually, Sam Ybarra came over to my position. I guess he felt that he had to talk. He asked me if I knew that Beck and Green were his friends from high school. I told him that someone had mentioned that. After a period, Ybarra returned to his position. The dead Tigers were nearby and covered with ponchos. I can't recall ever having to spend the night with a dead friend's body, let alone two dead friends' bodies.

I read a version of these events that had Sam Ybarra wailing Native American chants all night. I don't recall any of that, but mentally, I might have just cancelled it out.

Brief Summary of Operation Wheeler Phase 1 & 2[2]

Timeframe (Phase 1): 11–25 Sept 1967
          (Phase 2): 26 Sept–8 Oct 1967
Base camp: Chu Lai
AO for Operation: Northwest of Tam Ky, I Corps
Enemy Situation: Numerous enemy units in the AO, plus the headquarters of the 2nd NVA Division. As the initial phase developed, intelligence indicated that the 2nd NA Division's headquarters was located a further 17 kilometers to the west of the 1st Brigade's AO which necessitated the development of Operation Wheeler: Phase 2 starting on 26 Sept.
Mission Summary: Americal Division directed the 1st Bde of 101st Abn div to find, fix and destroy VC/NVA forces and to neutralize VC/NVA base camps.
After Action Summary Phase 1: The 2/327th and the 2/502nd suffered the most casualties when they air assaulted into the northern sector of the AO. Our battalion was initially assigned blocking ambush positions to the south of the two sister battalions.
Other Considerations: The 3/506th joins the 1st Brigade on 25 October giving the brigade its fourth maneuver battalion. The 1st Brigade would only maintain its "separate" status until December, when the entire 101st Airborne Division would arrive in country.

****

[1]Omar Khayyam, <u>The Rubayyat</u>, Verse VIII.
[2]Combat After Action Report – Operation Wheeler, 1st Brigade, 101st Abn Division, Period 11 September–25 November 1967 (U), AGAM-P (M), (25 April 1968).

Chapter 35

The LAW, 82 Refugees
Late September – Early October 1967

We weren't asked to count the cattle.

By October, our numbers had declined significantly from those we had in late June. The nature of our missions hadn't changed, just the scope. One morning as the team was preparing to move out, Sergeant Trout (who was drafted again into the platoon sergeant position) handed me the M-72 LAW he had been carrying the last couple months, and asked me to find a target for it. He had been packing it around through some pretty abusive weather and terrain. He stated that it might not function properly if we ever really need to engage enemy armor. If we "used" it, we could requisition a new replacement.

As we set out, I actually had a target in mind. We were returning to an area where, the day before, we had spotted a squad of VC lingering around a small farming community. The huts were tucked away in shaded woodland that stretched out into a very large open area--a peninsula of vegetation jutting out into flat, wide paddy land. Our opponents were exactly where we left them the day before, sitting on a low wall constructed of large river stones with the huts behind them to our left. Just shootin' the breeze!

The situation was as follows: The odds were against our sneaking up on these guys. They were outside effective rifle range. We considered using artillery, but that option wasn't available because of the possibility that civilians might be in the nearby farmstead. A direct fire weapon would work--ergo...the M-72 LAW.

Our infantry training had included familiarization with the M-72, but we had never fired one. I was familiar with arming and sighting the LAW, but the old 3.5 inch rocket launcher was the only anti-tank weapon I had ever fired. I was soon to find out that the M-72 projectile had a faster, flatter trajectory, and a deafening crack when launched.

Since we lacked tactical experience with the weapon, the contact we were about to initiate would offer an opportune learning experience. The learning part of the experience started even before I fired the weapon. The launcher extended and armed as the instructions on the tube illustrated. I crawled forward into the rice paddy and positioned myself to avoid hitting anyone with the back blast. I steadied myself and the launch tube on a low paddy dike. When I peered through the rear peep sight, I realized that I should have waited to extend the launcher. The front plastic sight was blurred with water from my crawl through the wet grass to the paddy dike. I tried wiping it clear with my Tiger hat, but the hat and my fatigues were wetter than the sight. The longer that I lingered in the open, the greater the chance that one of our opponents might notice the activity. So I decided against slithering back to fetch dry toilet paper from my rucksack, and instead selected the "Kentucky windage" option.

Behind the squad of VC (who were nestled on and near the stone wall) was a tall tree apart from the rest. I aligned the tube on the tree and elevated it to compensate for distance. The old 3.5 launcher needed quite a bit of elevation to lob the rocket onto a long-range target. The LAW rocket flew a much lower, straighter trajectory. Because of my inexperience with the weapon, I had aimed too high, and the round hit the tree about ten feet up. But when we made our way over to the wall, we found a blood trail. Not a lot of blood, more like bloody mucous. We moved as cautiously as possible. The little amount of blood present wasn't going to lead us to a dead body. Eventually a VC with a rucksack jumped up on our right and tried to outrun an M-16 round, but he lost the race. His rucksack was packed with high quality medical supplies, most with instructions written in French, and displaying the Canadian red maple leaf logo. Obviously Canada had a better relationship with North Vietnam than we did.

The other part of the M-72 learning experience began with the jarring crack right after I had touched off the round. The effect was only beginning to become apparent after the excitement quieted down. Nature's background noises were gone or muffled. Bird chirps, rustling foliage, hushed footsteps, moving water, etc., were no longer blatantly obvious. It was like being under water. If ever I faced the prospect of firing that weapon again, the action would occur only after I had found some sort of hearing protection. Wads of toilet paper had to be better than nothing at all.

*****

We returned to our patrolling tasks, navigating our way in a long convoluted route back to the base camp, which was on a wooded ridge that ran up to the battalion CP location. We had been occupying this defensive position over the past several days. Considering our proximity to the battalion CP group, with its ability to attract mortar rounds, we had dug fox holes. So, upon returning, we slipped into our formerly established positions and started to chow down. I returned the empty M-72 tube to Sergeant Trout for direct exchange. My next plan was to rest and give my body a chance to deal with my hearing problem.

I am of the nature that appreciates routine. After meals I always sprinkled the extra salt on my boots—leech prevention. When sleeping, my ruck was placed above my head and items arranged inside where I could find them easily in the dark. My weapon was always where I could lay my right hand on it, and usually suspended off the ground on top of my web gear. To say that the disturbance in my normal range of assessing sounds caused me some dismay is more than an understatement.

I was hoping to draw CP security the next day (which actually did happen), but not in the way I would have imagined. My wish for a night's rest was not in the cards either. The lieutenant had another mission for us. Battalion had noticed some activity in an abandoned farmstead, a couple kilometers to the north, and wanted it reconnoitered. My team had patrolled some of the trails in that area, so we were the obvious choice for the task.

*****

It was already dark when we set out, but we were familiar with the trails off the hill on which the CP was situated, so navigation wasn't an issue. In roughly an hour we were closing down on the objective, a small cluster of structures in a treed area surrounded by dry paddies. A trail led into the site where some people were congregated around a small fire. Our main concern was the large amount of Vietnamese chatter. We were dealing with more than just a few individuals.

Fern-like vegetation about two-feet high flanked both sides of the path that led into the village. I had the team wait while I low-crawled through the vegetation on the left of the path. I observed children, adults, elderly, and near the small fire there were some males of military age. The atypical feature of this gathering was the large number of individuals present, and that they were making no obvious effort at remaining indiscrete.

I continued inching my way through the ferns and grass beside the trail, focusing my attention on the group of men near the fire. Out of nowhere, a bare foot set down just to the right of my head. Because of the ringing in my ears, I hadn't heard the individual come up behind me. My anxiety level elevated another notch when it appeared that this person was carrying a weapon. The individual continued past me, displaying no sign he was aware of my presence. What I initially perceived as a "weapon," when illuminated by the firelight, turned out to be a small broom common to Vietnamese households. And the individual, when silhouetted against the light, turned out to be an elderly woman. She positioned herself with the people by the fire. From her demeanor it seemed that she had not noticed almost stepping on an American soldier. She probably wasn't aware that she had just avoided a brush with the Grim Reaper by the width of one panicky impulse, but I was.

Conversations continued unabated with everyone seemingly oblivious of my presence. I lingered there a while, then returned to update the rest of the team. What we had was a large group of Vietnamese, dispersed about an old hooch complex, around a small fire, and making no attempt to conceal their presence. All age groups were represented, from small children to seniors. Some males of military age were present, but no weapons were evident. And they were making no use of any of the structures. They were gathered in the commons areas--no one inside the hooches. We radioed this information to our lieutenant. Battalion had been monitoring our transmissions and they directed us to take control of the situation and find out why these people were in an area that was thought to be vacated. Battalion would arrange illumination for the operation. We were directed to get ready and they would give us an "up" when the illumination rounds were on their way.

Since there were only a few of us, our plan was fairly simple. Two men went around to the right and would approach the group at the fire from behind. And two of us would go in from the front on the main trail. The RTO and medic would follow us.

After a brief wait, battalion radioed "splash," which meant that the illumination round was about to arrive on target above us. When the flare burst overhead, we entered the hooch area. Almost immediately, several adult Vietnamese started frantically waving Chieu Hoi certificates. These certificates were cashier-check size leaflets, dropped by aircraft and littered the countryside. On the front side was printed the bright yellow flag of South Vietnam with the promise of safe conduct through the combat zone for the bearer.

Refugees could use the leaflets to be safely conducted out of a hostile zone to a relocation center. VC or NVA defectors could use them to surrender.

We were mobbed by fourscore of Vietnamese all trying to tell us something in a language which we were not in the least bit fluent. We lowered our weapons and made motions that we understood their intentions. I radioed our situation to battalion and requested that an interpreter be put on the "horn." The radio communications pattern went from me to the interpreter, then from the interpreter to one of the village elders near me, then back to the interpreter, then back to me. The process ran much smoother after the village headmen mastered the push-to-talk concept of using the radio. I might add that it wasn't just the headmen making the decisions; women were actively involved in the conversations that were taking place. Quite a bit of verbal chaos took place before the lights went out.

In a normal illumination fire-mission, flare rounds overlap in succession---each on the heels of the previous flare--to illuminate the target continuously. We had only received one mortar round, and then the lights went out. Later we learned it was a broken fire pin that ended the light show. While I was on the radio with the battalion trying to resolve the illumination problem, the situation changed. The team of Bill Carpenter and John Feeney had produced a Zippo lighter, and were moving among the males of military age to ascertain if any were armed. Although humorous to mentally revisit from a safe spot in the future, at the time, the lighter solution had some tactical drawbacks. When we started our movement the flare provided good observation of everyone. Now, with only the lighter, Feeney and Carpenter were the principal subjects of illumination. The tiny lighter display should have invited fire from anybody with hostile intentions, but nothing happened. So the people surrounding us were serious refugees. We resumed the mission.

Battalion wanted a head count. We had eighty-two "packs" that needed transportation out of the combat zone. Jockeying the radio handset around again, instructions were eventually delivered to the Vietnamese that the next morning, battalion would arrange for them to be airlifted from the adjacent dry rice paddy and delivered to a safe area. We were directed to remain in the area and provide security until the extraction at first light. When the communications were completed, we took our leave from the civilians and set up in an isolated area for the night.

The next morning, a CH-47 Chinook medium lift helicopter arrived with battalion staff onboard to oversee the evacuation. We remained out of sight in the tree line in case there was a problem. One obvious problem arose when the Vietnamese started to mount the helicopter's ramp. The pack count didn't include the cattle! Not only were there eighty-two civilians to be extracted, but also their prized livestock: several humped back bovines that resembled the Brahman bulls in American rodeos. A second Chinook was required in order to remove the remainder of the civilians and their animals. We hung tight in the shadows until we were instructed to leave. Once back at the CP location, we took up security positions. We kinda' had the day off.

Brief Summary of Operation Wheeler Phase 2[1]

Timeframe: (Phase 2): 26 Sept–8 Oct 1967
Base camp: Chu Lai
AO for Operation: Northwest of Tam Ky, I Corps
Enemy Situation: Numerous enemy units in the AO, plus the headquarters of the 2nd NVA Division. As the initial phase developed, intelligence indicated that the 2nd NA Division's headquarters was located a further 17 kilometers to the west of the 1st Brigade's AO which necessitated the development of Operation Wheeler: Phase 2 starting on 26 Sept.
Mission Summary: Americal Division directed the 1st Bde of 101st Abn div to find, fix and destroy VC/NVA forces and to neutralize VC/NVA base camps.

After Action Summary Phase 1: The 2/327th and the 2/502nd suffered the most casualties when they air assaulted into the northern sector of the AO. Our battalion was initially assigned blocking ambush positions to the south of the two sister battalions.

Other Considerations: The 3/506th joins the 1st Brigade on 25 October giving the brigade its fourth maneuver battalion. The 1st Brigade would only maintain its "separate" status until December, when the entire 101st Airborne Division would arrive in country.

****

[1]Combat After Action Report – *Operation Wheeler, 1st Brigade, 101st Abn Division*, Period 11 September–25 November 1967 (U), AGAM-P (M), (25 April 1968).

Chapter 36

Final Patrols
Early October 1967

*I don't understand your questing old knight,
Or why you have traveled so far.
To journey for years through regions of fear
To discover you are where you are.* –Leo Heaney[1]

We came upon two of Sergeant Kratzberg's team members taking cover behind an embankment. When we inquired where the sergeant could be located, they pointed down the trail to the right. Ward and I had been part of the CP security element when the contact was first reported. We didn't need the radio, however; the firing wasn't much beyond the base of the hill beneath the CP's location. The lieutenant immediately dispatched us to give a hand.

As our personnel numbers dropped, the fellows that had been around awhile were dispersed among the sub-forces to balance out the experienced/inexperienced ratio. Jim Ward, Dallas Rogers, and I had been together since Kontum, but lately the three of us seldom patrolled together. Usually I had to send one of them to another team. I appreciated Ward taking point down the hill again. He was one of the best, and he had no trouble finding and melting into the action that was demanding Sergeant Kratzberg's attention at that moment.

We came upon the sergeant's rucksack first, and next his M-16. The bolt was locked to the rear, the magazine was empty. About fifteen meters further ahead was Sergeant Kratzberg armed only with his forty-five. He was a little winded and bleeding from a minor bullet wound to the fleshy part of one hand. The sergeant pointed off to the left. Ward moved around in that direction. After a brief exchange of gunfire, Ward returned with an AK. The battalion C&C ship picked up Sergeant Kenneth Kratzberg and his gear and flew him off to get some medical attention for his hand. It wasn't until we were chowing down that evening that I realized that Ken had taken the end to the story with him.

Lately the sundry rations had started to include reading material (in addition to fresh fruit and other goodies). A custom developed among several of us to read after meals for ten or fifteen minutes before the word for moving out was delivered. On the last sundry resupply, I had picked out *"Beau Geste."* Ken asked to have it when I was done. After reconsidering his request, he offered an alternative proposal. Because he was the "faster" reader, why not let him start the book and tear out each page as he finished it, and then pass that page to me? Since he managed to convey his second proposition by delicately treading around my sensibilities without insulting my intelligence, I agreed. I didn't expect him to get shot and depart the field with the final pages of the book in his rucksack. Later in the States, I looked up the ending. Glad I did. The last few pages, in a way, clarified and certified the title.

That was the last operation I would work with Ken. I had transferred to Phan Rang before he returned to line duty. On the last day of his extension tour, the extraction chopper took some rounds while leaving the field. Ken was wounded in the abdomen. While in the hospital he had a severe allergic reaction to the antibiotic and was left completely deaf. We reunited about six years later. He came to visit me several times while I was stationed at Ft. Lewis. Generally, if he came in winter, we skied; in the summer, we hiked. Early attempts at communicating usually involved his failed attempts at lip reading and our improvised gestures. It almost always devolved into short written notes on our side of the communication exercise. Eventually he was fitted with a Cochlear implant, which created marked improvements in actual two-way verbal conversation. A few years back, we hiked a section of the Pacific Crest Trail together. And we thought Vietnam had mosquitoes! When he passed in 2016, his family released his ashes at one of his favorite camping spots.

*****

As the operation moved into October, the terrain changed. No longer did broad expanses of rice paddies dominate the landscape. Steeply sloped hills descended onto smaller paddies near narrower, faster moving streams. This was base camp territory. The trails were well used. Most of our opponents that we encountered wore NVA uniforms rather than black pajamas, and often carried new AK-47s. Caches of ammo and supplies were uncovered in the most unsuspecting, natural looking surroundings. It was not uncommon to stop for a short break or lunch and find items just off the trail under a light covering of vegetation: mortar rounds, small arms ammunition, gas masks and other equipment. At one innocuous looking spot, just below a layer of leaves, we recovered a brand new, unused, fully rubberized Soviet CBR suit.

Besides a shift in terrain, another change was imminent. Soon the company First Sergeant would send word for me to leave the field for out-processing. I didn't keep a "short-timer's" calendar. My extension tour was ending, and I would simply wait for the summons. Hartz had already left the field and accepted a cadre position at the Proficiency Training School at Phan Rang. He suggested that I do the same. I had entered the Army in order to get the military obligation out of the way. (The all-volunteer military didn't become effective until years later.) At that time, I hadn't given the prospect of going to college any real consideration. But now I realized that attending a university was an actual prospect and something I wanted to accomplish. My backwards planning sequence went something like this: leave Vietnam with less than ninety days left to serve so I would qualify for an early release from service. That meant returning to the States after the end of June; spend January to June as cadre at the Proficiency School; take leave over Christmas; secure the cadre position in November and start work with Hartz. In the meantime, continue with what I was doing until the First Sergeant sent for me to return to base camp. Now, the plan only had to come together...and the NVA cooperate.

*****

I wasn't aware of it at the time, but my tenure with Tiger Force was three days from termination. We rendezvoused at the battalion TOC, on the crest of a hill surrounded by waist deep elephant grass. LTC Morse briefed us about the previous night's mortar attack on his command post. Following his briefing, we departed the sandbagged enclosure that housed the large S3 operations map. Outside the TOC, the commander pointed downhill to the spot in the jungle where he felt the mortar crew had launched their attack. We were tasked to recon the area in question and locate the mortar tube and the crew if they were still about.

LTC Morse had only assumed command around the first part of August. We barely knew him, but what we saw, we liked. More so, we respected his style of leadership. He wasn't shy of ground action. He learned our names. He addressed us by rank and name. He spoke to us directly, soldier to soldier. There was no way we would let him down. He was doing his part; we were obligated to do ours. Accomplishing the mission was central to our sense of being. Of course at our age, few of us could express the concept in words. We resorted to actions.

Rogers took point down the hill, and I had slack. Once through the elephant grass, we dissolved into the tree line. Eventually we discovered a small trail that didn't display evidence that it was heavily used. We followed this trail until it intersected a larger trail that exhibited a much heavier use pattern. The lieutenant called a halt, stating that we'd be there for awhile, so we sat down for a coffee break. This turned out to be one of those indiscrete places where our opponents had stashed, under a light covering of leaves, some of their 82mm mortar ammunition. A few of the guys near the machine gun had uncovered rounds also. We discovered eighteen at our location, so there were probably twenty plus rounds scattered about in that area.

The security team at the trail junction dropped the first enemy, a single opponent armed with an M-1 carbine whose bad luck it was to stumble onto the machine-gun position. The general movement of our adversaries appeared to be from the lowlands to the highlands. The lieutenant directed my team plus a machine-gun section and an RTO to go down trail a ways and establish an ambush.

We set up an L-shaped ambush at a place where the trail turned to the right. The machine-gun team backed itself into some vegetation at the elbow where it could rake the trail. Rogers and I took the furthest position away from the gun, while the rest of the team positioned themselves in the vegetation on the high side of the trail between us and the gun. We barely settled into position when the next NVA arrived on scene, armed with an AK and dressed in black pajamas. Later we discovered his pressed khaki uniform sealed in plastic in his rucksack, along with documents and currency. After securing his weapon and ruck, we quickly began cleaning up the scene. We moved the body off the trail, concealed it under some brush, and cleaned the trail of any disturbances or blood. These were precautionary actions to disguise our presence. We then relocated immediately a few hundred meters in the direction from which he had come.

About two hundred meters further down the trail we repeated the process and established another ambush site. Rogers and I had barely nestled into position on our rucksacks, when to our right, the third uniformed adversary approached us. This individual was different from the first two opponents. He had no rucksack, no ammo belt or web gear. His base camp had to be near. He was moving cautiously with an M-1 carbine at the ready. He had heard the shots and was investigating.

We could have dropped him when we first saw him, but since he was inching our way, we let him approach. He became aware of our presence about the time he was just opposite of us. Naturally, he became fixated on Rogers and me, never gazing up trail at the machine-gun crew or the other men. He was paused on the trail about seven or eight feet directly across from us. It wasn't really a Mexican standoff because he never had a chance of shooting any of us, or of getting away. He started to move the weapon's stock toward seating it in his shoulder, then stopped. He repeated the movement, and stopped and lowered his weapon again. We were a few feet above him, so he would have to raise his weapon high in order to bring it in line with us. Neither Rogers nor I moved; we both had him covered. Our machine-gun team was tuned in also, yet no one was in a hurry to shoot. I briefly averted my gaze to check if he had any back up coming up the trail. He was alone. In order to survive the situation, he would have to drop his weapon. If he had reached that conclusion, he didn't choose to exercise the survival option. As he moved again to bring the barrel up and seat the stock of his weapon against his shoulder, several bursts hit him.

As we were cleaning up the area and getting ready to relocate to set up another ambush, I asked the gun crew if they thought that the enemy soldier might have surrendered if we had checked fire a little longer. Their faces registered a little disbelief at my inquiry. Their response was on the order of: "Jeeze Sarge, we thought that he was about to shoot you!" I was of the same conviction. *And, these were the guys that the sensationalized press had lump-labeled as "Rampaging GIs!"* In reality, they were some of the finest, most professional light infantry troops in country—my personal opinion perhaps, but I do speak from some experience.

When we radioed our intentions to move to another location, the lieutenant directed us to hang tight until the remainder of the Force could join us, and we would move together to a night location. Moving together made sense. We had fewer than twenty men now and there was probably an enemy camp close by. It turned out to be abandoned, probably as a result of the recent gun fire. Chambers were hallowed into the hillside similar to what we had witnessed at Phan Thiet. The remainder of the camp wasn't surrounded with the normal bunkered complexes associated with infantry troops. Some speculated that it was a medical facility. We set up a defensive perimeter and spent the night there.

Jim Ward joined Rogers and me at our position. He had been farmed out to another team during the move down the mountain, which was common at this point of the operation when personnel numbers were low. The three of us had been together since November a year ago. I'm sure that being with the right men, at the right time, at the right place, and doing the right thing was no secret to my personal survival rate. The next day that premise would be put to the test again. I was slated for a patrol without either Ward or Rogers. Fortunately their substitutes also proved to have the right stuff--which supports my premise.

*****

Battalion wanted activity around a certain hooch checked out. We hadn't encountered any civilians in the area, so the odds were that the activity was adversarial. The team was small. Richard Moore and I had worked together before. From the few remaining Tigers, Dan Clint and Steve Merrill joined us. I hadn't realized until I was compiling information for this book that the lieutenant had asked for volunteers to accompany us on the mission. Steve said he had waited for awhile, and when nobody else volunteered, he said, "I'll go."

The mission was straight forward: find the hooch in question, report what we find to higher and deal with whatever develops. It probably sounds over confident on our part, but we usually had the element of surprise on our side. Plus, lately the enemy traveled in small groups--a situation which tended to bode in our favor.

Sustaining a casualty, however, could present a challenging situation. Naturally, Fate opted for the challenge.

Richard had point; I had slack. We avoided trails, and used streams and wooded areas. The objective was easy to locate. The structure was rectangular with four "doorless" entrance ways, two at each end of the long matted walls. The short walls were solid, no entrances or windows. Merrill and Clint guarded the rear, while Moore and I moved on the structure. With Richard at the right entrance and me on the left, we entered the hooch simultaneously.

Richard Moore, photo courtesy of Tom Rosales

What greeted us was not a residential setting. Hearth, food preparation items, sleeping areas--there were none. Hanging on the wall near Moore were three sets of dripping web gear. What transpired next was a replay of two déjà vu episodes. Moore spun to his left and fired a shot out the entrance across from him…and his weapon jammed again! I dashed out the entrance across from me in time to see a uniformed NVA trying to escape on the path to the left. I got off a quick shot that hit him in the shoulder and flipped him over on his back. He sank beneath some vegetation causing me to lose sight of him. I ran forward, jumped over the shrubbery and became airborne! The bank down to the rice paddy had been subject of heavy erosion which washed away a portion of the path. I had about a seven or eight foot drop to the sloping bank that had replaced the former trail. I hit the ground in front of the NVA. Because of the slope and the fact I was right handed, getting my weapon quickly around on target was the next challenge. While I was airborne I noticed that the NVA was sporting a shoulder holster from which he was frantically trying to extract a pistol. While the NVA and I were jockeying to get position on one another, Moore came around and intervened on my behalf. Richard dashed into the fray and planted a well-timed kick into our opponent's head just as the pistol was coming up. It wasn't until after the NVA was dispatched that I realized he had discharged his pistol just as Moore had diverted the barrel of the weapon. Moore was hit in the leg.

If you have to get shot in the leg, this type of wound was the way to take it. The round had not penetrated the muscle to any depth but had followed the muscle's contour just under the surface. Against Moore's dark skin, a maroon-colored blood trace about a quarter inch wide ran about twelve inches up his calf to the shiny copper head of the 9mm round just under the skin. I was looking at the proverbial bullet that was meant for me. The round was still perfectly formed; no mushrooming. That was the good news. Moore knew the not-so-good news as well as I did. The dripping web gear in the hooch contained rifle magazine pouches. There were at least three wet NVA, unaccounted for, probably armed with AKs, in our immediate area.

I asked Moore if he could put pressure on his leg. He knew what I was insinuating; we couldn't endanger an air crew trying to medevac him in that area. We needed to find an LZ well outside of rifle range. The rest of the team had joined us by now, so we gathered everything of intelligence value. We then hobbled out with Moore using his weapon as a cane, and sometimes accepting a little help from Clint or Merrill. We skirted the rice paddy looking to put some distance between us and any other opponents that might be in the vicinity of the hooch.

As we moved along, we radioed our situation and intentions to the lieutenant. When the CO asked what kind of weapon the NVA had, I balked a moment, and then responded that it was one of those little ones that the person who sends it in usually never sees it again. Side arms were one of the few captured weapons that we were allowed to keep, to use, and to eventually take back to the States with us. Unfortunately, once they were surrendered into the intelligence and operations assessment system, quite often someone in the system "adopted" them as their own. My thought was that if any one of us really needed a back-up weapon, it was definitely Moore! I might also mention that, if Moore hadn't been wounded by it, the capture of that pistol probably never would have been reported.

At this point in time, "Ghost Rider Six" entered the picture. Battalion had been monitoring our radio traffic, which was common. The battalion commander understood what the context of our transmission was about, and he directed me to turn in the "little one" in question. He added that he would personally guarantee its return. We "rogered that" and continued our quest for an LZ.

Before long we found an area that suited our security concerns, and vectored in the battalion C&C ship which extracted Moore, the pistol, and the NVA's rucksack. We then made our way to the coordinates of the next proposed night location. The CP group was already there. I checked in with the lieutenant and was directed to take the next chopper, due in the morning, back to base camp. The first sergeant had sent word that I needed to start out-processing; my extension tour was just about over.

*****

As usual, I deferred to my comfort zone and hooked up with Ward and Rogers for my final night in the field. We had managed eleven months together. It wasn't total goodbyes. I shared my plans to try to join Hartz in Phan Rang until my enlisted time was up. So we had periodic contact over the next several months when either of them passed through the administrative rear area. Like a true friend, I passed on my extraneous team "hardware:" claymore mine, smoke grenades, blood expander, morphine syrette, compass, non-electrical blasting caps, the remainder of my C-4, parachute flares, smoke grenades, LRRP rations, and a can of fruit cocktail. I'm sure they welcomed the additional weight with unmitigated enthusiasm. Jim Ward was promoted to sergeant, so he was my de facto replacement. I'm sure Sergeant Trout had a hand in that.

The next morning, I bid my goodbyes and boarded a chopper that made one intermediate stop at the battalion CP. There, two former Tigers who had taken staff assignments met me and presented the Walter P-38 that we had captured the day before. LTC Morse was true to his word[3]. About a month later, after Moore was released from the hospital, he stopped on his way through the Phan Rang administration center to see me and Hartz. I retrieved his pistol from the company arms room and turned the weapon over to him. He hadn't expected to see it again. With any luck, when he got forward, he would also receive one of the new, reliable A1 versions of the M-16 that were making their way through the system.

*****

Brief Summary of Operation Wheeler Phase 2[4]

Timeframe: (Phase 2): 26 Sept–8 Oct 1967
Base camp: Chu Lai
AO for Operation: Northwest of Tam Ky, I Corps
Enemy Situation: The 2nd NVA Division
Mission Summary: The 1st Bde of 101st Abn div to find, fix and destroy VC/NVA forces and to neutralize VC/NVA base camps
After Action Summary Phase 1: The 2/327th and the 2/502nd suffered the most casualties when they air assaulted into the northern sector of the AO. Our battalion was initially assigned blocking ambush positions to the south of the two sister battalions.

Other Considerations: The 3/506th joins the 1st Brigade on 25 October giving the brigade its fourth maneuver battalion. The 1st Brigade would only maintain its "separate" status until December, when the entire 101st Airborne Division would arrive in country.

****

[1] Leo J. Heaney, *The Tao of Gao*.
[2] According the battalion radio logs. Exhibit 438, Original Confidential downgraded to For Official Use Only. 1/327th Inf. Reproduced at the National Archives, 72-CID046-27852, 10:45 - 12:50 hours, 7 October 1967.
[3] For the record, I did not find the weapon inventoried in on the battalion radio logs, but it was listed on the Operation Wheeler After Action Report, along with 186 other individual weapons captured, page 18.
[4] Combat After Action Report – *Operation Wheeler, 1st Brigade, 101st Abn Division*, Period 11 September–25 November 1967 (U), AGAM-P (M), (25 April 1968).

Chapter 37
Homeward Bound
July 4, 1968

*"...I was so much older then
I'm younger than that now."*—Bob Dylan[1]

I returned to the States with less than ninety days left to serve, so I qualified for an early out. The 4th of July, 1968, was my discharge date (after twenty-seven months in Vietnam), just ten days after I became eligible to vote or buy a beer legally in my own country. After arriving in the states, out-processing was accomplished in a few hours, and I was released to go home. A few of us pooled our money for a cab from the Oakland Personnel Center to the San Francisco Airport. If I had thought that my Vietnam experience was behind me, my sojourn through the airport would indicate my assessment was premature.

I was traveling light: summer khaki uniform, shaving kit, and a captured Mosin Nagant carbine--a brutish looking weapon with a long, folding, spiked bayonet. In those days, a weapon could ship as hold baggage--just affix a claim check tag on it and turn it over at the check-in desk. In route to process the weapon, I encountered three individuals about my age (a man and two women) all dressed in biblical garb and shouldering three lightweight, medium-sized crosses. As the group was passing by me, the last female turned to me, eyed the carbine, and stated, "That must be heavy." I countered with, "Not as heavy as the load you're bearing." Neither of us had employed a sharp or bitter tone. Actually the statements were on the cordial side, more on the order of a greeting. We acknowledged that perhaps we entertained diverging points of view, but could still share some basic concepts of civility. We were both products of a democratic system that encoded in our nation's basic governing document the right of an individual to peacefully protest. I hope that the young woman, as well as subsequent generations of Vietnamese, understood that most of us felt that our service would help insure that the Vietnamese people were the beneficiaries of similar democratic guarantees.

I never considered the young woman's demonstration as a personal affront. On the contrary, I accepted it as a sign that our system was functioning as originally designed. Vietnam is not a dark legacy in my memory that requires externalizing. My thoughts of Vietnam are mostly composed of bright spots such as cherished memories, humorous tales, vivid landscapes, and remarkable comrades. By the way, I believe that Stephen Ambrose (author of "Band of Brothers") was correct regarding the concept of "brotherhood."

Legacies are what they are: "mechanisms" for spanning from what was, to what is. Our nation was once bitter enemies with Germany and Japan. Then, we all discovered the advantages that economic rivalry offers over prolonged warfare. Likewise, our relationship with China varied from allies in WWII, to adversaries in the Cold and Korean Wars, to immense economic rivals. At which point in the relationship did bloodshed end? What about Vietnam? It has a wonderful climate with an ancient cultural legacy. And its recent history is not unlike ours. Like us, it also threw off a colonial yoke. Ho Chi Minh modeled his constitution after our Declaration of Independence. Vietnam, like the early United States, was tested during its formative period. If history repeats itself, anyone want to bet where our two nations are likely heading? A person with gambling instincts could probably net a can of fruit, or more, on that wager.

"Inward Season Three…Out"

****

[1] Bob Dylan, *My Back Pages* from the Album: *The Other Side of Bob Dylan, 1964,* later the Byrds, Album: *Younger Than Yesterday*, 1967.

Epilogue
The Orange Time Bomb

"All we have to decide is what to do with the time that is given us."
-- J.R.R. Tolkien

On 4 February 1983, a few months shy of his thirty-seventh birthday, Charles E. Hartz II died. His wife Judy phoned me with the news that he had passed quietly in his sleep. A few years earlier he had been diagnosed with terminal brain cancer. When Judy sensed the end was near, she contacted Bobby Jacobs and me. We rendezvoused at Hartz's home to spend a few days with Charley and his family.

In 1979, Charley had initiated a lawsuit which eventually evolved into one of the first class action suits against the manufacturers of defoliants (i.e. Agent Orange) used in Vietnam. Charley believed (along with many other suffering Vietnam War veterans and Vietnamese citizens) that exposure to the defoliants had caused their medical problems. Unlike typical battle wounds, the component dioxin (a known carcinogen) also causes damaging effects by altering genes in humans. Therefore genetic disorders

Charley E. Hartz II,
photo courtesy of Leo Heaney

can also be passed down to subsequent generations in the form of birth defects. Three of Hartz's four children were born with serious birth defects; two of them almost died.

His final fight was in the courts, but not the courtroom. Knowing that he probably would not live long enough to see the legal action presented in oral testimony, he preserved his story through one of the first videotaped depositions conducted in Pennsylvania. It was taped on August 25, 1980. Eventually, the effort became part of a nationwide multi-district litigation. In 1988 a monetary settlement was finalized with seven of the manufacturing companies regarding compensation claims by veterans or their survivors. The fund (ultimately worth $240 million) ran out in 1997 after addressing just 52,000 claims.

The Vietnam Red Cross estimates that Agent Orange affected over 3 million Vietnamese, of which 150,000 were children with birth defects. The Vietnamese government provides a stipend to those believed affected. The Department of Veterans Affairs reports that as many as 2.8 million military personnel stationed in Vietnam between 1962 and 1975 were exposed to the defoliants in question.[1] Congress stepped in by enacting legislation that established a service-connected entitlement to disability compensation for veterans who served during Vietnam and subsequently suffered from specific disorders. The Agent Orange Registry was established by the Veterans Administration to track the special health concerns of veterans who may have been exposed. And, the VA assumes that certain "presumptive diseases" are related to exposure. Currently, that list includes:

- AL Amyloidosis
- Chronic B-cell Leukemias
- Chloracne, or similar acneform disease
- Diabetes Mellitus Type 2
- Hodgkin's Disease
- Ischemic Heart Disease

- Multiple Myeloma
- Non-Hodgkin's Lymphoma
- Parkinson's Disease
- Peripheral Neuropathy, Early-Onset
- Porphyria Cutanea Tarda
- Prostate Cancer
- Respiratory Cancers, including lung cancer
- Soft Tissue Sarcomas[2]

Some veterans or their families are still unaware of the benefits available to them. The veteran's job is to get on the registry, not just for himself, but for possible surviving family members.[3] If a veteran dies from complications associated from Agent Orange exposure, the spouse may qualify for survivor benefits. However, once the veteran has passed away, it can become extremely difficult to establish a claim if the veteran was not on the registry. Once registered, several benefits may be available—to the veteran, spouse, and children—including medical and financial compensation. The American Legion and the Veterans of Foreign Wars are two of the local agencies available to guide individuals through the process.

The national character of a country is not solely assessed on political largess, international philanthropy or the ability to avoid strategic blunders. A more telling glimpse of a nation's character is on how its government handles its responsibilities to its citizens.

****

[1] www.agentorangerecord.com/images/uploads/modules/AODFAQ.pdf
[2] www.publichealth.va.gov/exposures/agentorange/conditions/index.asp
[3] www.stripes.com/news/veterans/health-care/agent-irabge-registry-health-exam-for-veterans-1.131876

Glossary

105mm howitzer	♦ Basic artillery piece supporting U.S. infantry battalions
AF FAC pilot	♦ Air Force Forward Air Control Pilot; pilots who coordinate tactical air strikes in support of infantry
airborne division	♦ Paratrooper or parachutist division
AK-47	♦ Basic infantry rifle of the North Vietnamese Army and Vietcong, manufactured by the Soviet Union or Communist China
anti-personnel round	♦ A round designed to produce shot-gun like fragmentation designed to injure ground personnel
AO	♦ Area of Operations
AP	♦ Anti-personnel
APO	♦ Army Post Office
army artillery FO	♦ Army artillery forward observer
Army Commendation Medal	♦ Awarded to any member of the Armed Forces of the U.S. (other than General Officers) who, while serving after December 6, 1941, distinguished themselves by heroism, meritorious achievement or meritorious service
artillery	♦ A combat branch of the service that provides fire support to the ground troops (i.e. cannon, howitzer, gunships)
ARVN unit	♦ Army of the Republic of Vietnam (Army of South Vietnam)

ASAP	♦	As soon as possible
AWOL	♦	Absent Without Leave
azimuth	♦	A compass direction usually expressed in degrees
B-3 can	♦	A C-ration can, about the size of a Campbell's soup can, that contained a cocoa packet, cookies, and a tin of jam
battalion	♦	An infantry battalion usually consists of around 900 soldiers; an artillery battalion about 500 soldiers. During the Vietnam War, battalions were much smaller.
battalion brass	♦	Higher ranking officers, field-grade rank, normally major or above
battalion CP	♦	Battalion command post
battalion mortars	♦	4.2 inch mortars
battery	♦	An artillery company
beehive round	♦	A direct-fire artillery round which used steel darts (fleshettes) and used as a main defense against a ground attack
bird colonel	♦	A full colonel who sometimes commands a brigade
bivouacked	♦	A temporary military encampment
boonies	♦	Term used by American soldiers to designate rural or remote areas of Vietnam
brigade	♦	During the Vietnam War, a division was organized into 3 brigades, each commanded by a colonel. It consisted of approximately 20,000 people.
brigade CO	♦	Brigade Commanding Officer

brigadier	♦	A 1-star general, the commanding officer of a brigade
Bronze Star Medal	♦	Awarded to members of the U. S. Armed Forces for either heroic achievement, heroic service, meritorious achievement, or meritorious service in a combat zone
buck sergeant	♦	In the army, first of the sergeant ranks: Sergeant E-5.
C&C	♦	Command and Control
C-4	♦	A stable plastic explosive carried by infantry soldiers
cav	♦	Cavalry. Fast moving tactical elements
CBR suit	♦	A hazmat suit for chemical, biological, radiological hazards
Charlie	♦	Another name for Viet Cong. It came from the military alphabet code for **V**iet **C**ong: **V**ictor **C**harlie
cherry	♦	A new troop replacement
chicom tracers	♦	Usually green tracers used by the enemy and produced by the Chinese
Chieu Hoi leaflets	♦	Leaflets dropped over enemy areas to serve 2 principal purposes: used by enemy soldiers to surrender and by civilians seeking safe passage through a combat area. "Open Arms"
choppered	♦	Moving troops via helicopter
CID	♦	U. S. Army's Criminal Investigation Command
CIDG forces	♦	Civil Indigenous Defense Group troops
claymore mine	♦	A popular fan-shaped antipersonnel land mine that used C-4 as the explosive

clusterfuck	♦	A chaotic situation where everything seems to go wrong
CMB	♦	Combat Medics Badge
CO	♦	Commanding Officer
commo wire	♦	Communications wire
CONEX	♦	A large metal cargo container used by the U.S. Army for shipping supplies, as to overseas bases; from con(tainer for) ex(port)
CONUS	♦	Continental United States
corporal	♦	The lowest non-commissioned officer rank in the army, 2 stripes, usually found in artillery units
CP group	♦	Command Post group
C-rations	♦	Canned meals used in military operations
D model Huey	♦	Also called a "slick"; a helicopter that carries troops
defilade	♦	To fortify to protect
DEROS	♦	A soldier's Date Estimated Return from Overseas
deuce and a half truck	♦	A 2.5 ton truck
DZ	♦	Drop zone
entrenching tool	♦	A collapsible spade or small shovel
field pieces	♦	Artillery pieces i.e. 105mm Howitzer
fire base	♦	A temporary artillery firing position; usually 4 howitzers with crews and a company of infantry
fire team	♦	Half of a squad or sub-force; usually 5 men

firefight	♦ A brief intense exchange of fire between opposing military units
flash suppressor	♦ A device on modern military small arms weapons which reduces the flash signature of the weapon to help obscure the location of the shooter
flechette round	♦ Pointed steel projectile with a vaned tail for stable flight
FO	♦ Forward observer
fox holes	♦ An individual below ground fighting position usually occupied by 2 men
fragmentation grenades	♦ A common army grenade designed to disperse lethal fragment on detonation
free-fire zone	♦ A combat area in which any moving thing is a legitimate target
friendlies	♦ U.S. troops, allies, or anyone not on the other side
fusillade	♦ A number of shots fired in rapid succession
GP medium tent	♦ General purpose medium tent
grunt	♦ A nickname for an infantryman in Vietnam
guidon	♦ Small flag used as a military unit marker
higher (headquarters)	♦ Refers to the administration above the level you are at
hooch or hootch	♦ A house, living quarters, or a native hut
hop	♦ A privilege to military members by letting them fill seats on Air Force air transport flights that would otherwise remain empty

horn	♦	Another word for a radio handset
howitzer	♦	A type of artillery piece that can achieve a high angle of trajectory
Huey	♦	Nickname for the UH-series of helicopters: utility helicopter
humping	♦	Slogging around on foot
in country	♦	i.e. "in Vietnam"
infantry	♦	The ground combat branch principally responsible for taking and holding terrain
JAG	♦	The **J**udge **A**dvocate **G**eneral's Corps is the branch of the military concerned with military justice and military law
jump stick	♦	The group of paratroopers in line and hooked up to a cable and ready to jump
jungle shirt	♦	The quick drying fatigue shirt, olive drab, issued in lieu of the heavier cotton fatigue shirt in the states
KIA	♦	A soldier that is killed in action
klick	♦	1 kilometer
light anti-tank weapons	♦	A weapon such as a LAW used against light armored vehicles
LP	♦	Listening post. A forward position set up to obtain early warning of enemy movement
LRRP	♦	Long range reconnaissance patrol
		Or, the term used for the light weight meals (usually freeze-dried) developed for reconnaissance patrols
LST Transport	♦	Tank landing ship to load and transport cargo, vehicles, and troops to a combat area

LT	♦	Lieutenant
LZ	♦	Landing zone
M-1 carbine	♦	World War II vintage American rifle
M-16	♦	The standard American rifle used in Vietnam after 1966; nicknamed the widow-maker
M-2 carbine	♦	A modified M-1 carbine that allowed fully automatic fiing
M-3 grease gun	♦	A submachine gun, 45 caliber
MACV	♦	Military Assistance Command, Vietnam
magazine	♦	Where ammunition was stored until placed in a weapon
Mauser 98K	♦	Standard bolt action infantry rifle of the German army in WWII
medevac	♦	Emergency evacuation of wounded from a combat zone
medevac Huey	♦	Helicopter used for medevac
mess hall	♦	A place where meals are regularly served to a group
meter	♦	A measurement that equals 39 3/8 inches
MG	♦	Machine gunner
MIA	♦	A soldier that is missing in action
mortar	♦	A muzzle-loading cannon used to throw projectiles
MOS	♦	An enlisted man's military occupation specialty i.e. 11B=Infantry
NCO	♦	Non-commissioned officer
NCOIC	♦	Non-commissioned officer in charge
NVA	♦	North Vietnamese Army

oak leaf cluster	Indicates an additional award of the same medal; worn attached to the original medal
old man	Infantry jargon for the company commander, regardless of age
OPCON	Placed under operation control of another military group
OPLAN	The big plan to start a military operation
OPORD	Operations order: describes the situation, the mission, and what supporting activities the unit will conduct in order to achieve their commander's desired end state.
OV-1 birddog	Single engine fixed wing Cessna used to direct tactical air and artillery
PAVN	People's Army of Vietnam
piss tubes	Male urination tubes: cylindrical shipping casings for artillery and anti tank rounds placed in the ground at a 45 degree angle
plastic explosive	Usually C-4; an explosive commonly found in claymore mines
platoon	Approximately 45 soldiers belonging to a company
PLF	Parachute Landing Fall. Platforms part of jump training; a safety technique that allows a parachutist to land safely
point man	Lead soldier in a tactical formation
poppin-caps	Slang term for shooting a weapon
POW	Prisoner of War
profundity	Deep wisdom; intellectual depth; profound

psy-ops	♦	Psychological operations
P-Training	♦	Proficiency training
punji stick	♦	A sharpened piece of bamboo used as a booby trap weapon by the Viet Cong. It was usually rubbed with feces to create infection in wounds.
Purple Heart Medal	♦	A combat decoration awarded to members of the U. S. armed forces who are wounded by an instrument of war in the hands of the enemy, and posthumously to the next of kin in the name of those who are killed in action or die of wounds received in action.
push	♦	Slang term for the operating radio frequency
PX	♦	Post Exchange; the store on an Army base that only sells goods to military personnel, their families, and authorized civilians
PZ	♦	Pick-up zone
quad-50	♦	WWII era anti-aircraft weapons system of four 50-caliber machine guns
R&R	♦	Rest and Recuperation (or relaxation or recreation); a soldier's free time while serving in a non-family duty station
rear or rear area	♦	Refers to the location away from front line tactical activity, usually a supply and administration base
rear security	♦	Last soldier in a tactical formation
recon by fire	♦	Speculative fire. A tactic where military forces fire on likely enemy positions to provoke a reaction, thereby confirming their position

red ball	♦	A high speed highway, usually paved
replacement	♦	New personnel to a unit
rookie	♦	A novice
RPD	♦	Enemy weapon; light machine gun
RPG	♦	Rocket propelled grenade
RTO	♦	Radio telephone operator soldier
S1	♦	Refers to staff personnel
S2	♦	Refers to intelligence
S3	♦	Refers to staff operations
S4	♦	Refers to staff supply
SALUTE	♦	Size, Activity, Location, Uniform, Time, Equipment
SFC	♦	Sergeant First Class
short-timer	♦	A soldier whose tour of duty is almost completed and is getting ready to return to the states
shower point	♦	The place in the base camp area where a shower was established
Silver Star Medal	♦	U. S. Armed Forces's third-highest personal decoration for valor in combat, awarded primarily for gallantry in action against an enemy of the U. S.
slack man	♦	Second soldier in a tactical formation
slick	♦	A D-Model Huey; a helicopter that carries troops
special forces	♦	Army soldiers called "Green Berets"
spider hole	♦	A modified fox hole only about waist deep, usually for a single occupant
squad	♦	Usually commanded by a sergeant and composed of two teams of four men each.

stand-down	♦	To go off duty; a temporary cessation of offensive action
TAC	♦	Tactical Air Command
tactical air	♦	A US Air Force command supplying direct air support to ground combat units
The Force	♦	Tiger Force
TOC	♦	Tactical operations center
tonsure	♦	The shaven crown worn by monks and other clerics
Top	♦	The First Sergeant (highest sergeant in the company)
trioxane	♦	Fuel tabs for cooking
V or Valor Device	♦	Worn on certain military decorations, it distinguishes an award for heroism or valor in combat, instead of for meritorious service or achievement
VC	♦	Viet Cong
wait a minute vines	♦	Term used for vegetation that snags and hinders progress through the jungle
water buffalo	♦	Asian buffalo native to Southeast Asia
web gear	♦	Canvas belt and shoulder straps used for packing equipment and ammunition on infantry operations
white phosphorous grenades	♦	Commonly referred to as Willie Peter; heavy anti-personnel grenades that produce casualties by causing severe burns
WIA	♦	A soldier that is wounded in action

About the Author

Leo Joseph Heaney: army sergeant, student, army officer, anthropologist, researcher, teacher, author. He grew up in Jim Thorpe, PA., and is the son of a WWII veteran who served as a radio operator/gunner on B-17s over Germany.

Leo enlisted and served in Vietnam from April 1966-July 1968. 17 months (June 1966-October 1967) were with Tiger Force, of the 1st Battalion, 327th Parachute Infantry Regiment. His highest rank was Sergeant E-5 attained at age 19. Citations included: Combat Infantryman Badge, Parachutist Badge, Silver Star, Bronze Star, Army Commendation Medal with Valor Device and Oak Leaf Cluster, Purple Heart with Oak Leaf Cluster, Four Overseas Service Bars, Presidential Unit Citation for serving with 1/327th Infantry during Operation Hawthorne and the relief of Toumorong--1966.

Leo Joseph Heaney, photo courtesy of Leo Heaney

While attending Penn State University he participated in the ROTC program, and placed first of 1600 cadets at the 1971 ROTC summer camp at Ft. Indiantown Gap. ROTC honors: Distinguished Military Student, 1971; Distinguished Military Graduate, 1972.

After graduation, he re-entered the service as a commissioned officer in the Regular Army: Primary branch--Military Intelligence; Combat Arms branch--Infantry. He later resigned his commission with the rank of Captain.

While pursuing a certificate in Education from the University of Puget Sound he helped research and write a narrative of the Cowlitz Indian Tribe which assisted the tribal historians in the tribe's petition for Federal recognition. He also served as tribal representative on several archaeological projects in Western Washington.

He retired after 30 years as a high school Social Studies teacher.

Author contact: heaneylj@gmail.com

Leo Joseph Heaney, photo courtesy of Leo Heaney

www.ingramcontent.com/pod-product-compliance
Lightning Source LLC
Chambersburg PA
CBHW052011070526
44584CB00016B/1702